The important trend of recent years for theological colleges in Africa to transition to Christian universities is here provided with a pioneering research study. Semeon Mulatu has elegantly surfaced the core issues and patterns relevant to assessment of this trend. The vital question going forward could be whether these institutions can sustain a genuinely Christian character, where all dimensions of the educational formation function within an integrated Christian worldview, or if such institutions may come to evidence their Christian character merely by elements of ownership and staffing. One road could leave African Christianity deeply enriched, the other could leave theological education in Africa deeply impaired. This study provides resources for recognizing and assessing these critical challenges.

Paul Bowers, PhD
Managing Editor, *BookNotes for Africa*
Former International Director,
International Council for Evangelical Theological Education (ICETE)

In this book, *Transitioning from a Theological College to a Christian University*, Semeon Mulatu gives a fitting and relevant resource on this contemporary movement of our day. The book highlights various reasons that continue to shape this phenomenon, challenges faced by institutions in transition, and its impact on the relationships with institutional sponsors and key stakeholders. The book shows how the East African context is distinct from such transitions that North America and the United Kingdom witnessed in the later part of the twentieth century. Using a multi-case approach of surveying five institutions spread across four countries in the East African region, that is, Uganda, Kenya, Democratic Republic of Congo, and Ethiopia, Dr Mulatu shows how factors ranging from changing government higher education policies, market competition for students, threats of secularism, and need for financial sustainability have contributed towards the dynamic shaping of curricula design, mission focus, role of theology faculty or department, and policies on student enrolment and staff hiring of these institutions.

Granted the contemporary nature of this issue in light of numerous theological colleges planning for, or already engaged in, the process of transitioning into university status, this book has been published at the most fitting time. It is a timely and relevant resource to guide numerous institutions into an informed engagement of this exciting, challenging and enriching process of transitioning into the university status. Its prevalent emphasis on how this transition shapes the institution's Christian evangelical identity, and its role and effectiveness in discipling its membership, highlights this book's unique and distinct contribution on the status and voice of the evangelical ethos in the ongoing transitions in African theological discourse. For this reason, we in ACTEA highly recommend this book for all readers interested in understanding the nature and scope of this emerging issue in the African theological landscape.

Rev Emmanuel Chemengich, DMin
Executive Director,
Association for Christian Theological Education in Africa (ACTEA)

My first personal experience with an African theological institution which transitioned to a Christian university was in South Africa over twenty years ago. Since that time, the movement has proliferated, with examples now across the continent, from Kenya and the rest of East Africa, to West Africa – led by schools in Ghana (Nigerian Christian universities have a different pattern of origin), to Central and Francophone Africa. Despite the diverse geographical distribution, the commonalities are striking, including the many challenges. Many of these new Christian universities, which began with a focused mission and operating under a particular financial model, have significantly changed as they have navigated the transition. New financial models are developed which rely on much larger student bodies with numerous faculties. This in turn affects the demographics, dynamics, and ethos of the campus. The original mission of the theological faculty can appear to be lost in the university's new, more expansive mission. Old stakeholders of the seminary, who supported the former mission, can become disillusioned. Implementation of the new mission can be difficult with faculty who are unfamiliar with the integration of faith, life and learning. Studies of these common patterns and challenges, relatively new to Africa, are rare. Therefore, Dr Mulatu's careful research, focusing on five institutions in East Africa, is a welcome and significant contribution, and should be regarded as essential reading for those who wish a better understanding of this very important phenomenon in Christian higher education.

Scott Cunningham, PhD
Interim President and CEO, Overseas Council

Transitioning from a Theological College to a Christian University is an important work for all theological education institutions, not only in Eastern Africa, but all of Africa and beyond. To an outsider it seems theological colleges in Africa have been transitioning to Christian universities like lemmings over a cliff, with seemingly no rational basis for such a move. This is an overstatement, but Dr Mulatu's research and analysis indicates that perhaps it would have been wise for some universities to examine more clearly the implications of their move. Unfortunately, up until this work, there hasn't been any reliable research for such institutions to use as a resource in initial discussions. But now there is and it behoves any theological college thinking of making a transition to clearly study this work. Indeed, even for Christian universities, working through the issues that Mulatu raises would be a good investment of time on their behalf. I thoroughly recommend the work to all theological education institutions of whatever ilk.

Roger Kemp, DTh
Deputy Director,
International Council for Evangelical Theological Education (ICETE)

ICETE Series

Transitioning from a Theological College to a Christian University

Transitioning from a Theological College to a Christian University

A Multi-Case Study in the East African Context

Semeon Mulatu

Series Editor
Riad Kassis

© 2017 by Semeon Mulatu

Published 2017 by Langham Global Library
An imprint of Langham Publishing

Langham Publishing and its imprints are a ministry of Langham Partnership

Langham Partnership
PO Box 296, Carlisle, Cumbria CA3 9WZ, UK
www.langham.org

ISBNs:
978-1-78368-318-5 Print
978-1-78368-319-2 ePub
978-1-78368-321-5 PDF

Semeon Mulatu has asserted his right under the Copyright, Designs and Patents Act, 1988 to be identified as the Author of this work.

All rights reserved. No part of this publication may be reproduced, stored in a retrieval system or transmitted, in any form or by any means, electronic, mechanical, photocopying, recording or otherwise, without the prior written permission of the publisher or the Copyright Licensing Agency.

All Scripture quotations, unless otherwise indicated, are taken from the Holy Bible, New International Version®, NIV®. Copyright ©1973, 1978, 1984, 2011 by Biblica, Inc.™ Used by permission of Zondervan.

British Library Cataloguing in Publication Data
A catalogue record for this book is available from the British Library

ISBN: 978-1-78368-318-5

Cover & Book Design: projectluz.com

Langham Partnership actively supports theological dialogue and an author's right to publish but does not necessarily endorse the views and opinions set forth here or in works referenced within this publication, nor can we guarantee technical and grammatical correctness. Langham Partnership does not accept any responsibility or liability to persons or property as a consequence of the reading, use or interpretation of its published content.

To Meaza, my dear wife and best friend,
always supporting and encouraging me,
and to our son, Bruk, a great joy of my life,
and my parents, who showed me the way of
following the Lord wholeheartedly.

Contents

	Preface	xiii
	List of Tables and Figures	xiv
	List of Abbreviations	xv
1	Introduction	1
	Christian Higher Education in Africa	4
	Research Purpose	10
	Delimitations of the Study	10
	Research Questions	10
	Terminology	11
	Procedural Overview	13
	Research Assumptions	14
2	Precedent Literature	15
	Biblical-Theological Foundations	15
	What Makes Higher Education Distinctly Christian?	19
	The Role and Purpose of Christian Higher Education	33
	Threats of Secularization	41
	Higher Education in Africa	43
	Church-Affiliated Higher-Educational Institutes in Africa	47
	Conclusion	52
3	Methodological Design	55
	Research Questions Synopsis	55
	Design Overview	56
	Population	58
	Sample and Sampling Technique	58
	Delimitations of the Sample	59
	Limitations of Generalization	59
	Instrumentation	60
	Procedures	61
4	Analysis of Findings	67
	Compilation Protocol	67
	Findings and Displays	69
	Mekane Yesus Seminary	71

	Africa International University	99
	St Paul's University	119
	Uganda Christian University	141
	Shalom University of Bunia	162
	Evaluation of the Research Design	183
5	Conclusion	187
	Research Purpose	187
	Research Questions	187
	Reasons for the Transition	188
	External and Internal Challenges	190
	Effects of the Transition on the Mission	193
	Effects of the Transition on the Relationship with Churches	195
	Effects of the Transitions on the Theology Program	196
	Research Implications	199
	Research Applications	201
	Research Limitations	202
	Further Research	202

Appendix 1: Semi-structured Interview Questions 205

Appendix 2: Expert Panel Selection 209

Reference List. 211

Preface

This book is a result of the dissertation I did for my PhD program at the Southern Baptist Theological Seminary (SBTS) in Louisville, KY. I would like to express my sincere appreciation to Dr Hal Pettegrew, my supervising professor, for his guidance, support, and encouragement.

I owe a great debt to Christian Fellowship Church in Evansville, Indiana, for supporting me and my family financially and for providing for our needs during the years I studied at SBTS. I am also very grateful to the Lamb Foundation for their financial support and encouragement.

I am also very grateful to Paul Bowers who saw the usefulness of this work to theological seminaries and colleges and has encouraged me to get it published. I am grateful to Langham and ICETE for their willingness to publish this work and make it available to a wider audience.

I do not have words to express my appreciation for my dear wife, closest friend, and partner for her encouragement and support, with great sacrifice, without which I would not be able to do my studies.

Finally, but most importantly, I praise my God and Savior Jesus Christ, who called me to work in his kingdom and for giving me this opportunity to study so that I can be better prepared for his work.

Semeon Mulatu
Addis Ababa, Ethiopia
August 2017

List of Tables and Figures

Tables

Table 1: Types of Church-Related Colleges 27
Table 2: Church-Affiliated Universities in Kenya 49
Table 3: Church-Affiliated Universities in Uganda. 50
Table 4: Changes Due to the Transition in MYS and MY-MLC 99
Table 5: Changes Due to the Transition from NEGST to AIU 118
Table 6: Changes Due to the Transition from SPUTC to SPU 140
Table 7: Changes Due to the Transition from BTTC to UCU. 163
Table 8: Changes Due to the Transition from ISTB to UBS 184
Table 9: Reasons for Transition 188
Table 10: External Challenges 190
Table 11: Internal Challenges. 192

Figures

Figure 1: Enrollment of Higher-Educational Institutions in
    Sub-Saharan Africa 46

List of Abbreviations

ACK	Anglican Church of Kenya
ACTEA	Accrediting Council for Theological Education in Africa
AEA	Association of Evangelicals in Africa
AEAM	Association of Evangelicals in Africa and Madagascar
AIU	Africa International University
DRC	Democratic Republic of Congo
EECMY	Ethiopian Evangelical Church Mekane Yesus
GER	Gross Enrollment Ratio
ISAR	Institute for the Study of African Realities
ISTB	Institut Supérior Théologique de Bunia (Buna Theological Seminary)
MCK	Methodist Church of Kenya
MKC	Meserete Kirstos College
MY-MLC	Mekane Yesus Management and Leadership College
MYS	Mekane Yesus Seminary
NCCK	National Council of Churches of Kenya
NEGST	Nairobi Evangelical Graduate School of Theology
PCEA	Presbyterian Church of East Africa
RCEA	Reformed Church of East Africa
SPS	School for Professional Studies
SPU	St Paul's University
SSA	Sub-Saharan Africa
UCU	Uganda Christian University
UNESCO	United Nations Education, Scientific and Cultural Organization
UIS	UNESCO Institute of Statistics
USB	Université Shalom de Bunia (Shalom University of Bunia)

1

Introduction

Several theological colleges and seminaries in Africa are transitioning or considering transitioning to Christian liberal arts colleges or universities. These are colleges originally established to train ministers in biblical, theological, and ministry skills for a vocational ministry in churches and Christian organizations. These institutions have expanded or will expand their purposes and programs in this transition.

Such transitions have taken place in many higher-educational institutes in the West. Many universities in the United States and England were originally established by faith communities to train ministers for the churches. Holmes says, "American higher education was the child of religion, and the history both of the church denomination and of the westward expansion can be traced through the history of America's colleges and universities."[1] Holmes mentions Harvard, Yale, Princeton, and Columbia as examples of such institutions.[2]

Though these and many other higher-educational institutions were started by churches, through the years many of them have abandoned their religious distinctiveness. Burtchaell, in his book *The Dying of the Light: The Disengagement of Colleges and Universities*,[3] gives an account of how colleges that began as denominational colleges have now become secular. Burtchaell gives a good summary of how these colleges slowly drifted away from their denominational roots to secular academic institutions.[4] He argues that the

---

1. Arthur F. Holmes, *The Idea of a Christian College* (Grand Rapids, MI: Eerdmans, 1975), 19.
2. Ibid.
3. James T. Burtchaell, *The Dying of the Light: The Disengagement of Colleges and Universities from their Christian Churches* (Grand Rapids, MI: Eerdmans, 1998).
4. James T. Burtchaell, "The Decline and Fall of the Christian College (II)." *First Things* (May 1991): 24–41.

drifting started when educators in these institutions, who felt that the leaders of the church might use their influence to hinder their reform agendas, managed to pull out the institutions from church governance. Reacting to the "sectarian" narrowness, they moved the intellectual and disciplinary life of their institutions away from any specific church to a generic Christianity. Burtchaell observes that these educators, who were themselves observant believers, failed to foresee "that the academy had no way to remain Christian without vital membership in an ecclesiastical fellowship."[5] These educators eventually brought secularization of their institutions.

The effects of secularization continued to grow when many academic institutions started emphasizing "scientific inquiry as separate from the development of character or moral precepts."[6] Describing how secularization impacted liberal arts college campuses, Gomes writes,

> The elite residential liberal arts colleges have responded to rapid social changes by distancing themselves from their more particular pasts, most noticeably in the role that religion is seen to play in the total mission of the institution, and by fashioning themselves as best they can in the image of the larger, secular research universities . . . The formative consensus of these institutions and the ethical dimensions that flowed from it has been broken, and for some time there has not been anything to take its place.

Not all schools that were started by faith groups followed the same path. There are some who kept their Christian traditions and religious vision. Benne explains how six institutions from different Christian traditions kept their religious vision. He argues that the strong religious traditions that sponsored those schools "have provided the resources for a compelling vision on the part of each college or university, which has become the organizing paradigm for the life and mission of each school. That religious vision constitutes a comprehensive, unsurpassable, and central Christian account of life and reality."[7]

---

5. Ibid., 24.
6. Julie A. Reuben, *The Making of a Modern University: Intellectual Transformation and the Marginalization of Modernity* (Chicago: University of Chicago Press, 1996), 126.
7. R. Benne, *Quality with Soul: How Six Premier Colleges and Universities Keep Faith with Their Religious Traditions* (Grand Rapids, MI: Eerdmans, 2001), 140.

By the middle of the twentieth century, several evangelical institutions had emerged that undertook the challenge of integrating knowledge and value that their secular counterparts have abandoned.[8] Describing the emergence of such evangelical colleges that have returned to the Christian commitment to education, Carlberg writes,

> Most evangelical institutions started as Bible colleges funded, supported, and guided by a denomination or strong independent Christian leader. Others began as smaller replicas of established liberal arts colleges or secular universities where research, service, and teaching were prominent. Whether rooted in the Bible school movement or modeled after the historic liberal arts college, most embraced Christian piety and required chapel attendance, prayer before class, mission outreach, and courses in Bible and Theology studies.[9]

Though these institutions are small, they have become an important force for diversity in the American educational system.[10] Mark Noll, pointing out the growth of such institutions, writes, "In the twentieth century, evangelical colleges and (since the 1960s) universities have constituted one of the most important alternatives to the burgeoning sweep of state-sponsored higher education."[11]

Secularization has also taken place in many higher-educational institutes in England. Until the 1990s England had four universities considered Christian: Oxford, Cambridge, Durham, and King's College, London.[12] Bebbington[13] and D'Costa[14] discuss in their books how these English universities were

---

8. Judson R. Carlberg, "The Evangelical Vision: From Fundamentalist Isolation to Respected Voice," in *The Future of Religious Colleges*, ed. Paul J. Drove (Grand Rapids, MI: Eerdmans, 2002), 228.
9. Ibid.
10. Ibid., 229.
11. Mark Noll, "The Evangelical Mind in America," in *Should God Get Tenure?*, ed. David W. Gill (Grand Rapids, MI: Eerdmans, 1997), 195–196.
12. P. Glanzer, "Searching for the Soul of English Universities: An Exploration and Analysis of Christian Higher Education in England," *British Journal of Educational Studies* 56, no. 2 (2008): 164.
13. D. Bebbington, "The Secularization of British Universities since the Mid-Nineteenth Century," in *The Secularization of the Academy*, ed. G. Marsden and B. J. Longfield (New York: Oxford University Press, 1992).
14. G. D'Costa, *Theology in the Public Square: Church, Academy, and Nation* (Malden, MA: Blackwell, 2005).

secularized. According to Bebbington, what makes the secularization of the universities in England different from those in the United States is the role played by the state.[15] The various laws that were passed by Parliament played a big role in changing these universities from Church of England universities to secular universities.[16] Since the state controls almost all of these institutions, they were forced to expand or contract according to the desires of the state.[17] These universities face constant pressure to accommodate all kinds of citizens in the UK. They cannot discriminate among students for admission on the basis of religion and in appointing academic staff unless they can clearly make a case that a certain belief is necessary to teach that specific subject. Regarding the place of theology in the curriculum of these institutions, Glanzer says, "Unlike America, the practice of general education or core curriculum that would allow universities to require all students to take theology classes does not exist in England."[18]

Describing the other two challenges higher-educational institutions founded by Christian organizations in England face, Glanzer says, "With the secularization of the English population, it is difficult for universities to market themselves as Christian institutions. Moreover, the Anglican and English culture appears to shy away from such overt claims to particularity. As a result, it would appear that the church's resources, influence and attention are too broadly scattered for it to create a number of institutions that retain a strong sense of Christian identity."[19]

Christian Higher Education in Africa

Africa, especially the region called sub-Saharan Africa, has the lowest enrollment in higher-educational institutions. The countries that this study focuses on, Ethiopia, Kenya, Uganda, and Democratic Republic of Congo (DRC), are part of sub-Saharan Africa. This region has one of the lowest gross enrollment ratios (GERs) in tertiary education. Explaining the situation in the region, Varghese says, "In 2000, the GER in higher education in SSA was only

---

15. Bebbington, "Secularization of British Universities," 265.
16. Ibid.
17. Glanzer, "Searching for the Soul of English Universities," 178.
18. Ibid., 173.
19. Ibid., 179.

3.5 percent... A majority of the African countries in 2000 have an enrollment ratio of less than 5 percent. More importantly, the distance between African countries and countries in other regions has widened due to the slow progress made in this region."[20]

Several higher-educational institutions in Africa have their roots and precursors in missionary ventures and religious organizations.[21] The church played a pivotal role in the establishment of several higher-educational institutions.[22] In most sub-Saharan countries, formal educational programs were part of the Christian mission for many years.[23] Many elementary and high schools were established and run by Christian organizations or churches, and these organizations included education as an integral part of the Christian mission. "In venturing into higher education at the tertiary level, therefore, the churches are building on a rich intellectual and religious heritage that has always seen formal education and Christian mission as inseparable entities in the building of society."[24]

There are twelve church-affiliated universities and Christian liberal arts colleges in Kenya.[25] Most of these universities and Christian liberal arts colleges started as Bible/theological colleges to train ministers for the church and Christian organizations. They eventually added other programs and transitioned to Christian universities and liberal arts colleges. Two of these universities, Africa International University (formerly Nairobi Evangelical Graduate School of Theology) and St Paul's University (formerly St Paul's United Theological College), are included in this multi-case study.

Uganda has six private universities and university colleges that are founded by churches and recognized by the government. Four of these universities were founded by the Church of Uganda, one by the Catholic Church and one

---

20. N. V. Varghese, *New Trends in Higher Education: Growth and Expansion of Private Higher Education in Africa* (Paris: International Institute for Educational Planning, 2006), 29.
21. W. Otieno, "The Privatization of Public Universities in Kenya," in *Private Higher Education: A Global Revolution*, ed. P. G. Altbach and D. C. Levy (Boston, MA: Sense, 2005), 75.
22. Ibid.
23. J. Kwabana Asamoah-Gyadu, "Christian Higher Education for Africa: Need, Relevance, and Value," paper presented at the meeting of the International Association for the Promotion of Christian Higher Education, 2007; http://www.iapche.org/gyadu-paper.htm; accessed 10 October 2009.
24. Ibid.
25. O. Abagi, "Private Higher Education in Kenya," in Varghese, *New Trends in Higher Education*, 75.

by the Seventh-Day Adventist Church (www.unche.or.ug). Uganda Christian University, which was founded by the Church of Uganda in 1991 as Bishop Tucker Theological College and transitioned to a Christian university in 1999 (www.ucu.ac.ug), is included in this study.

In Democratic Republic of Congo there are six Christian universities.[26] One of these institutions is Shalom University of Bunia which was first founded in 1961 as a Bible school owned by five different church denominations. Its name was changed to Institut Supérieur Théologique de Bunia (Bunia Theological Seminary) in September 1976. After five decades of existence, Bunia Theological Seminary made an important transition to Shalom University of Bunia in 2001 (www.unishabunia.org). Shalom University of Bunia is included in this multi-case study.

There are no Christian universities that are established in Ethiopia yet. However, two colleges that started as Bible/theological colleges have started the transition process to become Christian universities. The first one is the Mekane Yesus Seminary (MYS) that was founded in 1960. When MYS was established, its aim was "to assist in the extension of the Kingdom of God in Ethiopia by offering training to the church pastors, evangelists and church leaders."[27] In 1995 the seminary added a Leadership, Management, and Communication College to its Theology and Music programs. MYS have plans to add other programs in the future and become a Christian university (www.myes.org). MYS is included in this multi-case study.

The other theological college that is in the process of becoming a Christian university is Meserete Kirstos College (www.mkcollege.org). It was founded in 1994 as "Meserete Kirstos Church Bible Institute" for the purpose of "providing relevant and contextualized biblical training for pastors, evangelists, and lay leaders within Ethiopia."[28] In 1995 the institute was recognized as Meserete Kirstos College (MKC). Currently it runs diploma- and degree-level programs in Bible and Christian ministries. Its vision statement says, "The College envisions becoming a full 'Christian University,' offering a broad range of undergraduate and graduate programs relevant to impacting the Ethiopian

---

26. P. L. Glanzer, Joel Carpenter, and Nick Lantinga, "Looking for God in the University: Examining Trends in Christian Higher Education," *Higher Education: The International Journal of Higher Education and Educational Planning* 61, no. 6 (2011): 721–755.

27. www.myes.org.

28. www.mkcollege.org.

societies and beyond towards a more honest, just, and compassionate and prosperous future."²⁹

The Christian higher-educational institutes in Africa also face the challenge of secularization seen in the West. What happened to the University of Ghana gives an example of what is taking place in many similar institutes in Africa. Although the University of Ghana was established on Christian moral foundations, after independence, it was pressured by the government to broaden its divinity faculty to include the study of non-Christian religions. That eventually led to the religious neutrality of all its programs.³⁰

Christian higher-educational institutions also face competition from other private and public higher-educational institutions. In order to compete, expand, and stay financially viable in this environment, some Christian higher-educational institutions have chosen to be lenient on their religious requirements and to start programs that are in demand for job-oriented fields.³¹

Though the common trend in higher-educational institutes that were established by churches and Christian organizations is to gradually lose their religious distinctiveness over many years, there are exceptions in Africa. Levy argues that there are several higher-educational institutions that have kept their religious missions. Daystar University and the Kabarak Universities are two of the institutions he mentioned as examples.³² The mission statement of Daystar University says, "Daystar University seeks to develop managers, professionals, researchers, and scholars to be effective Christian servant leaders through the integration of Christian faith and holistic learning for the transformation of church and society in Africa and the world."³³

As many theological colleges and seminaries in Africa are rushing to transition to Christian universities, is secularization a possible unintended consequence for these institutions? Have the experiences of those institutions that have transitioned or are transitioning shown evidence of drifting away from their evangelical mission and values? In what ways has the transition affected the mission, evangelical values, and theological programs of the

---

29. Ibid.
30. Asamoah-Gyadu, "Christian Higher Education for Africa."
31. Daniel Levy, "A Recent Echo: African Private Higher Education in an International Perspective," *Journal of Higher Education in Africa* 5, no. 2–3 (2007): 206.
32. Ibid., 205.
33. www.daystar.ac.ke.

institutions? Considering the threat of secularization and other unintended consequences of such transitions, does the church in Africa need to use its valuable resources to transition her theological and Bible colleges to liberal arts colleges or universities? These and similar questions need to be addressed to determine if the church needs to involve itself in liberal arts education.

After a thorough research of the literature, this researcher has not found any significant research that has been done in the East African context on how transitions from a Bible/theological college to Christian liberal arts colleges or universities affect the transitioning institutions. This research is especially driven by the desire to find out the reasons for such transitions, the challenges of the transition process, and how such transitions affect the mission of the institutions, the theological training programs, and the relationships of the institutions with their founding or sponsoring churches.

The reason why this research focuses on how the transitions affect the mission of the institutions is that the institutional mission is where institutions articulate their identity and role in higher education that directs all educational activities of the institution. Changes in the institutional mission affect everything that goes on in the institution.[34]

This research also focuses on how the transitions affect the Theology program of these institutions because it is through their theology that Christian higher-education institutions articulate how their faith is integrated with learning that is offered in their institutions. Benne, explaining the importance of theology in Christian higher-educational institutions, says,

> Christianity as a living tradition is an account of life that is comprehensive, unsurpassable, and central. Theology gives an articulated account of that faith; it too aims to be comprehensive, unsurpassable, and central. One would think, then, that theology would be amply employed by Christian colleges and universities to articulate their identity and mission, to stipulate the relation of revelation and reason in their particular tradition, to gather a Theology department in which its members would gladly carry

---

34. Anthony Diekema, *Academic Freedom and Christian Scholarship* (Grand Rapids, MI: Eerdmans, 2000), 57.

that vision on behalf of the school and the faculty, to construct a curriculum, to elaborate a public justification for the school's ethos, and to provide a Christian intellectual tradition with which the whole school in its many departments could engage.[35]

This research also analyzes how transitioning from a theological college to a Christian liberal arts college or university affects the institution's relationship with its founding church or organization in the East African context. As indicated above, one of the reasons why secularization took place in many academic institutions in the West that were founded by churches and Christian organizations is that these institutions started distancing themselves from their particular past[36] and moved to a generic Christianity instead of relating to actual church.[37] On the other hand, those institutions that maintained their strong ties with their founding churches also kept their religious vision as central to their mission.[38]

For this study, the researcher selected five institutions from Ethiopia, Kenya, Uganda, and Democratic Republic of Congo that began as theological (Bible) colleges or seminaries and now are transitioning or have transitioned to Christian liberal arts colleges or universities. The researcher used certain key factors such as location, denominational affiliation, or sponsorship, and stages in the transition process to choose the institutions. These institutions are Mekane Yesus Seminary (Ethiopia), Africa International University (Kenya), St Paul's University (Kenya), Uganda Christian University (Uganda), and Shalom University of Bunia (DRC). Out of the five institutions, MYS is in transition to become a Christian university while the other four have already transitioned to Christian universities. All these institutions have added at least two additional programs to their Theology program and have made clear plans to add more programs in the next five to seven years.

---

35. Benne, *Quality with Soul*, 15.
36. Peter J. Gomes, "Affirmation and Adaptation: Values and the Elite Residential College," in *Distinctively American: The Residential Liberal Arts Colleges*, ed. Steven Koblik and Stephen R. Graubard (New Brunswick, NJ: Transaction, 2000).
37. Burtchaell, "Decline and Fall of the Christian College (II)."
38. Benne, *Quality with Soul*.

Research Purpose

The purpose of this qualitative multi-case study was to analyze and describe transitions from a theological college or seminary to a Christian liberal arts college or university in the East African context.

Delimitations of the Study

This study is limited to institutions in Ethiopia, Kenya, Uganda, and DRC that are transitioning or have transitioned from a theological college or seminary to a liberal arts college. Though a transition from a Bible (theological) college to Christian liberal arts college or university brings many changes to an institution, this study is delimited to the reasons for and challenges of the transitions and how such a transition affects the overall mission of the institution, its relationship with the founding or sponsoring churches, and its Theology program.

The study is delimited to institutions that have added at least two additional programs to their Theology program and have made clear plans to add more programs in the next five to seven years. This study is also delimited to Protestant evangelical Bible or theological colleges that have transitioned or are transitioning to liberal arts colleges or universities. The findings, therefore, do not generalize to church-affiliated institutions that belong to other Christian traditions. Though this qualitative study attempts to consider the phenomenon in several institutions in the region that are transitioning or have transitioned, it will be limited in its representation because all transitions are different and dependent on the nature of the institutions and their specific context.

Research Questions

The following five questions guided this study.
1. What are the reasons for the transition from a theological college to a liberal arts college or university?
2. What are the external and internal challenges these Christian higher-educational institutions face as they go through this transition?
3. In what ways is the mission of the institution affected by the transition from a theological college to Christian liberal arts college or university?

4. In what ways has the transition affected the relationship between the institution and the sponsoring church(es) or Christian organization(s)?
5. In what ways has the transition from a theological college to a Christian liberal arts college or university affected the Theology program of the institution?

Terminology

The following terms and definitions are presented to clarify the way they are used in this dissertation.

Bible college. "Bible college" has a similar meaning to "theological college" in this research. Some colleges use the title "Bible college" instead of "theological college" but they are similar institutions.[39]

Christian higher education. "Christian higher education" refers to education offered at postsecondary colleges and universities within an evangelical Protestant tradition where "the Christian vision is the organizing paradigm" and "Christian account of life and reality is publicly and comprehensively relevant to the life of the school by requiring that all adult members of the ongoing academic community subscribe to a statement of belief."[40]

Faculty. The word "faculty" is used in two ways in this research. Depending on the context, it refers to "the teaching and administrative staff and those members of the administration having academic rank in an educational institution" or "a branch of teaching and learning in an educational institution." For example: Faculty of Social Sciences.[41]

Christian liberal arts college. A "Christian liberal arts college" is a college that prepares students in arts and science from a Christian worldview perspective for life's work rather than for a specific profession or vocation.[42]

Evangelical. "Evangelical" is a noun or an adjective that refers to Protestant Christians who hold to doctrinal ideas such as the authority of the Scriptures, the completeness of the atoning work of Christ, justification by grace through

---

39. David S. Dockery, *Renewing Minds: Serving Church and Society through Christian Higher Education* (Nashville, TN: B&H, 2007), 9.
40. Benne, *Quality with Soul*, 50.
41. www.merriam-webster.com.
42. Holmes, *Idea of a Christian College*, 106.

faith, and the necessity of the work of the Holy Spirit in regeneration and change of the human heart.[43]

Institutional mission. The "institutional mission" of a higher-educational institution is a statement that defines the institution and its role in higher education. It directs all educational activities of the institution including student body, admission policies, faculty recruitment, and planning. The institutional mission has to be adopted by the governing board and all the administrators of the institution and appears in all appropriate publications of the institution, including its catalogue.[44]

Leaders. "Leaders" in this study refers to those people who are employed by an institution of higher education at the level of president (principal), vice-president, academic dean, and the board chairperson.

Liberal arts colleges. "Liberal arts colleges" are colleges that mainly have undergraduate programs offering a bachelor's degree. They are small (1,000–2,500 students). Their curriculum is aimed at imparting general knowledge and developing general intellectual capacities in contrast to a professional, vocational, or technical curriculum.[45]

Secularization. "Secularization" in higher-educational institutions refers to the activity of moving education away from the control or influence of religion.[46] It refers to the declining importance of faith, the diminished influence of religious organizations on the institution, and the diminishing of religious commitments.[47]

Theological college. A "theological college" is a college that is established for the purpose of preparing students for church-related vocations. They are generally undergraduate programs and their focus of study is Christian materials.[48]

---

43. Tom J. Nettles, "Evangelicalism," in *Evangelical Dictionary of Christian Education*, ed. Michael J. Anthony, Warren S. Benson, Daryl Eldridge, and Julie Gorman, Baker Reference Library (Grand Rapids, MI: Baker Academic, 2001), 265.
44. www.nwccu.org/standards.
45. www.about.com.
46. www.thefreedictionary.com.
47. Stephanie L. Mixon, Larry Lyon, and Michael Beaty. "Secularization and National Universities: The Effect of Religious Identity on Academic Reputation," *Journal of Higher Education* 75, no. 4 (2004): 403.
48. Dockery, *Renewing Minds*, 9.

Theological program. "Theological program" in this study refers to the program within a Christian higher-educational institution that focuses on biblical, theological, and ministry studies and prepares students for church-related vocations.

Procedural Overview

The research methodology that was used in this study is a qualitative, multi-case study method. This method was chosen because it helps to answer research questions that are descriptive in nature and that analyze the effects of change in the institutions that are selected for this study. For this multiple-case-study research, the researcher selected five institutions in Ethiopia, Kenya, Uganda, and DRC that started as theological colleges and have added at least two additional programs to their Theology program and made clear plans to add more programs in the next five to seven years. Four of these institutions have already become Christian universities and one of them is in transition. The researcher contacted the presidents of institutions that met these criteria and asked for their willingness to participate in this study, and selected the five institutions that were willing and accessible to the researcher. The data for this research was gathered from in-depth interviews, the official documents of the institutions, and from on-campus observation notes of the researcher.

The in-depth interviews were conducted with the president (principal, vice-chancellor, rector), the academic dean (deputy vice-chancellor for academic affairs), and the deans of the Theology programs and other senior leaders of each of these institutions. The interviews were designed to bring to the fore the experiences and perceptions of the leaders of these higher-educational institutions about the reasons for, and the effects, challenges, and impacts of the transitions. The data that was collected from the interview sessions was recorded and transcribed. The transcripts were sent to the interviewees for their validation. Once the validations were received, the data was analyzed and coded for patterns and themes, and the findings from the interviews are analyzed, summarized, and reported.

The document research was conducted by examining the institutions' catalogues, published newspapers, brochures, and official documents. The researcher also visited all five academic institutions to gain a perspective on the educational environment. While on campus the researcher attended campus activities such as chapel when in session, held informal discussions with faculty members and students, and made observations. The researcher collected resources through all these activities that would provide information on the effects of the transition on the institutions.

Research Assumptions

The following is a list of the assumptions that are central to the current study.

1. Christian higher education that is based on a biblical foundation that integrates faith and learning helps the church influence the culture for Christ.
2. Church-affiliated higher-educational institutions do not necessarily provide Christian higher education.
3. The commitment of a Christian higher-educational institute should be to the Lord and his Word, then to the church, and then to the society, in that order.[49]
4. The official published documents of the institutions give an accurate reflection of the institutions' ethos, vision, and curriculum emphases.
5. The leaders of the institutions that were interviewed for this research answered the questions in an accurate manner.

---

49. Ibid.

2

Precedent Literature

The precedent literature review in this chapter is presented in five sections. The first section reviews the biblical-theological basis for Christian higher education that is presented in the literature. The second section deals with the literature that describes the distinctive factors in Christian higher education. Section three focuses on the role and purpose of Christian higher education. The fourth section discusses the literature that describes how secularization became a threat to many higher-educational institutions that were started by churches and Christian groups. The context of Christian higher education in Africa, especially in East Africa, is discussed in section five.

Biblical-Theological Foundations

God has revealed himself to man in different ways. One of the ways he revealed himself is through his creation, and this revelation is available to all (Ps 19:1–4; Rom 1:20). This is what theologians call general revelation.[1] Erickson states that there are three traditional modes of general revelation: nature, history, and the constitution of the human being.[2] Through his creation, God has revealed his power and divine nature to all human beings (Rom 1:19–20). God created man with the capacity to perceive the existence of a Supreme Being from observing the universe around him.[3] Through general revelation, God calls mankind to "respond by acknowledging that there has to be behind it all

---

1. Wayne Grudem, *Systematic Theology: An Introduction to Biblical Doctrines* (Grand Rapids, MI: Zondervan, 1994), 123.
2. Millard J. Erickson, *Introducing Christian Doctrine* (Grand Rapids, MI: Baker, 1992), 34.
3. Charles Ryrie, *Basic Theology* (Chicago: Moody, 1999), 33; Henry C. Thiessen, *Lectures in Systematic Theology*, reprint (Grand Rapids, MI: Eerdmans 2006), 8.

a living, powerful, intelligent, super-human Being."[4] "The person who views the beauty of a sunset and the biology student dissecting a complex organism are exposed to indications of the greatness of God."[5]

The second way God revealed himself in general revelation is through history. Erickson, explaining how God revealed himself in history, says, "If God is at work in the world and is moving toward certain goals, it should be possible to detect the trend of his work in events that occur as part of history."[6]

The third means of God's general revelation is through human beings themselves. God has given human beings moral and spiritual qualities that help them make moral judgments. This has great significance for education. God's creation is a source of knowledge and through scientific studies of nature and interaction with people, human beings can learn about God and things he has created.

Though what God has revealed through general revelation is sufficient to lead people to some knowledge about God, it does not give sufficient information about God and our relationship with him. That is why God has also revealed himself in a *special* way through the Bible and his Son, Jesus Christ.

The Bible is God's written Word that comprises both the Old Testament (Rom 15:4) and the New Testament (2 Tim 3:16). Everything that is necessary for our salvation and Christian life and growth is clearly revealed in the Scriptures.[7] God's Word is truth (John 17:17), without error (Ps 12:6), sure (Ps 119:89), and the ultimate standard of truthfulness (Matt 4:4; 2 Pet 1:20–21).[8] Describing the authority of God's Word, Knight writes, "For the Christian, the Bible is the foremost source of knowledge and the most essential epistemological authority. All other sources of knowledge must be tested and verified in the light of scripture."[9]

The other way God has revealed himself in a special way is through his Son, Jesus Christ. The Bible teaches that Christ is the center of all things. One of the key passages that teaches Christ's centrality is Colossians 1:15–17, which

---

4. Ryrie, *Basic Theology*, 37.
5. Erickson, *Introducing Christian Doctrine*, 34.
6. Ibid.
7. Grudem, *Systematic Theology*.
8. Ibid.
9. G. Knight, *Philosophy and Education: An Introduction in Christian Perspective* (Berrien Springs, MI: Andrews University Press, 2006), 179.

says, "He is the image of the invisible God, the firstborn over all creation. For by him all things were created: things in heaven and on earth, visible and invisible, whether thrones or powers or rulers or authorities; all things were created by him and for him. He is before all things, and in him all things hold together." Christ, as this passage describes him, is the Creator of all things, the Sustainer of all things, the Goal of all things, the Redeemer of all things, and the Judge of all things.[10] Since Christ is the center of all things, all Christian education should be Christ-centered.

For many Christians, Christ-centered education is related to education that is offered in the church, Bible colleges, or seminaries that are mainly established to train people for evangelism, church ministry, and missions. Can liberal arts education be Christ-centered? Is it possible to teach chemistry, sociology, history, music, physics, and English literature in a way that is Christ-centered? Litfin says,

> To speak of Christ-centered liberal arts education is to make the claim that Jesus is the centerpiece of all human knowledge, the reference point for all our experience. It directs our attention to the only One who can serve as the centerpiece of an entire curriculum, the One to whom we must relate everything and without whom no fact, no theory, no subject matter can be fully appreciated. It is the claim that every field of study, every discipline, every course, requires Jesus Christ to be understood aright.[11]

Since God is the creator of everything and is the source of all true knowledge that is revealed through general revelation and special revelation, we can agree with the early church fathers who stated, "All truth is God's truth, wherever it is found."[12]

The Bible teaches that human beings are created in the image of God and are created to be God's vice-regents to rule and subdue the earth (Gen 1:26–27). Since human beings are created in God's image, they have the capacity to be rational, moral, and relational. Even though all these capacities are affected by the fall, human beings are still the bearer of God's image and God's image

---

10. D. Litfin, *Conceiving the Christian College* (Grand Rapids, MI: Eerdmans, 2004), 39–42.
11. Ibid., 64–65.
12. Arthur F. Holmes, *The Idea of a Christian College* (Grand Rapids, MI: Eerdmans, 1975), 25.

in them is not completely lost (Jas 3:9). Explaining the implications of this in relation to education Holmes says,

> Man has a God-given, God-preserved, God restorable potential, a potential to be developed, disciplined and invested in response to God. Such development, discipline and direction are the Christian's responsibility and stewardship. To educate the whole person, to encourage disciplined learning and the quest for excellence is a sacred trust. The Christian should give himself contagiously to looking around him and to thinking, to the exploration of nature and to the transmission of cultural heritage, as well as to teaching Christian beliefs and values. The educator's task is to inspire and equip individuals to think and act for themselves in the dignity of men created in God's image. There is no room here for a dichotomy between what is secular and what is sacred, for everything about men created in God's image belongs to God – that is, it is sacred.[13]

In what he called the first and the greatest commandment, Jesus said, "Love the Lord your God with all your heart and with all your soul and with all your mind" (Matt 22:37). This commandment includes loving the Lord with our minds and has implication for our mission in Christian higher education. "To love God with our minds means that we think differently about the way we live and love, the way we worship and serve, the way we work to earn our livelihood, the way we learn and teach."[14]

Many passages in the Old Testament wisdom literature declare that the beginning of all wisdom, knowledge, and understanding is the fear of the Lord (Prov 1:7; 2:5; 9:10; Ps 111:10; Job 28:28). These passages teach that a reverence for God, the maker of heaven and earth, has to be our beginning point for all our inquiries, thinking, learning, and teaching.

Christian higher education, therefore, is more than providing education in different subject areas. It is providing Christ-centered education to men and women so that they develop their God-given potential to learn and interpret

---

13. Ibid., 23–24.
14. David S. Dockery, *Renewing Minds: Serving Church and Society through Christian Higher Education* (Nashville, TN: B&H, 2007), 11.

the world around them with reverence for God, from "the vantage point of God's revelation."[15]

What Makes Higher Education Distinctly Christian?

Are Christian liberal arts colleges necessary? Should not the church's focus be on education that is offered in churches, Bible colleges, or seminaries that are mainly established to train people for evangelism, church ministry, and missions? If churches disciple their members, equip them well to serve God and his people, and train them to engage their culture with the truth of the Word of God, why can't believers use the secular colleges and universities to get education in arts and sciences? These and similar questions need to be addressed to determine if the church needs to be involved in liberal arts education.

Several reasons are proposed for establishing Christian liberal arts colleges or Christian universities. Holmes, in his book *The Idea of a Christian College*, gives some of these reasons.[16]

The first reason given for the need for Christian higher-educational institutions is that these colleges protect young people from the influence of sin and heresy. Some consider Christian colleges as "defenders of the faith"[17] that provide a safe environment for students where they receive answers to the questions raised by the critics of their faith and Christian values. Though this view has some truth in it, not all education offered in the Christian liberal arts colleges is designed to protect students against sin and heresy. Describing one of the weaknesses of this argument Holmes says, "The trouble with it is that there often are no ready-made answers, new problems arise constantly, and the critics are perplexingly creative."[18] The other shortcoming of this argument is that Christian higher-educational institutes cannot provide a sin-

---

15. David S. Dockery, and David P. Gushee, eds., *The Future of Christian Higher Education* (Nashville, TN: B&H, 1999), 13.
16. Holmes, *Idea of a Christian College*, 14–16.
17. Manning M. Pattillo and Donald M. Mackenzie, eds., *Church-Sponsored Higher Education in the United States: Report of the Danforth Commission* (Washington DC: American Council on Education, 1966).
18. Holmes, *Idea of a Christian College*, 14.

proof environment to students because sin is not just a problem coming from outside; it is also a heart issue.[19]

The second reason given for the need for Christian liberal arts colleges is that they offer courses in Bible and Theology in addition to good education in liberal arts in a Christian environment.[20] Though this is another good purpose, this need can be met by offering courses in Bible and Theology in churches or seminaries that are close to secular universities students attend. Churches can also provide spiritual support for students. A truly Christian liberal arts education should not just offer what is basically a secular education with Bible and Theology courses on the side without properly integrating faith with all the subjects offered.[21]

The third reason given by some is that Christian colleges provide social and extracurricular benefits to students.[22] It is true that most Christian colleges are smaller than the big secular universities, and that difference allows students and faculty to build closer relationships and provides opportunities to serve one another. As important as this reason is, it is not adequate for establishing such colleges because these needs can be met in other ways.[23]

The fourth reason given for Christian higher education is that it helps the church to withstand the waves of secularism that are taking over our culture and our higher-educational institutions. In the West and in most other regions of the world, secularism is becoming a dominant force in higher-educational institutes. Though this is a very valid reason, the church's involvement in higher education does not necessarily guarantee that the church will become capable of withstanding the waves of secularism. We learn from history that even those institutions that were established by church groups were taken away by secularism. Harvard, Yale, Princeton, and Columbia in the United States[24] and Oxford, Cambridge, Durham, and King's College, London, in the UK are only

---

19. Ibid.
20. Ibid., 15.
21. Stephen V. Monsma, "Christian Worldview in Academia," *Faculty Dialogue* 21 (1994): 146.
22. Holmes, *Idea of a Christian College*, 16.
23. Ibid.
24. Ibid., 19.

a few examples of such institutions.[25] This chapter later discusses how some higher-educational institutions were able to withstand the effects of secularism.

All the reasons given above are good reasons for establishing Christian liberal arts colleges or universities. However, they are inadequate and are not comprehensive enough. Identifying the key factors that make higher education distinctly Christian is important to clearly define the purpose of Christian higher education.

Robert B. Sloan, Jr., addressing the question, "What is distinctively Christian higher education?," lists the six ways in which the notion of Christian higher education is employed.[26]

1. When people refer to Christian higher education, they are simply making reference to the history and tradition of the institution. That could be a reference to their founding documents, intention of the founders, or founding organizations.
2. Others use the expression "Christian institution" simply to refer to the composition of the members of the governing board that meet certain religious qualifications for membership.
3. It is also used as a frame of reference for Christian higher education to describe the relationship the institution has with a church or Christian denomination.
4. Others use the expression "Christian higher education" as a reference to "the *atmosphere* or the *environment* of the institution," referring to the way things are done or the values that the institution holds.
5. Another way of thinking of Christian higher-educational institutions is in terms of the "Christian or religious *activities*" of the institution. These activities include chapel services, annual conferences, seminars, or extracurricular activities that have a Christian emphasis.
6. The sixth way Christian higher education is understood has to do with the curriculum, reflected in subject areas connected to the institution's Christian identity or required courses in Bible and Theology.

---

25. P. Glanzer, "Searching for the Soul of English Universities: An Exploration and Analysis of Christian Higher Education in England," *British Journal of Educational Studies* 56, no. 2 (2008): 164.
26. Robert B. Sloan Jr., "Preserving Distinctively Christian Higher Education," in *The Future of Christian Higher Education*, ed. David S. Dockery and P. Gushee (Nashville, TN: B&H, 1999), 26–28.

Though the six frames of reference given above to describe Christian higher education are legitimate, they are not comprehensive enough to describe Christian higher education. There are additional factors that make Christian higher education distinct.

Curriculum That Integrates Faith and Learning

Describing how the notion of Christian higher education is broader than what is mentioned above, Sloan writes, "Christian education comes ultimately into every classroom. It involves our worldview; it involves how we think and how we live. It involves not only how we teach and how we live, but also it involves what we teach. It involves the very substance of our intellectual pursuits."[27]

Holmes[28] argues that the work of a Christian college is different from Christian involvement in higher education and it is different from giving Christian witness in conjunction with secular education. Explaining what makes a Christian college distinct from other liberal arts colleges and why we need a Christian college, Holmes writes,

> Its distinctive should be an education that cultivates the creative and active integration of faith and learning, of faith and culture. This is its unique task in higher education today. While the reality is often more like an interaction of faith and learning, a dialogue, than a completely ideal integration, it must under no circumstance become a disjunction between piety and scholarship, faith and reason, religion and science, Christianity and the arts, theology and philosophy, or whatever the differing points of reference may be.[29]

On a similar note, Monsma argues that a truly Christian university "is marked by courses and curricula which are rooted in and are permeated by a Christian worldview, rather than a secular worldview (often disguised as a supposedly neutral worldview)."[30]

---

27. Ibid., 30.
28. Holmes, *Idea of a Christian College.*
29. Ibid., 16.
30. Monsma, "Christian Worldview in Academia," 146.

Leadership Committed to a Christian Mission

A leadership that is committed to a Christian vision and mission plays a major role in making a higher-educational institution distinctly Christian. Mark Schwehn's description of what a Christian university leadership should look like is helpful. Schwehn says, "It must have a board of trustees composed of a substantial majority of Christian men and women, clergy and lay, whose primary task is to attend to the Christian character of the institution. They will do this primarily but not exclusively by appointing to the major leadership positions persons who are actively committed to the ideal of a Christian university."[31]

Schwehn then lists the kinds of things the leadership needs to make sure are present in the institution.

1. A Department of Theology that offers courses in Biblical Studies and Christian Intellectual Tradition;
2. An active chapel ministry that offers worship service in the tradition of the faith community that supports the school but that also makes provision for worship by those of other faiths;
3. A critical mass of faculty members who in addition to being excellent teacher-scholars carry in themselves the DNA of the school, for the perpetuation of its mission as a Christian community of inquiry;
4. A curriculum that includes a large number of courses, required for all students, that are compelling as parts of a larger whole that constitutes a liberal education.[32]

The board of trustees and the senior leadership of a Christian higher-educational institution also play a crucial role in helping the institution to maintain a strong relationship with the founding or sponsoring church and its religious heritage.[33]

Old and Sponsoring Churches

The other vital element in Christian higher-educational institutes is their relationship with the founding or sponsoring churches. Merrimon Cuninggim,

---

31. M. R. Schwehn, "A Christian University," *First Things* (May 1999): 26.
32. Ibid., 26–27.
33. J. Arthur, "Faith and Secularization in Religious Colleges and Universities," *Journal of Belief and Values* 29, no. 2 (2008): 200.

in his book *Uneasy Partners: The College and the Church*, describes the shift that has taken place in the relationship between colleges and their founding churches in the United States in the twentieth century.[34] The first form of relationship between the colleges and the churches that arrived by the end of the nineteen century was that the church was the senior partner, and the college the junior. The second form of relationship, common between the 1930s to sometime in the 1960s, can be described as roughly even, neither having the upper hand over the other. The third form of relationship that exists to this day is that the colleges are in the primary position while the churches play the junior role.[35]

Summarizing the current relationship between church-related colleges and churches, Cuninggim says, "The overwhelming majority of the church-related colleges are still in genuine touch with their long-time founding churches, but for the last twenty-five years or so they have come to be the primary entity of academic decision-making for themselves, with the churches thereby relegated to playing, often unhappily, only a secondary role."[36] Most of these institutions, according to Cuninggim, openly state their church connections but they work as autonomous educational institutions and they rejoice in that fact.[37]

The relationship between the academic institutions and the founding or sponsoring churches can also be seen in how the academic institutions hold on to the religious heritage of the founding churches. Some of them have a nominal relationship with their founding churches and can no longer be considered Christian, while others maintain strong relationships and hold on to the religious heritage of the founding churches. O'Conell, describing what kind of influence the church should have on these institutions, says,

> The expression "religious colleges" refers to those institutions of higher learning where the religion of the founding or sponsoring religious group has some direct influence upon the institution itself. By "direct" I mean real, observable, clear, and effective, with an active connection between a particular religion and a particular

---

34. M. Cuninggim, *Uneasy Partners: The College and the Church* (Nashville, TN: Abingdon, 1994), 33.
35. Ibid.
36. Ibid., 38–39.
37. Ibid., 39.

academic institution. It is not a "religious college" simply because its origins were religious, or its founders were clergymen or other religious women or men, or because the campus is peppered with religious symbols and works of art, or because there is a chapel. The direct influence to which I refer can be seen in terms of institutional identity, mission, governance, administration, criteria for faculty hiring, curricula, student life, campus ministries, policies, operations and procedures, and so forth.[38]

Though Christian higher-educational institutions relate differently to their founding or sponsoring churches, their main purpose has to be serving churches. Discussing the relationship of Christian higher-educational institutions with churches, Dockery says,

We also need fresh thinking about the relationship of Christian higher education to the church, for it is central to God's working in history. The church is not only central to history but to the gospel and Christian living as well. Thus, theology is more than God's words for us, the community of faith. It is vitally important that we understand theology not merely in individualistic terms. We need to move to a corporate and community understanding of these ideas. For these reasons the early years of Christian higher education placed their focus first in terms of service for the churches and then more broadly for society.[39]

Different authors have tried to categorize institutions by the way they relate to their founding or sponsoring churches or religious groups. A report by Danforth Commission, *Church-Sponsored Higher Education in the United States*,[40] categorizes higher-educational institutions that are associated with religious bodies in the United States into four categories. The report categorizes institutions based on their "purpose, clientele, faculty, educational program, financial support, treatment of religion, and church affiliation."[41] The four

---

38. David O'Conell, "Staying the Course: Imperative and Influence within the Religious College," in *The Future of Religious Colleges: The Proceedings of the Harvard Conference on the Future of Religious Colleges*, ed. Paul John Dovre (Grand Rapids, MI: Eerdmans, 2002), 63–64.
39. Dockery, *Renewing Minds*, 175.
40. Pattillo and Mackenzie, eds., *Church-Sponsored Higher Education in the United States*.
41. Ibid., 196.

categories of church-related institutions, according to the report, are (1) "the defender of the faith college," (2) "the non-affirming college," (3) "the free Christian college," and (4) "the church-related university."[42] The report indicates that these categories do not cover all possibilities and some institutions may fall into more than one category.

Those that are described as a "defender of the faith college" are those institutions whose main purpose is providing education in arts and sciences for people who will later take lay or clerical leadership positions in a particular religious tradition. These institutions recruit exclusively from their sponsoring groups students and faculty "who will be staunchly loyal" to their tradition and go out to "defend and advance a clearly defined religious position in a secular society."[43]

The second institutional pattern, the "non-affirming college," refers to church-related higher-educational institutions that give relatively little attention to religion. They admit students and appoint faculty without giving consideration to their religious interest or faith. Although their publications may mention their church affiliation, their purpose or mission statements omit any reference to religious or spiritual values.[44]

The third institutional pattern is called the "free Christian college." This type of college is considered "free" because it does not tell its students what they must believe. However, it has a definite Christian commitment that is reflected in its focus on chapel, its strong department of religion that offers courses in religion, and the attention it gives to integrating faith with learning. The majority of the faculty members share the religious purposes of the institution and some of them hold positions of leadership in the sponsoring church. Prospective students are attracted to such institutions because of their dual emphasis on academic excellence and religious vitality. These institutions also have a close association with their sponsoring churches, and the churches make a substantial financial contribution to the institutions.[45]

The fourth pattern is the "church-related university." The institutions that belong to this category are large urban-based institutions with student

---

42. Ibid., 191–196.
43. Ibid., 192.
44. Ibid.
45. Ibid., 196.

enrollment between 5,000 and 20,000 and that provide programs in many professional and occupational fields. With regard to religion, they are pluralistic and they do not have religious requirements that apply to all students. They have a tenuous relationship with their sponsoring churches.[46]

Robert Benne, in his book *Quality with Soul*, proposes four categories of church-related colleges. They are *orthodox, critical mass, intentionally pluralist*, and *accidentally pluralist*.[47] Benne describes these categories using eight aspects of the institution's life: (1) public relevance of Christian vision; (2) public rhetoric; (3) membership requirements; (4) religion/theology department; religion/theology required courses; (5) chapel; (6) ethos; (7) support by church; and (8) governance.[48] Table 1 shows Benne's types of church-related colleges.

Table 1: Types of Church-Related Colleges

Major divide	Orthodox	Critical mass	Intentionally pluralist	Accidentally pluralist
	The Christian vision as the organizing paradigm	versus	Secular sources as the organizing paradigm	
Public relevance of Christian vision	Pervasive from a shared point of view	Privileged voice in an ongoing conversation	Assured voice in an ongoing conversation	Random or absent in an ongoing conversation
Public rhetoric	Unabashed invitation for fellow believers to an intentionally Christian enterprise	Straightforward presentation as a Christian school but inclusive of others	Presentation as a liberal arts school with a Christian heritage	Presentation as a secular school with little or no allusion to Christian heritage
Membership requirements	Near 100%, with orthodoxy tests	Critical mass in all facets	Intentional representation	Haphazard sprinkling

---

46. Ibid.
47. Benne, *Quality with Soul*, 49.
48. Ibid.

Religion/theology department	Large, with theology privileged	Large, with theology as flagship		Small, exclusively religious studies
Religion/theology required courses	All courses affected by shared religious perspective	Two or three, with dialogical effort in many other courses	One course in general education	Choice in distribution or an elective
Chapel	Required in large church at a protected time daily	Voluntary at high-quality services in large church at protected time daily	Voluntary at unprotected times, with low attendance	For a few, on special occasions
			(Dominant secular atmosphere)	
Ethos	Overt piety of sponsoring tradition	Dominant atmosphere of sponsoring tradition – rituals and habits	Open majority from sponsoring tradition finding private niche	Reclusive and unorganized minority from sponsoring tradition
Support by church	Indispensable financial support and majority of students from sponsoring tradition	Important direct and crucial indirect financial support; at least 50% of students	Important focused, indirect support; small minority of students	Token indirect support; student numbers no longer recorded
Governance	Owned and governed by church or its official representative	Majority of board from tradition, some official representatives	Minority of board from tradition by unofficial agreement	Token membership from tradition
		(College or university is autonomously owned and governed)		

Litfin suggests two categories of church-affiliated academic institutions, namely, the umbrella model and the systemic model, focusing only on those that can be called truly Christian higher-educational institutions.[49] In the umbrella model, though a variety of voices can thrive under the Christian "umbrella," the voice of the sponsoring Christian tradition that is represented by the "critical mass" remains a privileged one. Those with different voices are at least expected to "support the broad educational mission of the school."[50] Describing this model further, Litfin says, "In such institutions the sponsoring perspective will typically be kept more or less discernable. It may show itself in such things as the school's architecture, traditions, curriculum, and extracurricular activities, as well as in the makeup of its governing board, faculty, and student body."[51]

The second model Litfin talks about is the systemic model. Describing this model, Litfin writes, "As the name suggests, they seek to make Christian thinking systemic throughout the institution, root, branch, and leaf. Their curriculum is typically all-encompassing. Their goal is to engage any and all ideas from every perspective, but they attempt to do so from a particular intellectual location, that of the sponsoring Christian tradition."[52] These institutions recruit their faculty exclusively from those who embody their own tradition. "What is true of the critical mass in the Umbrella model is to be true of all of the scholars in the Systemic model. They seek to live and work as Christians."[53] Litfin's umbrella model and systemic model roughly correspond to Benne's *critical mass* and *orthodox* categories respectively.

Though both the umbrella model and the systemic model are acceptable models for Christian higher-educational institutions, institutions that follow the umbrella model may face serious challenges as they try to be more open to students and employees from different backgrounds. Describing how this has eventually led toward secularization for some schools, Benne says,

> One of the most obvious characteristics of the colleges and universities that have moved toward pervasive secularization is their flight from what they called a "sectarian" identity and approach. Their fateful move toward openness in personnel,

---

49. Litfin, *Conceiving the Christian College*, 14.
50. Ibid., 14–15.
51. Ibid., 15.
52. Ibid., 18.
53. Ibid.

vision, and ethos was prompted by, among other things, a felt need to expand their appeal to many sorts of students. While some of the colleges began with large majorities from their own traditions, they in time noticed that they had competition for those students from many sources, not least of which were the public institutions of higher education. Many also decided that students from their own traditions alone could not long make for a valuable enterprise in a competitive environment, so they opened themselves to all comers. Something similar could be said for the failure to recruit administrators and faculty of the sponsoring tradition, though that would have seemed a more feasible task.[54]

This comment shows that the board and administration of Christian higher-educational institutions should be very careful in making policies regarding faculty hiring and student recruitment in order to avoid these pitfalls and to stay focused on their Christian mission.

Clearly Stated Christian Mission

Another vital element in a Christian higher-educational institute is its mission statement. Anthony Diekema, a former president of Calvin College, says that Christian colleges should give "constant attention to institutional mission and its extensive articulation."[55] The mission of the college must permeate everything done in the college in a way that gives "internal consistency to teaching, scholarship, student life, administration, community relations."[56]

Christian higher-educational institutions that deliberately avoid mentioning their religious identity or vaguely define their Christian mission in their mission statements in order to become acceptable to the secular public may find themselves on the slippery path that led many institutions to generic Christianity and eventually to total secularization.[57] Arthur argues, "This process, when it goes unchecked, results in a loss of the institution's raison

---

54. Benne, *Quality with Soul*, 20.
55. Anthony Diekema, *Academic Freedom and Christian Scholarship* (Grand Rapids, MI: Eerdmans, 2000), 57.
56. Ibid.
57. Arthur, "Faith and Secularization in Religious Colleges and Universities."

d'être and renders it almost impossible to identify, or determine, what it means to be a religiously affiliated college or university."[58]

It is possible that the mission statement of higher-educational institutions may not always reflect the true identity of the institution and its role in higher education. Arthur writes, "To take any college's or university's claim for mission at face value would be both naïve and simplistic. The mission has to be evidenced in the decision-making and policies of an institution, in particular in the actions and commitment of senior management. Any religiously affiliated institution can sever its connections or freely choose to move towards a stronger identification and connection with the religious heritage of its sponsoring religious tradition."[59]

Therefore, a truly Christian higher-educational institution is distinguished not only by a mission statement that clearly articulates the Christian worldview, but also by implementing it "throughout the curriculum, and by faculty whose scholarship is anchored in that same worldview."[60]

Committed Christian Faculty

Next to the leadership of the institution, the faculty plays a key role in making a college a Christian college. A truly Christian college needs faculty members who are committed Christians who faithfully implement the mission of the school in their teaching and research roles. Faculty members in a Christian liberal arts college or university have the privilege and the responsibility of passing on the Christian intellectual traditions that integrate faith and learning in all the subjects they teach.[61]

Hiring faculty members who do not share the faith of the founding organization would seriously affect the institution's attempt to bring religious perspectives into all the subjects taught. Faculty members who do not share the faith of the Christian higher-educational institution they work for would "see every effort to connect with the sponsoring religious heritage as a coercive and repressive move."[62]

---

58. Ibid., 201.
59. Ibid., 200.
60. Diekema, *Academic Freedom and Christian Scholarship*, 57.
61. Dockery, *Renewing Minds*, 101.
62. Benne, *Quality with Soul*, 29.

A Strong and Central Faculty of Theology

Another distinctive factor of a Christian higher-educational institutions is the role that the department of theology plays in the overall program. Benne argues that theology enables Christian higher-educational institutions to articulate their faith, identity, and mission, and to "stipulate the relation of revelation and reason in their particular tradition."[63] Sullivan also argues, "Many Christian universities in practice give far too little support to the position and healthy functioning of theology, thereby undercutting the capacity of the institution to articulate its identity and to communicate intelligently its raison d'être."[64]

Theology departments that are alive and central to the whole curriculum help Christian liberal arts colleges or universities to stay focused on their core missions. Board of trustee members, administrators, faculty, staff, and students need to learn to think theologically. Dockery, describing the need to develop a theology for Christian higher education, says, "Since one of the goals of Christian higher education is to help students live in the world with a lifestyle that issues in glory to God, then we must think – and think deeply – not only of personal ethics but the implications of the biblical faith for social, economic, and political ethics as well. Such necessities touch the heart of the life and mission of Christian higher education."[65]

The Department of Theology plays a key role in creating interconnectedness and interdisciplinary dialogue among the different disciplines within a Christian university.[66] Theologians who fail to engage in such a dialogue fail to influence the culture of their academic environment and "relinquish [the] right to pose the central questions, redefine limits, set priorities, or offer alternative answers to society's questions of ultimate concern."[67] Emphasizing how theologians can play this key role, Tanner writes, "One cannot be a constructive theologian for the present day without familiarity with the currency of the other intellectual or cultural fields of the day, and it is through the assessment of how other

---

63. Ibid., 15.
64. John Sullivan, "Connection without Control: Theology and Interconnectedness in the University." *Christian Higher Education* 6, no. 2 (2007): 154.
65. Dockery, *Renewing Minds*, 172.
66. Sullivan, "Connection without Control," 150.
67. J. E. Hull, "Aiming for Christian Education, Settling for Christian Educating: The Christian School's Replication of a Public School Paradigm," *Christian Scholars Review* 13 (Winter 2002): 216.

theologians of the past and present have dealt with comparable material of their own times and places that one develops a sense for what needs to be done now."[68]

The Department of Bible and Theology also plays a key role in offering courses in biblical studies and Christian intellectual tradition that are required of students of all programs in the institution. Faculty members in the Bible and Theology Department can provide biblical and theological insights on different issues to fellow faculty members and students. Tanner argues that theologians can help their academic institutions focus on the most pressing problems and challenges of contemporary life.[69]

A Christian university or liberal arts college with a strong theology department helps its faculty and students to discern "how the Gospel impinges upon all humanistic and scientific questions," such as "what constitutes the human person, the quality of the good life, the purpose of social existence, the nature of the physical universe, the structure of political and social order."[70]

The Role and Purpose of Christian Higher Education

The discussion above showed the factors that make Christian higher education distinctly Christian. The next section looks closely at the key factors that define the purpose of Christian higher education.

Integration of Faith and Learning

One of the key roles higher-educational institutions play is helping the Christian community to integrate faith and learning. Explaining the importance to the church of integrating faith and learning, Litfin writes,

> The Church's inability or unwillingness to work at bringing faith and learning together meant that it ceased to think Christianly about all the realms of life, which in turn meant that in those realms it ceased to matter . . . To refuse the challenge to think

---

68. K. Tanner, "Theology and Cultural Contest in the University," in *Religious Studies, Theology, and the University*, ed. L. E. Cady and D. Brown (New York: State University of New York Press, 2002), 210.
69. Ibid., 206.
70. R. Wood, *Contending for the Faith* (Waco, TX: Baylor University Press, 2003), 120.

Christianly about every dimension of life, to allow the realms of faith and learning to remain sealed off from one another, is to cease to think, and thus to cease having any contribution to make.[71]

Higher-educational institutions, therefore, have the responsibility of helping the Christian community by integrating faith and learning.

Ken Badley, in his article "The Faith/Learning Integration Movement in Christian Higher Education: Slogan or Substance?", indicates that integration of faith and learning has been a favorite topic of discussion among Christian scholars.[72] Giving the typical definition of curricular integration seen in the literature, Badley says, "Curricular integration is the organization of teaching material to interrelate or unify subjects usually taught as separate academic courses or departments."[73] He presents a summary of the literature on integrating faith and learning, and identifies five paradigms of integration in the literature. He calls them *fusion integration, incorporation integration, correlation integration, dialogical integration,* and *perspectival integration.*[74]

Fusion integration refers to integration of two elements in which the elements retain some of their original characteristics. *Incorporation integration* occurs when one of the elements infiltrates the other and becomes its subset. In *correlation integration,* "someone, usually a teacher, shows the relationship between two subjects by noting points of intersection or common interest."[75] *Dialogical integration* refers to a "sufficiently high and continuous degree of correlation that we can properly claim a conversation had begun between two areas."[76] The paradigm that Badley supports is *perspectival integration,* in which "a worldview supplies the coherence, in the sense that disparate and even conflicting elements cohere as they fit into a larger framework of thought and practice."[77] According to this paradigm, the academic institution's desire

---

71. Litfin, *Conceiving the Christian College*, 145.
72. Ken Badley, "The Faith/Learning Integration Movement in Christian Higher Education: Slogan or Substance?", *Journal of Research on Christian Education* 3, no. 1 (1994): 13.
73. Ibid., 26.
74. Ibid., 24.
75. Ibid.
76. Ibid.
77. Ibid., 25.

for each student is to develop a uniformly Christian worldview which relates that perspective to all the disciplines of the curriculum.[78]

Hamilton and Mathisen also discuss four different views on how Christian higher education should integrate faith and learning.[79] The first model is called the *convergence model*. This model assumes that evangelical Christianity and higher learning lead to the same conclusion, and they do not need reconciliation. Knowledge discovered through natural means and knowledge that is revealed by God are complete in themselves and confirm each other.[80]

The second model is the *triumphalist model*. This model argues that the existing intellectual culture is flawed by its underlying secular assumptions and it ultimately leads to self-destruction.[81] However, the Christian faith will endure and triumph over learning because it is true. According to this model, religious ways of knowing are always superior to secular ways of knowing.[82]

The third model, the *value-added model*, assumes that faith and learning are not in conflict with each other nor change each other in fundamental ways because they occupy different spheres.[83] Faith supplements learning by bringing an ethical dimension, "an appreciation for the transcendent, and answers to the questions of meaning," while "learning can enrich faith – helping one to understand how God and his creatures have responded to each other in the past, filling in the details of God's creative handiwork, and so forth."[84]

The fourth model is the *integration model*. This model starts with the assumption that all academic inquiry begins with a set of assumptions that are rooted in the student's worldview, and Christian scholarship should begin with a Christian worldview and presuppositions.[85] Academic inquiries that are based on secular worldviews lead to distorted outcomes. This model also argues that discovered knowledge and revealed knowledge are incomplete by

---

78. Ibid., 28.
79. Michael S. Hamilton and James A. Mathisen, "Faith and Learning at Wheaton College," in *Models for Christian Higher Education: Strategies for Success in the Twenty-First Century*, ed. Richard T. Hughes and William B. Adrian (Grand Rapids, MI: Eerdmans, 1997).
80. Ibid., 268.
81. Ibid.
82. Ibid., 269.
83. Ibid., 270.
84. Ibid.
85. Hamilton and Mathisen, "Faith and Learning at Wheaton College."

themselves and they are both needed for full understanding. The integration model is similar to Badley's perspectival integration paradigm.

Knight argues that proper integration of faith and learning starts by acknowledging that the Bible is the prime source of knowledge and the indispensable epistemological authority, and that all other sources of knowledge should be tested and verified in the light of the teachings of the Bible.[86] True integration of faith and learning also acknowledges that there is unity in true knowledge because all true knowledge comes from the Creator who created it all.

Litfin argues that the slogan "All truth is God's truth" that is commonly used in Christian higher-educational circles encapsulates a set of convictions that are crucial to the task of Christian higher education. He gives ten important implications embedded in this phrase:

1. God exists.

2. Through the agency of his son, God created the universe and all that is in it.

3. We can therefore entertain an intellectual construct called "reality."

4. This reality is complex and multi-dimensional.

5. This reality, though complex and multi-dimensional, is also coherent and unified, centered upon the person of Jesus Christ.

6. God has created humans with the capacity to apprehend, however fallibly and incompletely, this reality.

7. Genuine knowledge is therefore feasible for humans.

8. Human knowledge of reality stems from two prime sources: special revelation and discovery.

9. We can therefore maintain a distinction between faith and error.

---

86. Knight, *Philosophy and Education*, 179.

10. All that is truthful, from whatever source, is unified, and will cohere with whatever else is truthful.[87]

Explaining what integration of faith and learning entails, Holmes writes, "Integration also transcends awkward *conjunctions* of faith and learning in some unholy alliance rather than a fruitful union. What we need is not Christians who are also scholars but Christian scholars, not Christianity alongside education but Christian education."[88]

Integration of faith and learning requires hard work. It requires a thorough understanding of methods, materials, concepts, and theoretical structures in order not to make superficial and unsatisfactory integrations.[89] This must be a major engagement of Christian higher-educational institutions, and they must do it with a strong commitment to their faith. Faculty members in Christian higher-educational institutions have the major responsibility of integrating faith and learning by developing a uniformly Christian worldview in students, one which relates all subjects they teach with that perspective.

Developing a Christian Worldview in Students

Another important purpose of Christian higher education is helping students to develop a Christian worldview. J. Mark Bertrand, in his book *(Re)Thinking Worldview*, defines "worldview" as "an interpretation of influences, experiences, circumstance and insight. In fact, it is an interrelated series of interpretations – and it becomes a method of interpreting, too."[90] Knight says, "One doesn't have to be especially brilliant to realize that the biblical worldview and the predominant mentality of the larger culture are often at odds, or that there are different religious and even different Christian worldviews."[91]

Since one's worldview is how one interprets and understands reality, it is very important that Christians have a worldview that is biblically and theologically sound. Dockery explains the significance of developing a Christian worldview:

---

87. Litfin, *Conceiving the Christian College*, 86–95.
88. Holmes, *Idea of a Christian College*, 17.
89. Ibid., 17.
90. J. Mark Bertrand, *(Re)Thinking Worldview: Learning to Think, Live, and Speak in This World* (Wheaton, IL: Crossway, 2007), 26.
91. Knight, *Philosophy and Education*, 234.

> Christians everywhere recognize that there is a great spiritual battle raging for the hearts and minds of men and women around the globe. We now find ourselves in a cosmic struggle between a morally indifferent culture and Christian truth. Thus we need to shape a Christian worldview and life view that will help us learn to think Christianly and live out the truth of Christian faith.[92]

Therefore, Christian higher-educational institutions have the responsibility of providing education that integrates faith and shapes a Christian worldview in their students. Graduates who have developed a Christian worldview and are well equipped with the truth can go out and challenge secular worldviews and be witnesses of Christ in the secular world.

Helping the Church to Withstand the Waves of Secularism

Christian higher-educational institutions also play a key role in helping the church to withstand the waves of secularism. As mentioned above, secularism is a growing threat for churches as well as for Christian higher-educational institutions. Describing the challenge evangelicals are facing and suggesting a possible solution, Nathan O. Hatch says,

> In recent years, evangelicals have come to raise the alarm about the pervasive secularism of modern intellectual life and its repercussions in legislation, ethics, and jurisprudence; yet they have done almost nothing to address the root of the problem. The battle for the mind cannot be waged by mobilizing in the streets or on Capitol Hill, nor by denouncing more furiously the secular humanists. If we are to help preserve even the possibility of Christian thinking for our children and grandchildren, we must begin to nurture first-order Christian scholarship. This means, of course, freeing Christian scholars to undertake what is a painstakingly slow and arduous task, one that has almost no immediate return on investment. The support of Christian scholars is a selfless enterprise indeed, because it is investing

---

92. Dockery, *Renewing Minds*, 50.

current resources to ensure that we do not mortgage the future intellectually for the next generation.[93]

As Hatch argues, Christian higher-educational institutes need to work towards developing and maintaining Christian scholars who shape the intellectual life of evangelical believers. This war waged for the mind can be won only by the truth that is based on God's Word. Paul says,

> For though we live in the world, we do not wage war as the world does. The weapons we fight with are not the weapons of the world. On the contrary, they have divine power to demolish strongholds. We demolish arguments and every pretension that sets itself up against the knowledge of God, and we take captive every thought to make it obedient to Christ. (2 Cor 10:3–5)

Spiritual Formation of Students

What has been emphasized so far is the role Christian higher-educational institutions play in the development of the intellectual aspect of the faith of their students, yet equally important is the role these institutions play in the character (spiritual) formation of their students. Developing a Christian worldview and getting an education that integrates faith and learning has to lead to a changed life that honors the Lord. Classes, chapel services, and other extracurricular activities should all be designed in such a way that they contribute to the spiritual development of students.

Faculty and staff members play a key role in the spiritual development of students. Christian higher-educational institutions need faculty and staff members who think and live as Christians in order to create a community that encourages spiritual development in students. Pressnell writes, "The future of Christian higher education starts in the hearts of those who fill the faculty and staff ranks of our campuses. The potential of our scholarship and our institutions will only be fulfilled if the inner life is sufficiently transformed. Much of our heritage as evangelicals is a tapestry of intellectualism and inward

---

93. Nathan O. Hatch, "Evangelical Colleges and the Challenge of Christian Thinking," in *Making Higher Education Christian: The History and Mission of Evangelical Colleges in America*, ed. Joel A. Carpenter and Kenneth W. Shipps (St. Paul, MN: Christian University Press, 1987), 158.

experience. The challenge before us is to strive actively for the wisdom that is found in practicing the presence of Christ in our scholarship."[94]

Therefore, the role of faculty members in Christian higher-educational institutions is more than just teaching, doing research, or investing in the lives of students – but also building a Christ-centered community.[95] It is in a Christian community that spiritual development occurs. "A Christian university is not a church, yet it is a faith-informed, faith-affirming, and grace-filled community – a distinctive community."[96]

Preparing Students for a Life of Service

As academic institutions that train students, one of the main goals of Christian higher-educational institutions is preparing students for a life of service to the church and society. These institutions need to prepare students in such a way that they become well-equipped servants in the marketplace and agents of change in the world around them.

Gordon Smith,[97] in his research on spiritual formation in Christian higher-educational institutions, shows how spiritual formation of students relates to their preparation for service.

> Spiritual formation happens when there are activities designed for specific ends in the formation of character that complement the formal academic program. Spiritual formation within the academic setting is most effective when the classroom is both affirmed and complemented, and where vital elements of the spiritual life are nurtured, taught, and encouraged in settings other than the classroom. There is nothing quite like service to test the inner person and potentially inform not only our spiritual

---

94. Claude O. Pressnell, Jr, "The Spiritual Life of the Christian Scholar: Practicing the Presence of Christ," in *The Future of Christian Higher Education*, ed. David S. Dockery and David P. Gushee (Nashville, TN: Broadman & Holman, 1999), 134–135.
95. Dockery, *Renewing Minds*, 128.
96. Ibid., 141.
97. G. T. Smith, "Spiritual Formation in the Academy: A Unifying Model," *Faculty Dialogue*, 26 (1996); www.iclnet.org/pub/facdialogue; accessed 20 November 2010.

growth but also the classroom. There is a strong awareness of the interconnection of field experience with classroom reflection.[98]

Preparing students to become active and engaged members of society is a major part of the mission of Christian higher-educational institutions.[99] Holmes writes, "The Christian college embodies a strategy for Christian involvement in the life of the mind and the life of a culture."[100]

Therefore, the purpose and mission of Christian higher-educational institutions should include integrating faith and learning, shaping a Christian worldview and Christian character in students, and equipping them to serve the church and society. Describing what Christian higher education involves, Dockery says, "The mission of Christian higher education involves providing Christ-centered higher education that promotes excellence and character development in service to church and society."[101]

Threats of Secularization

As mentioned in the first chapter, many of the higher-educational institutes in the West were founded by church denominations. These educational institutions were first established by churches with the purpose of propagating faith and morality in addition to educating people in different areas of study.

However, many higher-educational institutions that were started by churches have through the years lost their evangelical distinctiveness, while fewer institutions have kept their evangelical identity. Burtchaell,[102] in his book *The Dying of the Light: The Disengagement of Colleges and Universities*, investigates those colleges in the United States that began as denominational colleges but are now secular colleges. There are similar stories of higher-educational institutes in England. As mentioned in chapter 1, until the 1990s England had four universities considered Christian: Oxford, Cambridge,

---

98. Ibid., 3.
99. Benne, *Quality with Soul*.
100. Holmes, *Idea of a Christian College*, 116.
101. Dockery, *Renewing Minds*, 31.
102. James T. Burtchaell, *The Dying of the Light: The Disengagement of Colleges and Universities from their Christian Churches* (Grand Rapids, MI: Eerdmans, 1998).

Durham, and King's College, London.[103] Bebbington[104] and D' Costa[105] discuss in their books how these English universities were secularized.

Ringenberg, explaining the gradual move to secularism of higher-educational institutions in the US, writes, "Very few, if any, institutions have moved quickly from being predominantly Christian to being predominately secular. Almost invariably they have gone through an intermediate step in which they seek to promote religious values in general without giving specific preference to the Christian religion."[106] Ringenberg then lists seven marks that indicate a move to secularization in those institutions. These marks are:

> 1. The public statements about the Christian nature of the institution begin to include equivocal rather than explicit phrases; these statements often describe Christian goals in sociological but not theological terms.

> 2. The faculty hiring policy begins to place a reduced emphasis upon the importance of the scholar being a committed Christian, and subsequently fewer professors seek to relate their academic disciplines to the Christian faith.

> 3. The importance of the Bible and the Christian religion in the general education curriculum declines.

> 4. The previously strong official institutional support given to religious activities in general and the chapel service in particular decline.

> 5. The institution begins to reduce and then perhaps drop its church affiliation or, if it be an independent institution, it tends to reduce its interest in identifying with interdenominational and parachurch organizations.

---

103. Glanzer, "Searching for the Soul of English Universities," 164.

104. D. Bebbington, "The Secularization of British Universities since the Mid-Nineteenth Century," in *The Secularization of the Academy*, ed. G. Marsden and B. J. Longfield (New York: Oxford University Press, 1992).

105. G. D'Costa, *Theology in the Public Square: Church, Academy, and Nation* (Malden, MA: Blackwell, 2005).

106. William C. Ringenberg, *The Christian College: A History of Protestant Higher Education in America*, 2nd ed. (Grand Rapids, MI: Baker, 2006), 120.

6. Budget decisions begin to reflect a reduced emphasis upon the essential nature of Christian programs.

7. An increasing number of students and faculty members join the college community in spite of rather than because of the remaining Christian influences, and the deeply committed Christians begin to feel lonely.[107]

Ringenberg's marks of secularization listed above are very helpful in identifying key areas to look for to find out if a Christian higher-educational institution is moving towards secularization. The key areas include changes in the mission statement, faculty hiring policy, the place of Bible and Theology courses in the overall curriculum, and the relationship of the institution with the founding or sponsoring churches.

Is secularization a threat for Christian higher-educational institutions in Africa, especially in Eastern Africa? How can these institutions prevent a drift from their core evangelical mission? These are the questions that this research attempts to address and they are discussed later. The next section gives an overview of higher education in Africa, especially Christian higher education.

Higher Education in Africa

Gary and Hayward indicate that higher education has undergone a rapid transformation throughout the world in the last quarter of a century. These forces of change are "the expansion of higher education and the push for greater access, the problems of declining resources and the challenge of diversifying funding sources, the expectation that higher education will make a greater contribution to economic and social development, the pressures to be accountable to an increasingly skeptical and demanding public, the conflicts surrounding institutional autonomy, the growth of technology and the drive for internalization."[108] In addition to these challenges, higher-educational

---

107. Ibid., 120–121.
108. Madeleine F. Green and Fred M. Hayward, "Forces For Change," in *Transforming Higher Education: Views from Leaders around the World,* ed. Madeleine F. Green (Phoenix, AZ: American Council on Education/Oryx Press, 1997), 3.

institutions in Africa face political unrest, war, lack of freedom, and the interference of the government.[109]

The governments in most African countries keep a tight control of the public universities and crack down on any that are critical of the government. The leadership positions in these institutions are highly politicized and are usually given to those who are loyal to the government.[110] Those who seek to promote academic and institutional freedom face serious challenges and may be forced to resign.[111] This political unrest affects everything that occurs within these institutions. The private institutions also face most of these problems.

Lack of financial resources and well-qualified faculty members are the other challenges higher institutions in Africa face. Well-educated people in these countries leave their home countries because of the lack of freedom they experience in their academic work and in the search for a better life in the West.[112] That greatly affects the quality of education in these higher-educational institutions.

Explaining the challenge of demand and expectations, Hayward says, "Part of the crisis in African higher education grows out of the rapid expansion of postsecondary education – an expansion that continued after the economies began to decline. Growth in the number and size of tertiary institutions was fueled by government expectation that university education would provide the base for national economic development and the public's expectation that a university degree would guarantee economic and social success for their children."[113]

Talking about the role higher education plays on the continent of Africa, former United Nations Secretary General Kofi Annan said, "I believe the university must become a primary tool for Africa's development in the new century. Universities can help develop African expertise; they can enhance the analysis of African problems; strengthen domestic institutions; serve as a model environment for the practice of good governance, conflict resolution

---

109. Fred M. Hayward, "Higher Education in Africa: Crisis and Transformation," in *Transforming Higher Education: Views from Leaders around the World*, ed. Madeleine F. Green (Phoenix, AZ: American Council on Education/Oryx Press, 1997), 87–88.
110. D. Teferra and P. G. Altbach, "African Higher Education: Challenges for the 21st Century," *Higher Education* 47, no. 1 (2004): 21–50.
111. Ibid.
112. Ibid.
113. Hayward, "Higher Education in Africa: Crisis and Transformation," 89.

and respect for human rights; and enable African academics to play an active part in the global community of scholars."[114]

As mentioned in chapter 1, Africa, especially the region called sub-Saharan Africa, has the lowest enrollment of higher-educational institutions. The countries on which this study focuses, Ethiopia, Kenya, Uganda, and Democratic Republic of Congo (DRC), are part of sub-Saharan Africa (SSA). This region has one of the lowest gross enrollment ratios (GERs) in tertiary education. "In 2000, the GER in higher education in SSA was only 3.5 percent ... A majority of the African countries in 2000 have an enrollment ratio of less than 5 percent. More importantly, the distance between African countries and countries in other regions has widened due to the slow progress made in this region."[115] Figure 1 shows how enrollment of higher-educational institutions in sub-Saharan Africa compares with that in other regions.[116]

Taking Ethiopia as an example, in 2004, out of the total population of 73,000,000, only 77,727 were enrolled in any variety of higher-educational institution.[117] That means only 0.001064 percent, or 1 in every 939 Ethiopians, attended college. Statistics also show that the proportion of people who graduated from some form of higher-level educational program was 1 in 3,181.[118]

Recent development in these countries has helped the expansion of elementary- and secondary-school education. The expansion of secondary-school education in Africa has increased the number of students who desire to go on to higher education. Since the public universities are not in a position to meet the growing demand, governments have privatized some of the public universities and opened the door for starting privately owned higher-educational institutions.[119]

---

114. United Nations, "Information Technology Should Be Used to Tap Knowledge from Greatest Universities to Bring Learning to All, Kofi Annan Says," United Nations Press Release SG/SM/7502 AFR/259, 2 August 2000; http://www.un.org/press/en/2000/20000802.sgsm7502.doc.html; Accessed 5 October 2009.

115. N. V. Varghese, *New Trends in Higher Education: Growth and Expansion of Private Higher Education in Africa* (Paris: International Institute for Educational Planning, 2006), 29.

116. UNESCO Institute for Statistics, "*Trends in Tertiary Education: Sub-Saharan Africa*" (UNESCO Institute for Statistics, July 2009), 2; www.uis.unesco.org; accessed 2 February 2011.

117. Central Statistical Authority, *Ethiopian Statistical Abstract 2004* (Addis Ababa: Central Statistics Authority, 2004), 332–339.

118. Ibid.

119. Varghese, *New Trends in Higher Education*, 19.

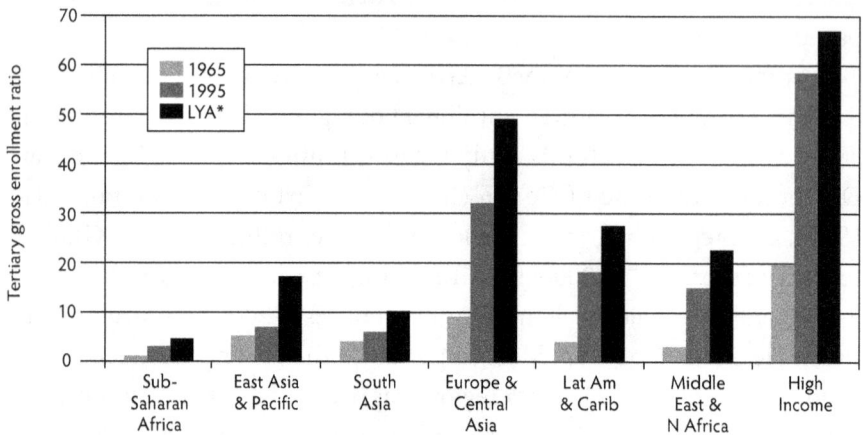

Figure 1: Enrollment of Higher-Educational Institutions in Sub-Saharan Africa[120]

Osokoya gives four reasons for the growth of privatization of higher education in the developing states of Africa.

> Firstly, there is the inability of the public sector to satisfy the growing social demand for higher education, hence the need for the private sector to expand students' access to higher education. Secondly, there are the de-regulation policies of the governments on the provision of education and thus giving adequate opportunities for private participation in education. Thirdly, in many African countries, the demand for employment oriented courses and subjects of study has changed and public universities seem unable to respond adequately to this phenomenon, hence it becomes imperative that private sector should increase. Fourthly, in most African countries, public education is criticized for inefficiency while the private sector is increasingly promoted for its efficiency in operation.[121]

---

120. *LYA (latest year available) means that for each country, the most recent data available are used, and those data are then aggregated by region. For most countries LYA is 2002/2003. The range is 1998/1999 to 2003/2004. *Source*: UNESCO and World Bank.

121. Israel Olu Osokoya, "Privatization of University Education in Africa: Lessons from the Theories and Practices of the United States of America and Japan," *International Journal of African & African American Studies* 6, no. 2 (2007): 1; ojcs.siue.edu; accessed 20 December 2010.

Varghese categorized private higher-educational institutes into four groups, namely: transnational, collaboration with foreign institutions, collaboration with public universities, and religious affiliation.[122] The transnational institutes of higher learning are those that are owned by foreign organizations and operate like multi-nationals. Higher-educational institutions that belong to the second category are those that operate in collaboration with foreign institutions of higher education. In the third category are those institutions that function in collaboration with other institutions within the same country. The fourth group of higher-educational institutions includes those institutions that are owned and operated by Christian denominations or Muslim organizations.[123]

Some of the private institutions were established as business endeavors; therefore, they are for-profit institutions. However, many of the private higher-educational institutions are not-for-profit institutions, and they are supported by religious organizations. The majority of these institutions are affiliated with churches or Christian organizations, while some are Islamic universities. These religion-affiliated universities "offer courses focusing on religious epistemologies – either on Islamic or on Christian beliefs and traditions."[124]

Church-Affiliated Higher-Educational Institutes in Africa

As briefly mentioned in chapter 1, many of the higher-educational institutions in Africa were founded by mission or other religious organizations, including churches.[125] In most sub-Saharan countries, formal educational programs were part of the Christian mission for a long time.[126] Therefore, when the Christian mission organizations and churches ventured into the tertiary level of education, they were building on their rich intellectual and religious heritage.[127]

---

122. Varghese, *New Trends in Higher Education*, 20–21.
123. Ibid.
124. Ibid., 22.
125. W. Otieno, "The Privatization of Public Universities in Kenya," in *Private Higher Education: A Global Revolution*, ed. P. G. Altbach and D. C. Levy (Boston, MA: Sense, 2005), 175.
126. J. Kwabana Asamoah-Gyadu, "Christian Higher Education for Africa: Need, Relevance, and Value," paper presented at the meeting of the International Association for the Promotion of Christian Higher Education, 2007; http://www.iapche.org/gyadu-paper.htm; accessed 10 October 2009.
127. Ibid.

Writing about the role of religious institutions in African higher education, Levy says, "A striking finding of the global private higher education literature is the potent presence of religious institutions in early development. Since African private higher education is still in its youth, we might expect a strong religious presence, and that is what we find. As noted, religious institutions counted prominently among the continent's precursors, including in Kenya, South Africa, and Uganda."[128]

Unlike Latin America and other regions where Catholic churches played a crucial role in establishing universities, it is the Protestant churches that took the lead in Africa.[129] In recent years many evangelical universities have been established by evangelical churches in sub-Saharan Africa, and there are many more to come. Joel Carpenter writes, "The environment for creating evangelical universities is ripe to bursting point in parts of sub-Saharan Africa. I found 10 colleges and universities formed over the past two decades by evangelicals from a variety of traditions and movements."[130] A number of these Christian universities and colleges were originally established as theological colleges/seminaries.

The focus of this study is on church-sponsored higher-educational institutes in Eastern African countries, namely, Ethiopia, Kenya, Uganda and Democratic Republic of Congo, that offer degree programs (bachelor-, master's- or doctoral-degree-granting colleges or universities). Institutions that offer only studies related to church vocations are not included.

No Christian universities have been established in Ethiopia yet. However, the Mekane Yesus Theological Seminary, which was founded in 1960 and was mainly a theological seminary, is now transitioning to become a Christian university.[131] The other theological college in the process of becoming a liberal arts college is Meserete Kirstos College,[132] which was opened in January 1994 for the purpose of providing training for pastors, evangelists, and lay leaders within Ethiopia. The college "envisions becoming a full 'Christian University,'

---

128. Daniel Levy, "A Recent Echo: African Private Higher Education in an International Perspective," *Journal of Higher Education in Africa* 5, no. 2–3 (2007): 205.

129. Ibid.

130. Joel A. Carpenter, "Universities on the Mission Field? Part I: New Evangelical Universities: Cogs in a World System, Or Players in a New Game?", *International Journal of Frontier Missions* 20, no. 2 (2003): 57.

131. www.myts.org.

132. www.mkcollege.org.

offering a broad range of undergraduate and graduate programs relevant to impacting the Ethiopian societies and beyond towards a more honest, just, compassionate and prosperous future."[133]

Table 2 lists church-affiliated Christian colleges and universities in Kenya.[134] Table 3 lists the private church-affiliated universities that are licensed by the government of Uganda.[135]

Table 2: Church-Affiliated Universities in Kenya

University and date founded	Founder
St Paul's University, 1903	Anglican, Presbyterian, Methodist, Reformed Church, and National Council of Churches in Kenya (NCCA)
Kenya Highlands Evangelical University, 1953	The World Gospel Mission
United States International University (USIU), 1969	United States International University in the USA
Daystar University, 1974	Mr S. E. M. Pheko (African), Dr Donald and Mrs Faye K. Smith (Americans) – affiliated to Daystar University in USA
Pan Africa Christian University (PAC), 1978	Pentecostal Assemblies of Canada
Africa International University (AIU), 1980	Association of Evangelicals of Africa (AEA)
University of Eastern Africa Baraton, 1980	Africa/Middle East division of Seventh-Day Adventists
Catholic University of Eastern Africa (CUEA), 1992	Association of the Member Episcopal Conference in Eastern Africa (AMECEA)
Africa Nazarene University (ANU), 1994	The Nazarene Church
Kenya Methodist University, 1994	Methodist Church

---

133. Ibid.
134. O. Abagi, "Private Higher Education in Kenya," in *New Trends in Higher Education: Growth and Expansion of Private Higher Education in Africa*, ed. N. V. Varghese (Paris: International Institute for Educational Planning, 2006), 75; P. L. Glanzer, Joel Carpenter, and Nick Lantinga, "Looking for God in the University: Examining Trends in Christian Higher Education," *Higher Education: The International Journal of Higher Education and Educational Planning* 61, no. 6 (2011).
135. www.unche.or.ug.

Table 3: Church-Affiliated Universities in Uganda

University and date founded	Founder
Ndejje University, 1992	Luweero & other dioceses
Uganda Martyrs University, 1993	Catholic Church
Bugema University, 1994	Adventist Church
Busoga University, 1999	Busoga Diocese
Uganda Christian University, 1999	Church of Uganda

The following institutions are identified by Glanzer, Carpenter, and Latinga[136] as Christian universities in the DRC: Shalom University of Bunia, Université Catholique de Bukavu, Université Catholique du Congo, Université Catholique du Graben, Université Notre-Dame du Kasayi, and Université Protestante au Congo.

In most cases, the institutions listed above were started as Bible/theological colleges that were mainly training ministers for the church and Christian organizations. They eventually added other programs and transitioned to Christian universities. Since several other institutions are also preparing to make this transition, the number of Christian universities in Africa will continue to grow in the coming years.

Is secularization a threat for Christian higher-educational institutions in Africa? The answer one gets for this question is mixed. There are some who are forced to compromise on their mission and evangelical values, while others stand strong against the influence of secularization.

What is seen in one institution in Ghana, as described by Asamoah-Gyadu, gives us a good picture of what is taking place in many similar institutes in Africa.

> Although Ghana's universities could be said to have been established on Christian moral foundations, the institutions are not Christian in orientation as such. At the University of Ghana even the former Divinity Faculty was, following the attainment of independence, prevailed upon to broaden its outlook to include the study of non-Christian religions or risk the loss of support by the government of Dr Kwame Nkrumah. In response the name of the

---

136. Glanzer, Carpenter, and Lantinga, "Looking for God in the University."

Divinity School had to change to reflect the religious neutrality of its new programs, hence the current name, Department for the Study of Religions. Christian influence on the lives and future of university students in Ghana has thus mainly come from the churches and Parachurch organizations, many of them evangelical in orientation, that have proliferated on the campuses since the 1960s.[137]

Other Christian higher-educational institutions choose to be lenient on their religious requirements for faculty and students in order to compete, expand, and stay financially viable in their competitive environments.[138] That has opened the door to secularization.

Though the trend for higher-educational institutes that were established by churches and Christian organizations is to gradually lose their religious distinctiveness over many years, there are exceptions in Africa. Levy argues that several higher-educational institutions have kept their religious missions.[139] Giving some examples of such institutions, Levy writes,

> While Kenya's Daystar University does not proselytize students, it does require that faculty and especially administrators are members of Pentecostal churches. Ugandan faculty and students must commit to their universities' basic mission of promoting Christian values. A "compassionate" tone can be noted for Nigeria's Pentecostal institutions, notwithstanding their primal capitalist hue. Generally, Africa's religious higher education has an explicit mission of character-building, but this need not mean a vague religious mission. A sharp religious mission is evident at some institutions; Kenya's Kabarak University aspires that all hear the call of Jesus Christ as Lord. In Kenya, all the religious universities have explicitly Christian content.[140]

As mentioned above, the focus of this study is on institutions that transitioned or are transitioning from a Bible/theological college or seminary

---

137. Asamoah-Gyadu, "Christian Higher Education for Africa."
138. Levy, "A Recent Echo," 206.
139. Ibid., 205.
140. Ibid.

to a Christian liberal arts college or university. Such transition requires a big change in the overall structure of the organization and needs careful leadership and management of change. Ramley[141] suggests a series of questions leaders of academic institutions should ask before beginning a change process.

> 1. Do you have a mandate for change? If so, from whom?

> 2. Do you understand the factors in the institutional culture and history as well as in the external environment that can support or resist change?

> 3. Is the campus ready to change? If not, what might you do to create a more receptive climate for change?

> 4. Have you thought through a strategy to manage institutional response as the change process unfolds?

> 5. Can you undertake and lead change?[142]

Conclusion

The expansion of Christian higher-educational institutes helps the churches in Africa to have a better influence in their societies in addressing the physical, social, economic, and political issues. It also has the potential of bringing transformation in these countries if it is done properly. However, as Holmes argues, the work of Christian colleges or universities should not be just an involvement in higher education.[143] It requires the integration of faith and learning at every level. "This uniting of faith and learning then is the essence of Christian higher education. This is the call of the hour and the distinctive approach to education where all teaching and learning must take place with a view toward reality found only in the glory and grandeur of God."[144]

Christian higher-educational institutes that are considering transitioning to Christian liberal arts colleges or universities need to plan carefully and make

---

141. J. Ramley, "Moving Mountains: Institutional Culture and Transformational Change," in *Field Guide to Academic Leadership*, ed. R. Diamond (San Francisco: Jossey-Bass, 2002).
142. Ibid., 59.
143. Holmes, *Idea of a Christian College*.
144. Dockery, *Renewing Minds*, 115.

sure they are becoming truly Christian universities, not just Christians who are involved in liberal arts education. Learning from history, evaluating the influence that comes from government, donor organizations, and accrediting agencies, and having the financial resources and qualified faculty who are committed to the vision of a Christian higher education are some of the issues that need careful consideration.

3

Methodological Design

This chapter describes the methodology and procedures used in this research. It also defines the population, the samples used, the delimitations of the sample, and the limitations of generalizations of this research.

The purpose of this qualitative multi-case-study research was to analyze and describe transitions from a theological college or seminary to a Christian liberal arts college or university in the East African context. The study focused on five selected institutions in Ethiopia, Kenya, Uganda, and Democratic Republic of Congo that began as theological (Bible) colleges or seminaries and are now transitioning or have transitioned to Christian liberal arts colleges or universities. The schools that were selected for this study were institutions that had added at least two additional programs to their Theology program and had made clear plans to add more programs in the next five to seven years and become liberal arts colleges or universities.

Research Questions Synopsis

The following five questions guided this research:

1. What are the reasons for the transition from a theological college to a liberal arts college or university?
2. What are the external and internal challenges these Christian higher-educational institutions face as they go through this transition?
3. In what ways is the mission of the institution affected by the transition from a theological college to Christian liberal arts college or university?
4. In what ways has the transition affected the relationship between the institution and the sponsoring church(es) or Christian organization(s)?

5. In what ways has the transition from a theological college to a Christian liberal arts college or university affected the Theology program of the institution?

Design Overview

The methodology employed in this study is qualitative, multi-case-study research.[1] Qualitative research attempts to understand a phenomenon that occurs in a natural setting.[2] Researchers conduct qualitative case studies in order to "describe, explain, or evaluate particular social phenomena."[3]

The qualitative research method is employed in this research because it helps to answer research questions that are descriptive in nature. It is also used because the amount of information that exists on the topic of this research is very limited.[4] Using the qualitative case-study research method, this study investigated the reasons for such transitions from theological colleges to universities, the challenges of the transition process, and how such transitions affect the mission of the institutions, the theological training programs, and the relationships of the institutions with their founding or sponsoring churches.

Writing about the case-study method, Leedy and Ormrod indicate that it is a useful method "for investigating how an individual or program changes over time, perhaps as a result of certain circumstances or interventions."[5] For this multi-case study, the researcher chose five institutions from Ethiopia, Kenya, Uganda, and Democratic Republic of Congo that were willing to take part in the study and were accessible to the researcher. The researcher also used certain key factors such as location, denominational affiliation or sponsorship, and stages in the transition process to choose the institutions. Selecting multiple cases that are different in certain key areas helps the researcher "to make comparisons,

---

1. J. W. Creswell, *Research Design: Qualitative, Quantitative, and Mixed Methods Approaches*, 3rd ed. (Thousand Oaks, CA: Sage, 2009), 73.
2. Paul D. Leedy and Jeanne Ellis Ormrod, *Practical Research: Planning and Design*, 9th ed. (Boston, MA: Pearson, 2010), 135.
3. M. D. Gall, W. R. Borg, and J. P. Gall, *Educational Research: An Introduction* (White Plains, NY: Longman, 1996), 289.
4. Leedy and Ormrod, *Practical Research*, 135.
5. Ibid., 137.

build theory, or propose generalizations"[6] and see how the research subject can be illustrated in multiple cases.[7]

The data for this research was collected from multiple sources, including interviews, documents, reports, and printed materials.[8] The researcher also spent time in each of the five institutions conducting interviews, interacting with people, and gaining a perspective on the educational environment. While on campus the researcher attended campus activities such as chapel, and held informal discussions with faculty members and students of the Theology department, with the approval of the administration. The researcher also recorded the information he gathered that related to the topic of the research.

The researcher conducted interviews with the leaders of the selected institutions in face-to-face interactions.[9] The interviewees included presidents (vice-chancellors, principals, rectors), vice-presidents (deputy vice-chancellors, deputy principals), academic deans, heads of schools of theology or departments of theology, and heads of the other newly added programs of the institutions. The interviews were designed to bring to the fore the experiences and perceptions of the leaders of these higher-educational institutions regarding the reasons for and the effects, challenges, and general impact of the transitions.

The researcher focused on the perspectives the participants held regarding the problem.[10] Using the qualitative study method, this research presents multiple perspectives held by the participants of the study regarding the effects of the transitions in their institutions.[11] Driven by the research questions, this study inquires into the meaning the leaders of the selected institutes ascribe to the effects of the transition on their institutions.

In addition to the data collected through the interviews, the researcher collected data from other sources of information,[12] such as field observations, documents, and published materials, including catalogues, mission statements,

---

6. Ibid.
7. Creswell, *Research Design*, 74.
8. Ibid., 73.
9. Ibid., 37.
10. Gall, Borg, and Gall, *Educational Research*, 289.
11. Creswell, *Research Design*; E. Guba and Y. S. Lincoln, "Do Inquiry Paradigms Imply Inquiry Methodologies?", in *Qualitative Approaches to Evaluation in Education*, ed. D. M. Feeterman (New York: Praeger, 1988).
12. Creswell, *Research Design*, 75; Leedy and Ormrod, *Practical Research*, 137.

vision and value statements, public announcements, strategic plan documents, official reports, doctrinal statements, and course description of class syllabi. All these documents supplemented the data that was gathered through interviews.

Population

The population for this qualitative study consists of Protestant/evangelical higher-educational institutions that are transitioning or have transitioned from theological (Bible) colleges to Christian liberal arts colleges or universities in Ethiopia, Kenya, Uganda, and Democratic Republic of Congo.

Sample and Sampling Technique

The sampling strategy used for this study is purposeful sampling.[13] Explaining purposeful sampling in a qualitative research, Creswell says, "The inquirer selects individuals and sites for study because they can purposefully inform an understanding of the research problem and central phenomenon in the study."[14] The institutions selected for this study represent other former Bible colleges in Ethiopia, Kenya, Uganda, and Democratic Republic of Congo that are transitioning or have transitioned to liberal arts colleges or universities. These are institutions that are evangelical, have added at least two other programs to their Theology program, and have made clear plans to add more programs in the next five to seven years and become liberal arts colleges or universities.

The researcher contacted different organizations and leaders of theological seminaries in Africa to get their recommendations of institutions that could be included in this multi-case study. One of the organizations that the researcher consulted was Overseas Council, an international organization that partners with theological institutions around the world, with thirty partners in Africa.[15] The researcher visited the headquarters of Overseas Council in Indianapolis, Indiana, USA, and talked to its leaders, asking for their recommendations for potential institutions that have transitioned or are transitioning to Christian

---

13. Creswell, *Research Design*, 125.
14. Ibid.
15. www.overseas.org.

universities that could be used as cases for the study. He received their recommendations and started with that list.

On May 2011 the researcher also attended All African Leadership Institute, a regional institute organized by Overseas Council in Addis Ababa, Ethiopia. At the meeting forty-five different theological institutions from twenty-four African countries were represented. This researcher was able to meet face-to-face with the leaders of six institutions that are transitioning or have transitioned to Christian universities and leaders of other institutions that are considering the transition. Three of those are included in this study. The researcher used certain key factors, such as location, denominational affiliation, and stage in the transition process, in selecting the five institutions in this study in order to get a wider representation that would help him to make comparisons and propose generalizations.

Delimitations of the Sample

The researcher has delimited the sample for this study to five selected evangelical higher-educational institutions in four Eastern Africa countries, namely, Ethiopia, Kenya, Uganda, and Democratic Republic of Congo, that have transitioned or are transitioning from theological colleges to Christian liberal arts colleges. The sample is also delimited to Protestant Bible or theological colleges.

Limitations of Generalization

This study is limited in generalization to Protestant Bible or theological colleges that transitioned to liberal arts colleges or universities. The findings, therefore, do not generalize to church-affiliated institutions that belong to other Christian traditions. Though this qualitative study attempts to consider the phenomenon in institutions in the region that are transitioning or have transitioned, it will be limited in its representation because all transitions are different and are dependent on the nature of the institutions and their specific contexts.

Instrumentation

The instrument that was used in this qualitative study was a set of interview questions, prepared by the researcher, which were open-ended and designed for a face-to-face in-depth interview.[16] The questions revolved around the research questions of this study.

In developing the interview questions and classifying the responses, the researcher used Robert Benne's table, presented in his book *Quality with Soul*.[17] Benne's table "Types of Church-Related Colleges," presented earlier in Table 1,[18] was very helpful in categorizing church-related colleges' connections to their religious heritage. In his chart Benne listed eight aspects of an institution's life that help to examine its connection with its religious heritage. They are (1) public relevance of Christian vision; (2) public rhetoric; (3) membership requirements; (4) religion/theology department; religion/theology required courses; (5) chapel; (6) ethos; (7) support by church; and (8) governance. Benne divided church-related colleges into four types: *orthodox, critical mass, intentionally pluralist,* and *accidentally pluralist*. He admits that his chart does not take into consideration all nuances, and that schools do not necessarily fall into one neat category.[19]

The researcher used these eight aspects of the life of the institutions to see how transitioning from a Bible college to a Christian liberal arts college or university has affected the life of the institutions in this study. The questions prepared for the interviews were used to draw out responses from the leaders of the institutions on their perspectives on the changes they see in their institutions in these eight areas. These questions were also designed to get answers to the research questions.

The interviewer followed the prepared questions during the interviews but also added questions that were necessary to clarify or expand some ideas raised by the interviewees. The responses provided by the interviewed leaders have helped the researcher to gather important information regarding the leaders' perspectives on the transitions of their institutions from theological colleges to Christian universities.

---

16. Leedy and Ormrod, *Practical Research*, 148.
17. Benne, *Quality with Soul*, 48–49.
18. See above, p. 27.
19. Benne, *Quality with Soul*, 48.

The prepared questions were reviewed by an expert panel that commented on the clarity and suitability of the questions for the research. The researcher submitted the names and qualifications of the members of the panel to his supervisor for approval. After receiving the approval of the members of the expert panel, the researcher sent his interview questions to the members of the panel. After revising and making necessary corrections on the questions based on the comments received from the expert panel, the researcher submitted a written copy of the questions to the Dissertation Committee and Research Ethics Committee of the Southern Baptist Theological Seminary for approval. Once the interview questions were approved, they were sent out to the leaders of the institutes that were chosen for this research prior to the interview sessions.

The data from the interviews was audio-taped and then transcribed as Word documents. The researcher then sent to each interviewee the transcript of the interview, so that he or she could make any necessary notations and changes. The researcher gave each interviewee a period of three weeks to look at the transcript and make necessary corrections.

After making the corrections that were raised by the interviewees, the researcher coded all the data on the interview transcripts using NVivo 9 software. This software helped the researcher to code the data of each transcript according to the key themes identified in the literature review and the research questions of this qualitative study.

Procedures

The section below describes the process that was used to gather, categorize, and analyze the research data. The researcher used a qualitative multi-case-study research method for this study.

Interview Questions and Protocol

As indicated above, the researcher prepared the questionnaires that were used in this study from the information gathered through the literature review. The interview questions were open-ended and designed for a face-to-face in-depth interview.[20] The semi-structured interviews allowed the researcher to

---

20. Leedy and Ormrod, *Practical Research*, 148.

ask questions in addition to the standard questions for clarification or to probe the interviewee's reasoning.[21]

The researcher also prepared an interview protocol that stated the title of the project, time of the interview, date, place, name of the interviewee, position of the interviewee, interviewee's academic institution, interviewee's email address, and the length of time the interviewee had worked in that position and in higher education. It also asked for a signature from the participant to show his or her agreement to allow the researcher to record the interview and use the data in his research. The researcher has included the interview questions at the end of the interview protocol (see appendix 1).

Expert Panel Review

To ensure the appropriateness of the interview questions, the researcher used an expert panel. The members of the panel included three members who are experts in different aspects of the topic of this research. After contacting the potential members of his expert panel to ask about their willingness to be involved, the researcher submitted the names and qualifications of the three experts to his dissertation supervisor (see appendix 2 for the listing and qualifications of the expert panel). Upon receiving the approval of the dissertation supervisor, the researcher sent the interview questions to the members of the expert panel. The function of the interview panel was to review and evaluate the appropriateness of the interview questions for gathering the appropriate data in a way that answered the research questions.

The researcher made the necessary amendments to the interview questions based on the evaluation and comments he received from the expert panel. The researcher then submitted the updated instrument to his dissertation committee supervisor for his final approval.

Ethics Approval

After making the corrections based on the comments of the expert panel and the pilot interviews, the interview questions were submitted to the Dissertation Committee and Research Ethics Committee of the Southern Baptist Theological

---

21. Ibid., 188.

Seminary for approval. Upon receiving the approval of the instrument, the researcher initiated the actual research process.

Seeking Permission and Arranging Visits

The researcher contacted the leaders of the institutions selected for this study to ask about their willingness to take part in this multi-case study. He was able to make face-to-face contact with the leaders of three of the institutions and email contact with the leaders of the other two organizations. The researcher sent a formal letter to each institution with an attachment containing the interview protocol. Upon receiving confirmation of their willingness to take part in the study, the researcher contacted the leaders of each of the institutions to secure permission to conduct interviews. Interview questions were then sent out to the respondents who had expressed their willingness to participate in the interview. The researcher then visited each of the five institutions at the agreed time to conduct interviews and gather the necessary data for the research.

Conducting the Interviews

The interviews were conducted according to the interview protocol discussed above. The interview sessions took an average of fifty minutes. At the beginning of each interview session, the researcher thanked the participants for taking the time to participate in this research. He then asked the interviewees to fill out and sign the consent forms that had been sent to them earlier to give permission to the interviewer to record the data. Upon receiving consent from the interviewees, the researcher asked the questions that had been sent to the interviewees in advance. The questions were open-ended and the researcher listened closely to each participant and took notes as necessary. The semi-structured interview also allowed the interviewer to ask follow-up and probe questions.[22]

At the end of the interview, the researcher thanked each of the interviewees and explained that the interviewee would receive the transcription of the interview so that he or she could make any necessary changes or corrections. The researcher also reminded interviewees that he would send them a summary of the research findings at the end of his research.

---

22. Ibid., 141.

Transcribing the Interviews

Once the interviews were completed, the researcher transcribed them all into Word documents. Then the researcher sent the transcripts of the interviews to the interviewees with a personal letter expressing appreciation for their participation. In the letter, the researcher asked each of the interviewees to look at the transcript of his or her interview and make any necessary corrections. The researcher also indicated that he would give the interviewees a period of three weeks to review their transcripts, make changes and notations, and send them back to him as email attachments, and that if he did not hear from them in those three weeks he would assume that they validated the interview transcript.

Visitation and Collection of Other Data

During his visits to the five institutions to do the interviews, the researcher spent an average of six days on each campus. During his visit the researcher collected sources of data such as documents, published materials such as catalogues, mission statements, vision and value statements, public announcements, strategic plan documents, official reports, and doctrinal statements that the institution made available. He also took observation notes. During his visit, the researcher was also able to have informal conversations with teachers, students, and staff members, and attend chapel services at two of the institutions. The researcher's goal was to look for the convergence of the data that was collected through the different sources.

Analyzing the Data

All the data that was gathered was analyzed according to the five steps given by Creswell[23] and one step by Leedy and Ormrod:[24]

1. The researcher organized and prepared the data for analysis. This included transcribing interviews, typing up the field notes, and sorting out and arranging the data in a logical order.[25]

---

23. Creswell, *Research Design*, 184–190.
24. Leedy and Ormrod, *Practical Research*, 138.
25. Creswell, *Research Design*, 185.

2. The researcher then read through all the data in order to obtain a general sense of the information gathered and started recording his general thoughts about the information.[26]
3. The researcher then imported all the data into NVivo 9 software. This software helped the researcher to code the data of each transcript according to the key themes identified in the literature review and the research questions of this qualitative study. Through coding, the researcher organized the material into chunks or segments of text before bringing meaning to the information.[27] The data was coded according to the topics raised by the research questions and those that had relevance to the research.
4. Using the coding process, the researcher then generated a number of themes or categories. The themes were then analyzed for each individual case and across all the cases. The themes were also used to identify multiple perspectives.[28]
5. The researcher then gave a "detailed discussion of several themes (complete with subthemes, specific illustrations, multiple perspectives from individuals, and quotations) or a discussion of interconnected themes."[29]
6. The final step was constructing an overall portrait of the cases. Conclusions were drawn that might have implications beyond the specific cases included in this research.[30]

After these steps, the researcher developed an overall description of the effects of the transition in the Christian higher-educational institutions that have transitioned or are transitioning from theological colleges to Christian liberal arts colleges or universities.

---

26. Ibid.
27. G. Rossman and S. F. Rallis, *Learning in the Field: An Introduction to Qualitative Research* (Thousand Oaks, CA: Sage, 1998), 171.
28. Creswell, *Research Design*, 189.
29. Ibid.
30. Leedy and Ormrod, *Practical Research*, 138.

4

Analysis of Findings

This chapter presents the findings of the study that analyzed and described transitions from a theological college or seminary to a Christian liberal arts college or university in the East African context. This multi-case-study methodology enabled the researcher to have an in-depth look at five selected institutions in four countries in East Africa that have transitioned or are going through transition from a theological college or seminary to a Christian university.

In this chapter the researcher describes the means that were used to compile the data. The researcher also presents and analyzes the data that pertains to the reasons for the transitions, the challenges of the transitions, and how the transitions affected the mission, the relationship of the institutions with their founding churches, and their Theology programs. The findings of this study will be presented in the form of descriptive analysis.

Compilation Protocol

The researcher utilized four means of obtaining data. The data was obtained through interviews, informal discussions, official documents, and site observation of the researcher. The data that was gathered through the semi-structured interviews was the primary data that was used for analysis. The data that was gathered through the informal discussions, the documents, and observation notes was used to triangulate the data that was supplied through the interviews.

The collection of data was conducted in four different phases. In the first phase, the researcher developed a population sample of higher-educational institutions that are transitioning or have transitioned from a theological college or seminary to a Christian university or liberal arts college. Out of those institutions, the researcher identified five institutions that met the criteria that are outlined in chapter 3.

In phase two, the researcher traveled to each of the selected institutions to do interviews with the top leaders of the institutions. The visits gave the researcher an opportunity to talk to people directly in their own context[1] and to have contextual exposure.

The interviews were conducted face-to-face with the top leaders of the institutions of this multi-case study (see appendix 1 for interview protocol). The questions that were used in the interviews were open-ended. Interviews took an average of fifty minutes. For the purpose of accuracy in reporting findings from the interviews, all interviews were digitally recorded and then transcribed by the researcher into Word documents.

During the visits to the institutions, the researcher collected sources of data such as documents, published materials, catalogues, mission statements, vision and value statements, public announcements, strategic plan documents, official reports, and doctrinal statements that the institution made available. The researcher also was able to have informal conversations with teachers, students, and staff members, and attend chapel services at two of the institutions. The goal of the researcher was to look for the convergence of the data that was collected through the different sources.

In phase three, the researcher analyzed the data using the data analysis method described by Creswell[2] and Gall, Borg, and Gall.[3] The first step was importing all the transcribed interviews into the NVivo 9© software. NVivo 9 allowed the researcher to manually code the content of the transcribed interviews using category headings called "nodes" in the software. The researcher created parent nodes (major categories) that were related to the five research questions and coded the interview references that corresponded to each node. After the initial coding, the researcher created child nodes (subcategories and subthemes) that appeared in the interviews and related them to the parent node that they belonged to.

---

1. J. W. Creswell, *Research Design: Qualitative, Quantitative, and Mixed Methods Approaches*, 3rd ed. (Thousand Oaks, CA: Sage, 2009), 175.
2. Ibid.
3. Gall, Borg, and Gall, *Educational Research*, 358.

In phase four, the researcher analyzed the content that was gathered through websites, printed advertisements, and published materials such as catalogues, mission statements, vision and value statements, public announcements, strategic plan documents, official reports, and doctrinal statements that the institution made available. The researcher then imported the data collected into NVivo 9 and coded them according to the nodes created in phase three.

Then the researcher attempted to get a sense of the whole data. In that process, the researcher looked for categories or interpretations and labeled them. After identifying general categories or themes, the researcher looked for subcategories and subthemes and classified each piece of the data accordingly. Once a clear sense of the whole data appeared, the researcher integrated and summarized the whole data.

Findings and Displays

In this section, the researcher introduces each higher-educational institution that participated in this research with a brief history of the institution and its transition process. Then he presents the summary of the findings from data that was collected from each institute through the interviews and the other documents under the five primary categories that are based on the research questions. The analysis of the data is displayed in selected quotes from the interviewees as stated in the transcribed documents of the interviews.

Each case study is presented and followed by a summary of the findings that pertain to the five research questions. The presentation of the findings of each of the five institutions helped the researcher to clearly display the emerging patterns that are the basis for his conclusions presented in chapter 5. The researcher used Benne's eight categories of institutional life,[4] mentioned above, to develop the five research questions and the subquestions that were used to further explore the transition phenomenon.

The first research question focuses on the reasons given by the institutions for the transition from a theological college to a liberal arts college or university. Under this research question, the researcher investigated how the consideration for the transition was initiated, whether there was consensus about the change,

---

4. Benne, *Quality with Soul*.

and the roles played by the administration, board, and faculty members of the institutions.

The second research question looks at the external and internal challenges the institutions are facing due to the transition. The follow-up questions attempt to identify the major challenges and the sources of these challenges. In addition, the steps taken by these institutions to tackle the challenges are also described.

The third research question focuses on the effects of the transition on the mission of the institution. Questions related to this research question explore if there is a change in the institution's mission, its ethos, its hiring policy, and how the school presents itself to the public. Steps taken to protect the institution's Christian identity are also explored.

The fourth research question explores how the transition affected the institutions' relationships with their founding or sponsoring churches. Under this question, the researcher explored if and how the relationship of the institutions have changed during the transition. The other factors that help to shed light on those relationships, such as the churches' representation on the board and the churches' financial support of the institutions, were explored.

The fifth research question inquires about the effects of the transition on the Theology program. This research question explores the opportunities and the challenges the transition to a Christian university brought to the institutions. It explores how the institution attempts to integrate theology into the overall curriculum (integration of faith and learning). It also explores the role of chapel and other spiritual programs in the life of the institution.

The following section presents the analysis of the five institutions that transitioned from a theological college to a Christian university: the Mekane Yesus Seminary (Addis Ababa, Ethiopia), Africa International University (Nairobi, Kenya), St Paul's University (Limuru, Kenya), Uganda Christian University (Mukono, Uganda), and Shalom University of Bunia (Bunia, DRC). Each of these higher-educational institutions is presented in turn, with contextual information such as their geographical context, brief history, time of transition, and a summary of the research findings that pertain to the reasons for the transition, the challenges of the transition, and how the transition affected the mission, the relationship of the institution with its founding churches, and the Theology program of the institution.

Mekane Yesus Seminary

The MYS was established in Addis Ababa, Ethiopia, in September 1960 as a result of a joint venture of the newly established Ethiopian Evangelical Church Mekane Yesus (EECMY) and three mission organizations, namely, the Swedish Evangelical Mission, the American Lutheran Mission, and the German Hermansbur Mission.[5] It was established "under the legal personality of EECMY as a self-governing body corporate [sic] with the major tasks of training pastors, evangelists, church leaders, administrators and educators in different fields of the Church's holistic ministries."[6]

It started by offering a diploma program in Theology. In 1970 the Theological Education by Extension Department was added to offer courses at three different levels, Basic, Award, and Diploma. The program was established to train local Christian leaders who for different reasons were not able to attend the seminary as residential students.

In 1971 a Bachelor of Theology (BTh) program was started. The seminary also started a Music department in 1979. The department was closed in 1986 through lack of students and finances. In 2003 it was reopened as EECMY School of Music.[7] The school offers an Advanced Diploma in Musicology and its purpose is to equip candidates "with musical skills in contemporary and traditional instruments with emphasis on conceptualized music . . . to become professional musicians in and out of the church environments."[8]

In 1995 a Leadership, Management, and Communications department was added. This department was later upgraded to a college and was named Mekane Yesus Management and Leadership College (MY-MLC). "Currently, the college offers degree programs in General Management, Leadership and Development Studies, and Level III and IV programs in Accounting, Human Resources Management, Gender and Development, and Information Technology."[9] These programs are offered as regular, evening, and summer courses. The college has

---

5. www.myes.org.
6. Mekane Yesus Seminary, *Self-Evaluation Report of Mekane Yesus Seminary, Addis Ababa, Ethiopia* (Addis Ababa: Ethiopia, 2007), 136.
7. Magarsaa Gutta, *From a Humble Beginning to Advanced Standing: A History of Mekane Yesus Seminary 1960–2010* (Addis Ababa, Ethiopia: United Printers, 2011), 104–105.
8. www.myes.org.
9. Ibid.

plans to add degree programs on Gender and Development and Accounting and Finance.

In 1997 the Diploma program in Theology was phased out and transferred to the four regional seminaries of EECMY. In 1998 MYS founded the Ethiopian Graduate School of Theology in cooperation with the Evangelical Theological College of Addis Ababa. Currently the Mekane Yesus Seminary has a Department of Theology, Department of Theological Education by Extension (TEE), Mekane Yesus Management and Leadership College (MYMLC), Mekane Yesus Jazz Music School, and the recently opened college, College of Distance Education.

Mekane Yesus Seminary is currently working on the establishment of the Mekane Yesus University. Preliminary work has begun to implement the vision. The school has formed a steering committee that oversees the progress, and assigned an expert to work on the needed preliminary work.[10] The process of transitioning to a university and the challenges that are coming with it are discussed in the next section.

The researcher made several trips to the MYS over a period of three weeks to do interviews with the senior leaders of the seminary, to make observations, and to collect documents that are relevant to his research. The researcher interviewed the principal, the vice-principal, the dean of the Department of Theology and the dean of the Management and Leadership College. The interviews with the leaders ranged from forty minutes to an hour. The researcher provided the interview protocol to each of the interviewees before the day of the interview and conducted each interview in the office of each of the interviewees.

With the permission of the leadership, the researcher was also able to hold informal discussions with faculty members, staff members, and students of the seminary. The section below presents the findings of the researcher through the interviews, his own observation, and documents and publications he gathered during his visit at the MYS in relation to the five research questions.

Reasons for the Transition

The first research question asked, "What are the reasons for the transition from a theological college to a liberal arts college or university?" The

---

10. Gutta, *From a Humble Beginning*, 266.

researcher attempted to identify the different reasons MYS is transitioning to a Christian university.

The main reason that the MYS considered transitioning to a Christian university, according to one of the leaders interviewed, is the long-time dream of the leaders of the Ethiopian Evangelical Church Mekane Yesus to provide Christian education up to a university level (Interview A). The EECMY is the oldest and one of the fastest-growing evangelical churches in Ethiopia. The church had fought illiteracy from its very inception. "EECMY is the first institution that started adult literacy campaign in the country" (Interview A). The church also founded many elementary and high schools, and starting a university "had always been among the topics mentioned in its General Assembly that meets once in every four years. Finally, at the 17th General Assembly, the church resolved to begin a university" (Interview A).

Writing about the 17th General Assembly of EEMCY, Gutta writes, "The 17th Assembly was held from January 25–28, 2005 under the theme 'Arise and Shine' (Isa 60:1). It was at this Assembly that the policy directive was given to work towards *upgrading the MYS to university level* [Italics his]."[11]

Though establishing a fully-fledged university has not yet become a reality, the MYS had been adding additional programs to its Theology program even before the decision to establish a university was made by the General Assembly. Because of the growth of the church membership and the expansion of the church's holistic ministry in doing relief work, rehabilitation, and development, there was a growing need for trained leaders in different fields. Realizing that need, the seminary started a leadership department in September 1995. Gutta writes, "The MYS Department of Leadership, Management, and Communication began its training program in September 1995 on a diploma level under the auspices of the Mekane Yesus Theological Seminary."[12]

The department faced a budget problem when two sources of support for the program stopped their funding.[13] To meet its financial needs and to become self-reliant, the department first tried to generate income by offering short courses and doing consultancy work. However, these efforts did not generate enough funds to make the department self-reliant. Therefore, the

---

11. Ibid., 121.
12. Ibid., 174.
13. Ibid., 211.

dean of the Management and Leadership Department presented a proposal for the program to be upgraded to degree level. Gutta, quoting the minutes of the board, writes, "The promotion of the Department to a Degree level can only be done by designing a new curriculum which has major and minor secular subjects to get accreditation from the government's Ministry of Education, and then open the department to the general public in the country and the sub-region [of Africa]."[14]

After hearing the proposal of the dean, the board of Mekane Yesus Theological Seminary decided that the department be upgraded to a college and be named "EECMY Management and Leadership College," with the board of the seminary having the overall responsibility of leading the new college.[15] The decision to upgrade the department to a college was then endorsed by the EECMY executive committee.[16]

Explaining the reason for the decision to upgrade the Leadership and Management Department to a college, Leader A said, "Originally, we were offering leadership courses in the Theology department. However, when support from outside was decreasing, and when we saw the income generated by other private colleges, the church decided to upgrade the department into an independent Management and Leadership College accredited by the Ministry of Education and owned by the church so that it would generate income for the church and for the seminary" (Interview A). Therefore, one can conclude that the second reason why MYS considered expanding its programs by adding more non-theological courses is that it would be able to attract more students from the wider community and generate enough funds to help the college be self-sustaining.

Explaining further the reasons for upgrading the Department of Leadership and Management to a college, Gutta writes,

> The underlying reason for seeking the promotion of the Department to a College level was not only to solve a financial problem, but also to realize the original vision of the MYS to train qualified leaders for the EECMY and other churches and interested groups. There was a demand from the Church units that further

---

14. Ibid., 212.
15. Ibid., 213.
16. Ibid.

education be offered on Degree level to those who were already trained at Diploma level. Furthermore, the MYS, as the pioneer and leading training institution, was being underutilized and was not more open to the public service when it comes to rendering training in leadership on a status recognized by the Ministry of Education of the Country. Thus, concrete plans were made to ask for accreditation from the National Ministry of Education.

This shows that the third reason why the MYS considered expanding its programs was to get recognition from the government, be more open to the public, and to serve as a training institute for leaders in governmental and non-governmental organizations, in addition to training leaders for churches and Christian organizations.

Currently, MYS runs a Department of Theology, Department of Theological Education by Extension (TEE), Mekane Yesus Management and Leadership College (MY-MLC), Mekane Yesus Jazz Music School, and the recently opened College of Distance Education. These departments and colleges have plans to expand their programs and the degrees they offer. Gutta writes, "The Management and Leadership College, the Theology Department, and the TEE Department have plans to start trainings on MA and BA levels in the near future. The Music Department has a plan to start BA programme."[17] The expansion of these programs and the directives given by the 17th General Assembly of EECMY to start planning to establish the "Mekane Yesus University" are also factors that are leading to the transition to a Christian university.

From the above discussion, one can see five main reasons why MYS considered transitioning from a theological seminary to a Christian university. The first was born out of a long-term dream of the leaders of the EECMY to provide Christian education up to university level as part of the church's mission of serving the whole person. The second reason was that with the growth of the church and the expansion of the church's ministry in relief work, rehabilitation, and development, the church felt the need to train more leaders that could serve in all areas of its ministry in addition to the spiritual ministries of the church. In addition to that, they also aimed to provide education at a higher level for church leaders who did their training at lower levels.

---

17. Ibid., 262.

The third reason was that by expanding more programs and increasing the student body, the institution wanted to generate more income for the institution so that it became self-reliant at a time when financial support coming from outside the country was decreasing. Fourth, the seminary wanted to open up its ministry to general society to train leaders for governmental and non-governmental jobs in different fields of study. The fifth reason was to accommodate all the programs that are run by the seminary under the umbrella of a university. The section below discusses how that became a challenge and the different ways that have been considered to implement the idea of establishing the Mekane Yesus University.

External and Internal Challenges

The second research question asked, "What are the external and internal challenges these higher Christian institutions face as they go through this transition?" Presented below is what the researcher found from the interviews he conducted with the leaders and the materials published by the seminary.

The first challenge raised by one of the leaders during the interview was a lack of clear direction on how the transition should be implemented. Although the General Council of EECMY made a unanimous decision to establish a university, "there has not been a study done or a clear direction proposed on how it should be established" (Interview A). That is one of the reasons the implementation of the decision took so long (Interview A).

Though there is consensus about the establishment of the Mekane Yesus University, there have been different views on how to implement it because of the challenges discussed above. There are some who want MYS to be part of the university that is to be established, while others prefer to keep MYS as it is and establish an entirely new institute (Interview C). In January 2010, the board of MYS held a workshop to discuss the future of the seminary and the university. At this occasion different papers were presented. One of those papers was presented by a faculty member from the Theology department and reflected the concern of the members of the Theology faculty.

In the paper he presented the reasons why he thought the seminary should not be upgraded to a university. His argument was that seminaries and universities have different purposes and they meet different needs. The purpose of the seminary is training pastors, ministers, and teachers for church/Christian ministry to meet human, spiritual, and physical needs through biblically, theologically, and pastorally oriented disciplines, while the university's purpose is training professionals with various academic disciplines (including religious studies) for general social service (Interview E).

After the discussion, an agreement was made that "The Seminary and the University will grow independently without one engulfing the other."[18] It was also decided that it would be the Mekane Yesus Management and Leadership College that would transition to Mekane Yesus University, not the Mekane Yesus Seminary.[19]

Though the decision was made to develop the university as a separate institution from the seminary, there are leaders at MYS who are now asking the leadership of the church to reconsider that decision. One of the leaders said,

> Before I came to this office, a decision had been made to make the University a separate institute. But now we also are challenging the church officers if that can be profitable because the church already has a higher learning institute. Now the seminary itself is starting different departments like the Linguistic Department in collaboration with the Evangelical Theological College, Cinema and Film, and Communication and Media Departments. In the coming couple of years we will have these departments in place. So the question is, "Isn't the seminary already becoming a university on its own?" (Interview C)

The second challenge MYS is facing due to this transition is an administrative challenge. The Management and Leadership College was organized as an independent college and accredited by the government, but it is still functioning under the leadership of the seminary. Explaining the administrative challenge that created, one of the leaders said, "It is like having two different schools. We who are in the leadership are responsible for working with all the departments. But generally, they [the Management and Leadership College and the School of Theology] have little in common. I would say they are mutually co-existing. That is definitely one area where we need to work very hard in order to maintain a proper relationship" (Interview C).

---

18. Ibid., 263.
19. Ibid.

Another leader agreed. He said, "The structure is not functional" (Interview C). As a college accredited by the government, MY-MLC has its own logo, mission and vision statement, and relates to the government on its own. However, internally MY-MLC is still part of the Mekane Yesus Seminary. The dean of MY-MLC reports to the principal and vice-principal of MYS, as do the deans of the Theology Department and the School of Music. The board of MYS is also in charge of all the schools.

In addition to the administrative challenge, the transition has also created a conflict of purpose within the different schools of MYS. Leader B says, "There is a kind of dichotomy between the Theology program and the Management and Leadership program because they are so different in their purposes. The first purpose of the institution was to train leaders for the church. Now we see a shift from that vision to a secular vision" (Interview B).

The third challenge mentioned by the leaders is the seminary's inability to design the curriculum of the MY-MLC according to the desire of the church. As mentioned above, in 1995 MYS started a Department of Leadership and Management to train leaders for the church and Christian organizations. What started as a department eventually grew to a college and was named Mekane Yesus Management and Leadership College (MY-MLC). In order to attract more students from the general public and to get an income that would enable the college to be self-sustaining, the college sought accreditation from the Ministry of Education of Ethiopia and was granted it. Getting accreditation from the government helped the college to attract students from EECMY and from other evangelical churches in the country. It was also able to attract students from other religions.[20]

Getting accreditation from the government and forming an independent Management and Leadership College brought its own benefits and challenges. With the accreditation, the institution is able to attract students from the general public and increase its enrollment. The other benefit is that the graduates of the programs of MY-MLC have a better chance of getting jobs in different kinds of organizations as graduates of government-accredited programs. However, the institution has lost full control of running its programs as it sees fit (Interview A).

---

20. Ibid., 216.

The Management and Leadership College has to follow strictly the government guidelines because of its accreditation from the government. The regulations affect the curriculum of the college, its student recruitment policy, and its overall mission. MY-MLC cannot discriminate among applicants for the Management and Leadership program on the basis of their religious backgrounds. The website of the college states, "The programs offered have been fully accredited by the Ministry of Education and are open to all students, irrespective of religion, language, race, or sex."[21]

The college also does not offer Bible or Theology courses as part of the Leadership and Management program because it is required to keep its curriculum secular. All the programs that are designed by the college need to get approval from the Ministry of Education. Strictly following those guidelines makes it hard for the college to be distinct from other secular higher-educational institutions accredited by the government because the same rule applies to all.

Unlike in Kenya, Uganda, and DRC, the Ministry of Education of Ethiopia does not recognize or give accreditation to private higher-educational institutions that offer religious courses as part of their curriculum. The Higher Education Proclamation No. 650/2009 states that the proclamation "shall not apply to institutions under religious organizations and whose objectives and curricula are primarily religious."[22] Theological colleges in Ethiopia get their accreditations from accrediting organizations outside the country. The Mekane Yesus Seminary is accredited by the Accrediting Council for Theological Education in Africa (ACTEA). How the mission of the college and its curriculum are affected is discussed below in a later section.

Another challenge the institute faces during this transition is financial. Expressing the challenge of raising funds for the project, Leader A says, "We are already going through donor fatigue. No matter what we do, we are not getting financial support as we used to" (Interview A). Another leader also indicated that opening up the Management and Leadership College to the general public and starting more programs has not solved the financial challenges the institution is facing (Interview C).

---

21. www.myes.org.
22. http://www.ethiopian-law.com/federal-laws.

From the above discussion, one can see that there are at least five major challenges the institution is facing as a result of the transition. The first one is a lack of clear direction on the transition and establishment of the Mekane Yesus University. Though a decision has been made to transition only the MY-MLC to a university, some in the leadership still argue that it should be the whole seminary that should transition to a university. The second challenge is administrative, because the MY-MLC is organized as an independent college accredited by the government while it is under the leadership of the seminary. The third challenge is related to the second one: it is a lack of unifying purpose for the whole institution. The fourth challenge is the inability of the institution to design a distinctly Christian purpose statement and curriculum for the programs of MY-MLC because of government regulations that apply to the institutions it accredits. The fifth challenge is lack of financial resources to expand the facilities and programs.

Effects of the Transition on the Mission

The third research question asked, "In what ways is the mission of the institution affected by the transition process from a theological seminary to a Christian university?" Different aspects of the institution's life that are related to its mission, such as the public relevance of the Christian vision, ethos, and public rhetoric that Robert Benne[23] discusses, are also explored in this section.

The seminary uses "Purposes and Objectives" instead of a "Mission Statement" or "Vision Statement." The Constitution of the Joint Theological Seminary (the original name of Mekane Yesus Seminary) that was approved in 1960 states under "Article 3: Purpose,"

> The seminary shall strive to serve the Triune God, His Church and His people through:
>
> Section 1: The dissemination of the Gospel to all men through a right teaching and preaching of God's Word.
>
> Section 2: The establishment and nurture of congregations through the training and retraining of pastors and evangelists.

---

23. Benne, *Quality with Soul*, 49.

Section 3: The building of God's Church through the development of consecrated capable Ethiopian leadership of the church.

Section 4: The confrontation of the Ethiopian citizen with the Gospel message in such a way that it is meaningful to his needs and problems in his culture.[24]

This purpose statement in the MYS constitution has been revised from time to time. However, "the seminary's objectives have remained virtually unchanged."[25] The revised constitution of MYS in 2006 had made changes to the Purpose Statement to accommodate the changes that took place in the institution. "Article 7: Purposes and Activities" of this revised constitution states,

The Seminary is established with a purpose to serve the Triune God, His Church and His people in performing the following activities.

1. It contributes in the building of God's Church through the development of consecrated capable Ethiopian leadership for the church.

2. It promotes the nurture of congregations and the other church units through the training and the continuing education of pastors, church leaders, musicians, and teachers by conferring Degrees, Diplomas, and Certificates in various theological and professional streams.

3. It participates in the proclamation of the Gospel through a right teaching and preaching of God's Word in such a way that it becomes meaningful to the Ethiopian Citizens and others in their particular cultural settings.

4. It prepares and equips the Christian believers in view of the holistic Ministry of the Ethiopian Evangelical Church Mekane Yesus academically, vocationally, and spiritually for Christian ministry in an African context and in general.

5. It works on the provision of:

---

24. Gutta, *From a Humble Beginning*, 275.
25. Mekane Yesus Seminary, *Self-Evaluation Report*, 9.

a) knowledge of the cultural background for the Christian ministry,
b) theological education to fellow Christians in preparing them for Christian ministry,
c) continuing education to those already engaged in the Christian ministry,
d) management, leadership, and other professional training for persons preparing for or already engaged in the services of churches, organizations, and society in general, and
e) researches and publications relevant to Christian ministry and other social services.[26]

The current mission statement of the Department of Theology is very similar to the original mission statement of Mekane Yesus Seminary. It states,

> The Theology Department serves the mission of God by preparing men and women for Christian ministry in Ethiopia and the wider world. This is achieved through programs and activities which promote 1) a sound theological and biblical understanding of God's mission; 2) the development of ministry skills needed in God's mission; and 3) a mature commitment to God's mission. Faithful participation in God's mission requires an informed mind, skills for service, and dedicated hearts. These form the three priorities of the Theology Department.[27]

As mentioned above, what was started as the Leadership and Management Department of the MYS was upgraded to a college and named Mekane Yesus Management and Leadership College (MY-MLC). MY-MLC has been accredited by the Ministry of Education of Ethiopia. That required the college to follow the secular guidelines of the higher-educational policy of the country. As can be seen from its mission statement, other than the fact that it is owned by a church body, there is nothing that indicates the Christian nature of the college.

The vision statement of the college says, "Learning to grow, Learning to transform." The mission statement of the college says, "MY-MLC, as

---

26. Ibid.
27. Theology Department Five-Year Strategic Plan 2007–2011.

an institution of the Evangelical Church Mekane Yesus (EECMY), aims at training mature and competent citizens who will be able to make [a] significant contribution to the well-being and development of their country. We educate and empower students to become competent professionals in their respective fields of study."[28]

When Leader A was asked, "Has there been any change in the way the institution has presented itself as a Christian institution since the transition? How did the transition change the ethos of the institution?" he answered,

> It is important to notice some of the difficulties we are experiencing. When other private colleges were showing high growth in financial income, our MLC also wanted to join the club and thus applied to the government for accreditation. The government recognized our Management and Leadership College and yet forced us to leave out any biblical courses from our curriculum. That has left a scar in our mission. Now we want to take back our institution from the Ministry of Education and seek accreditation from other accrediting bodies. (Interview A)

The MY-MLC is still a college under the MYS as far as the EECMY is concerned. The principal and vice-principal of MYS are in charge of all the programs of MYS, including the MY-MLC. However, as far as the government is concerned, the Management and Leadership College is a college independent from the Mekane Yesus Seminary (Interview C).

That has created a tension. Although the mission statement of MYS has not changed and still focuses on preparing people for different ministries of the church, MY-MLC, which is considered part of the MYS, has a different mission statement. A leader said, "The mission statement of the Management and Leadership College is very similar to the mission statement of any secular college. Because of that, it has a distinct mission statement from that of the seminary" (Interview C).

The researcher asked another leader if the MY-MLC is helping to fulfill or complement the mission of MYS. He answered, "Yes and no." He said "yes" because the students that come to the Management and Leadership College are able to study in a Christian environment and can take Theology courses

---

28. www.myes.org.

if they like. This would not be the case if they had chosen to go to other private colleges or universities. However, these courses do not show on their transcripts. He said "no" because the Ministry of Education does not allow the college to include any Theology courses in the curriculum of the Management and Leadership College programs because they have to strictly follow the secular guidelines provided by the Ministry of Education.

Another leader argues that the mission of the seminary overall has not changed but expanded. Explaining what he meant by that, he said, "Previously the entire seminary was training human power for the consumption of the church. Now the MLC of Mekane Yesus is training human power for the church as well as the entire society of Ethiopia and beyond. Therefore, the mission of the institution has not changed; rather the ministry horizon of the seminary has expanded from church community to the entire Ethiopia community and beyond" (Interview D).

Leader C sees it differently and argues that the way the programs of MY-MLC are run is contrary to the mission of the church. He says, "The program in my opinion is against the position of the church. The church has a policy of giving holistic ministry and holistic development. Now we see a dichotomy here, secular and spiritual, and we are not giving holistic training" (Interview B).

The researcher also attempted to find out if there were things that made the programs of MY-MLC distinctly Christian. When he asked how the MY-MLC was different from other secular colleges that offered similar programs, a leader answered, "One of the values that we have is honesty. So we hope that our students are more honest than those of the other secular institutions because we are sharing with them certain Christian values. We expect from our students values of honesty, transparency, and faithfulness. Sometimes we do research and the performance of our students is much better than the graduates of other institutions" (Interview D). He added that the morning devotions that are open to all but not required of MY-MLC students was one of the ways that reflected the college's Christian identity. The prayers of teachers at the beginning of class and the clubs, such as the Spiritual Club, Environmental and Sanitation Club, and Gender and Development Club, also reflected the Christian faith and identity of the programs (Interview D).

Leader A agreed. He said, "We are Christ-centered – it is our big difference. We are not trying to construct the 22nd Ethiopian university. We are working towards training humble servant leaders like Christ" (Leader A). However, another leader disagreed. He said,

> Currently, except the fact that all of the professors and instructors are born-again Christians, there is no difference in terms of the curriculum. In fact, they try to insert some Christian elements, but the curriculum is the same as the curriculum that other secular institutes use because they are accredited by the Ministry of Education. The Ministry of Education has its own standards, and the Management and Leadership College's curriculum has to meet those standards. In that sense it is not different. Currently a series of debates is going on [as to] whether we should sacrifice our Christian identity for the sake of getting accreditation. I hope things will change soon because we are reconsidering it. We are asking, "What is the value we are adding as a church? Is it just adding another management and leadership college?" Definitely that is not the intention of the church. So we definitely are going back to preparing leaders for the church. (Interview C)

As discussed above, EECMY has made a decision to establish Mekane Yesus University. A foundation stone has been laid for the university complex. "An expert has been assigned to work on the needed preliminary work, and a steering committee has been appointed to oversee the steady progress of the work."[29] The vision, mission, and goals of the Mekane Yesus University are stated on the seminary's website as follows:

> VISION: To be a premier academic institution to articulate a Holistic African view of man under a Scholarship of excellence.

> MISSION: An Ethiopian university which is truly dedicated to academic excellence, innovative and with commitment to honest research, passionately engaged with society and demographically representative, advancing the cause of the disadvantaged and caring for God's creation and recognizing the Lordship of God, the creator and redeemer of the World.

---

29. Gutta, *From a Humble Beginning*, 266.

Goals of the University

- Promote an environment of higher learning which will expand a Holistic view of man as created by God, and provide access to learning that will expand educational and employment opportunities and support the transformation of the society socially and spiritually.
- Create and develop a God-fearing environment for all learners, and scholarship to pursue their studies in accordance with the principles of academic freedom and the pursuit of happiness.
- Engage in global academic competitive teaching, and create an environment conducive to dynamic interactive teaching and learning, advancing high levels of research and innovative engagements in scientific investigation.
- Foster an academic atmosphere that promotes critical thinking, in the development of Tradition, Change and Modernity and reappraisal of traditional views of the world of students and educators.
- Engage across continental academic undertakings, to enrich students' critical thinking and enhance the advancement of regional development across the African continent.[30]

As it can be seen from the vision and mission statement of the future university, the Christian elements of the mission are not boldly stated. The statement may have to go through further revision when the government demands that all the programs need to be secular to meet the requirements of the Ministry of Education. Though the current decision is to develop the MY-MLC into a university and seek accreditation from the government, allowing the MYS to grow independently to protect it from being engulfed by the university,[31] as indicated above, some of the leaders have been suggesting alternative options of getting accreditation for the university. One of the options suggested by the leaders is seeking accreditation from external accrediting agencies or

---

30. www.myes.org.
31. Gutta, *From a Humble Beginning*, 263.

working in partnership with other universities abroad and negotiating ways that their degrees could be offered for graduates of the seminary. Using these alternatives could enable the seminary (the future university) to design a distinctly Christian mission with a curriculum that fulfills the mission of the church (Leader A). One of the issues under discussion is whether the institution really needs accreditation from the government or not. So far, the Mekane Yesus Seminary does not have government accreditation as an institute, but its graduates are being accepted at different public universities in the country for post-graduate programs, including at Addis Ababa University. This shows that the universities that accept their graduates are recognizing the education offered at Mekane Yesus Seminary. The leaders hope that they can build a good reputation by producing graduates who can compete with the graduates of other government-accredited institutions (Interview C).

As mentioned above, the Ministry of Education of Ethiopia does not give accreditation to religious higher-educational institutions. MYS has its accreditation with ACTEA. A leader explained that they may consider similar options for the programs that are offered in the Management and Leadership College. They are looking for an international accrediting agency that would not only give them accreditation but also allow them to include Bible and Theology courses as part of their curriculum. The leader said, "We want to make sure that theology is part of all the programs that we have here. We do not want to be just another university in the country. Mekane Yesus University will be a different university. It will be like its name, Mekane Yesus University, Yesus [Jesus] at the center. The center of the university shall be Jesus" (Interview A).

Another leader expressed his doubt that the government would allow the establishment of a Christian university without proper accreditation from the Ministry of Education. He argued,

> Even if we plan to start a Christian university, I don't think we can do it as we plan because of the policy of the country. We must ask for accreditation from the Ministry of Education. We cannot be outside of the policy of the Ethiopian government, and it is quite different here from other countries. We cannot be independent; you have to abide by the regulation and laws of the country. Even if we dream about becoming a Christian university, the government would intervene for sure and push us to get accreditation from the

Ministry of Education because of their concern for the graduates of the university. The government wants students to study at institutions that are accredited by them because they want to make sure that they will be hired by the government, by NGOs, or other organizations at the end of their training. Those who hire the graduates want to see that they come from accredited academic institutions. (Interview B)

As one can see from the above discussion, the Mekane Yesus Seminary's mission statement clearly states that the institution's mission is preparing men and women for Christian ministry in churches, Christian organizations, and society in general in Ethiopia and the wider world. However, the vision statement, the mission statement, and core values of the MY-MLC do not clearly state a Christian mission other than indicating that it is owned by EECMY. The vision and mission statements of the future Mekane Yesus University can be described as a "straight-forward presentation as a Christian school but inclusive of others."[32] The mission and vision statements of the university may have to go through further revision, as happened to the MY-MLC, if the university seeks accreditation from the government and adopts its mission to the laws of the country. If that happens, the university could not have a distinctly Christian mission, and that works against the very reason why the church wants to establish a Christian university.

Effects of the Transition on the Relationship with EECMY

The fourth research question asked, "In what ways has the transition affected the relationship between the institution and the sponsoring church(es) or Christian organization(s)?" As indicated above, the EECMY owns Mekane Yesus Seminary (MYS). The board members and staff members of MYS are all members of EECMY.[33] MYS "primarily serves the various units of EECMY (synods, work areas, parishes, and congregations). Historically, this has been the case almost exclusively. However, in recent years MYTS has sought to include students from other denominations within Ethiopia and from churches of other African countries."[34]

---

32. Benne, *Quality with Soul*, 49.
33. Mekane Yesus Seminary, *Self-Evaluation Report*, 1.
34. Ibid., 2.

The MYS governing board is the body that governs both the Mekane Yesus Seminary and the Mekane Yesus Management and Leadership College (MY-MLC) and is appointed by the EECMY executive board.[35] The board operates according to the Constitution of Mekane Yesus Theological Seminary that always gets its approval from the highest administrative body of EECMY executive committee. "The Board was composed of one representative from the Synods, Presbyteries, and Work areas of EECMY, in addition to the EECMY General Secretary and Gospel Ministries Director, who were appointed by the EECMY Executive Committee and the MYTS Principal, who served ex-officio."[36]

EECMY has also been fully engaged in all the discussion about establishing Mekane Yesus University. As indicated above, the decision to establish MYU was made at the General Assembly of EECMY. Before it got to the assembly, the issue was discussed "among the seminary management committee, among students, the seminary board, and it was only after that was passed that it comes to the attention of the assembly" (Leader A).

The researcher asked how the future relationship of the university or MY-MLC will be affected considering all the limitations of what the church can do regarding the curriculum of the MY-MLC and the secular influence from the government. A leader explained that he does not see any negative consequences in the relationship between the church and MY-MLC because the church still has the power to run the program or to close it down if it decides to do so. The highest body of administration is still the church, and it is the owner. The church can close the school if it is convinced that it is not helping the mission of the church (Interview B).

Regarding the financial support EECMY gives to the different departments of MYS, a leader indicated that it is not the national church as such that is supporting the Theology faculty (Interview C). It is rather the sending bodies like the congregations and synods that support the program by sending their own evangelists, pastors, and candidates for these positions and paying for their fees and living expenses. They support MYS by sending their own people to study there and by paying for them. The leader said, "I would say, 99 percent of the theology graduates are sent by congregations, synods, and others, and they are guaranteed a job after graduation" (Interview C).

---

35. Gutta, *From a Humble Beginning*, 247.
36. Mekane Yesus Seminary, *Self-Evaluation Report*, 14.

MY-MLC gets support from different church bodies. For instance, the Women's Ministry Coordination Office of EECMY has supported the MY-MLC. Other donor agencies, like the Norwegian Church Aid, and a number of other mission organizations have also supported the MLC program. Some of these organizations are increasingly interested in supporting development areas rather than Theology programs. So they are trying to show their encouragement by supporting MY-MLC (Interview C).

Two of the leaders interviewed confirmed that there has not been any change in the current and future hiring practices of the seminary. All the full-time faculty members of the institution are born-again Christians, and a large majority of them are members of EECMY. Though the MY-MLC is not allowed to discriminate among students based on their religious background, the law of the government so far has not required the same regarding the institute's staff and faculty hiring policy.

However, there are some non-believers teaching at the School of Jazz Music. The reason for hiring these individuals, according to the school, is that there are few professionals in certain areas and those they can find are unbelievers (Interview C). There are also some exceptions at MY-MLC. A leader said,

> At the beginning we used to employ only members of EECMY. But later on, when finding qualified members of EECMY for all our needs became a challenge, we revised our approach and opened up our employment opportunities especially to those who are members of other Protestant denominations. So far we have employed two instructors from other denominations. But when it comes to employment of the part-time faculty, we hire anybody. It could be a Muslim, a Protestant or a non-Protestant. What we look for is their academic qualification and their expertise and that to some extent they share some of our Christian values. (Interview D)

The Mekane Yesus Seminary, as an institution owned by the EECMY, mainly serves the members of Mekane Yesus Church. However, in recent years they have opened up the school to students from other denominations. The MY-MLC and the new programs of the future Mekane Yesus University will be open to all, according to Leader A. Explaining that, he said, "This is Mekane

Yesus Church's school, so we believe that serving the body of Mekane Yesus Church is our priority. Mekane Yesus Church has over 5 million members; therefore, one university will not be enough for its own people, let alone for serving other denominations. However, Mekane Yesus believes in ecumenical relationships. It will always open its doors to whoever comes from whatever religious background, both nationally and internationally" (Interview A).

When asked about student recruitment at the MY-MLC programs, Leader C said, "At the Management and Leadership College, we accept everybody. As I said, it is accredited by the Ministry of Education and the Ministry of Education requires by law that the college be open to all students. There are also some Muslim students attending the program" (Interview C).

The researcher asked Leader A if the student recruitment policy of the Management and Leadership College and the future university would change if the government changes its policy and allows the institution to discriminate among applicants based on their religious backgrounds. He indicated that the university would not make changes to the entrance requirements for students. However, they would require all students to take Bible and Theology courses as part of their curriculum. That would give all students at least a chance to hear about Christ and the gospel message (Interview A).

In summary, from the above discussion one can conclude that there is a close relationship between the MYS and the owner EECMY. In terms of leadership, the governing board of MYS is appointed by the executive committee of EECMY and the board reports to it. All the members of the governing board are also members of EECMY. The board also has overall responsibility for the MY-MLC and the university that is going to be established.

Though for many years the students of MYS used to come almost exclusively from EECMY, in recent years the seminary has started accepting students from different denominations. However, the majority of students still come from EECMY. In addition, all the full-time faculty members of the institution are born-again Christians, and a large majority of them are members of EECMY.

EECMY also provides financial support to the institution, though the support mainly comes from congregations and synods that send their people for training and pay for their fees and living expenses. The Management and Leadership College also is supported by different church bodies and other donor organizations that work with the church.

However, as indicated above, MY-MLC's mission statement and curriculum are not in line with the mission statement of the seminary because the college has to follow the government's secular guidelines for higher-educational institutions to be an institution accredited by the government. That may also affect the mission of the university that is being established if it seeks accreditation from the government as MY-MLC did.

Effects of the Transition on the Theology Program

The fifth research question asked, "In what ways has the transition from a theological college to a Christian liberal arts college or university affected the theology program of the institution?" The answer to this research question comes from the replies given by the subjects of this research regarding how the role of the Theology department in the institution, the place of theology in the overall curriculum, and the role of chapel programs have changed because of the transitions.

The idea of establishing a university that makes the Mekane Yesus Seminary a part of it is not accepted by some members of the Faculty of Theology. They fear that such a move would undermine the effectiveness of the seminary in training ministers for the church. They point to the experience they have with the MY-MLC as an indication of what is to come if the seminary is transitioned to a university. When asked if there is a fear of secularization in the long run and if that is the cause for such concern, a leader from the Theology department said,

> Oh yes. That is why the Faculty of Theology has shown disappointment, even fear. When we trace the history of institutions that started as Christian universities, many have become secular institutions. Those of us at the Theology Department fear that if the secular programs continue to grow and occupy more and more space and keep taking the resources of the Theology Department, that eventually may diminish the Theology program. They are opening new departments year after year and they are expanding. So there is a kind of resource conflict here. They haven't constructed any building for their programs but they are expanding on the resources that the Theology program owned. That is a big challenge and then we say that this may lead

to a similar experience that is seen in many institutions that were secularized in the West. (Interview B)

The transition has also changed the campus life of students of Theology. When the institution only had a Theology program, it had fewer than 100 students and they had a pleasant dormitory life. Currently the number of students has grown to 700, and students of Theology can be assigned a dorm with students of the other programs, and they may even be unbelievers. A leader said, "The seminary has developed a number of rules and regulations, but still, to some extent, the campus life is affected because we can no longer manage the seminary with solely biblical principles" (Interview C).

The people living around the seminary campus know the place as Mekane Yesus Seminary, where pastors and leaders are trained for the church, and they have a high regard for it. Now the School of Theology and the Management and Leadership College share the campus, and there are both Christians and non-Christians on the campus because the MY-MLC accepts non-believers onto its program. Some of the non-Christians behave and act differently from those that are part of the School of Theology, and that frustrates the members of the School of Theology. A leader said, "Whenever non-Christian behavior is seen on campus, people say that students of Mekane Yesus Seminary did this or that. Seeing that kind of behavior on our campus is a concern for us" (Interview B).

The Theology department offers Theology courses for the students of the School of Jazz Music. It also attempts to have an influence on the Management and Leadership College's program, although it is limited. Explaining the efforts the Theology department makes, Leader B said, "For instance, yesterday and the day before, the Management and Leadership College had a curriculum review meeting, and both Theology and Management and Leadership instructors were together. The attempt is there to help the department to keep its Christian integrity, but it is not easy because of the secular nature of the school" (Interview C).

The seminary also invites the faculty and students of MLC to seminars that it prepares. That gives the students of MLC exposure to how the church can respond to contemporary issues from a biblical perspective (Interview B). The School of Theology also invites students of all programs to its "community day," where special spiritual programs are presented (Interview C).

Other than these kinds of involvement, the Theology department does not offer any courses in the programs of MY-MLC because the Ministry of Education does not allow the college to have theology as part of its curriculum. When the researcher asked if there are any efforts taken to integrate faith and learning in the courses that are offered at MY-MLC, Leader D replied,

> With regards to the curriculum, there is no integration of theology into our curriculum in an open way, but there are a few courses like Counseling in the African Context and Holistic Development that relate to theology. We teach counseling from the perspective of the African context, Ethiopian context and even the church context. So we invite instructors from the Theology department to offer courses in counseling. In regards to holistic development, we teach about developing a person holistically from a spiritual, psychological, and physical point of view. There are a few chapters and few lessons that talk about the Christian way of transforming a person, a community, or a society. We raise examples of development approaches from the Christian, Muslim, and non-Christian points of view. There are certain values we reflect in our curriculum, but we do not teach courses of theology. (Interview D)

MY-MLC uses the faculty members of the Mekane Yesus Seminary to teach courses such as Civics and Ethical Education, Psychology, Communication, Counseling, Holistic Development, and Business Ethics. Faculty members of MY-MLC also teach Information Technology courses to the students of Theology and Church Music (Interview D). There is a sharing of human resources between the departments, though it is not systematized and well planned (Interview D).

The researcher asked how the transition process has affected the enrollment of students in the School of Theology. Leader A answered, "Even though the number of students in the Theology department is less than the number of students in the MY-MLC, their number has been increasing every year since the establishment of the Management and Leadership College" (Interview A). Since the transition, the department has seen an increase in the number of lay leaders who are joining the program to study theology. These lay leaders are professionals in their fields, such as medical doctors, lawyers, musicians, and engineers (Interview A). Therefore, the changes that have taken place have helped the Theology department to increase its student enrollment.

The Theology department has not only increased its number of students. It has also expanded its programs. That is partly motivated by the competition that exists between the department and the Management and Leadership College. A leader explains it this way:

> The Department of Theology is coping with this competitive environment. We are expanding our programs. We have different divisions and we plan to call them departments in the future. They are Biblical Studies, Systematic Theology, Church History, Practical Theology, and Christian–Muslim Relations. We have started a Summer Institute of Diaconia. We have also started evening classes for our degree and diploma programs. We are planning to start Family Therapy in Counseling. We will start a summer bachelor of Theology program next month, and as of September 2011, we are planning to start a master's program in Practical Theology. So in one way we are expanding. Sometimes a challenge can also become an opportunity to grow. (Interview B)

The seminary has a chapel service every morning from 8:00 to 8:30. Attending chapel is a requirement for Theology students who live on campus. Those who live off campus are not required to attend chapel. Chapel is not required for students of MY-MLC. The college has some Muslim students. As students of MY-MLC, they are not required to attend chapel. Leader A said, "We have witnessed that when we pray and preach, they sit and listen to us, and when they graduate [some of them have already graduated], they promise to come back for their further studies and say they have enjoyed studying with us." The fact that the chapel service is scheduled early in the morning, and that it is required only for students living on campus, shows that chapel does not have a prominent role in the life of the institutions.

As indicated above, there are different views about the transition of the seminary to a university. Some have a real concern about the negative effect on the Theology program if it becomes part of the future university. A leader, expressing his concern, said,

> If we are training accountants with the same purpose and values as other secular academic institutions, why do we need the program

here? Why don't we send our students to those secular institutions? If we don't have a Christian purpose in our education, if we don't have a Christian flavor in our education; and if, as a Christian, I cannot go and lecture there, let us say, on holistic development from the Christian perspective or on many other topics, then what is the use of having the program? We do not have the right to teach biblical courses or other courses from a biblical perspective because the Ministry of Education's policy says that we cannot teach religious education in the department. All education has to be secular in the MLC. (Interview B)

The fear of these faculty members is that if the new university that is going to be established seeks accreditation from the government, it will be difficult to maintain the Christian identity of the whole institution. They prefer to see the seminary separated from the university. Leader B again says,

My point is that the purposes of a seminary and a university are quite different. When we talk about a seminary, its purpose is training pastors for the church. That is our first purpose. The purpose of a Christian university is quite different. That is training people for the marketplace and the community. It is training students to graduate and serve in the society with their Christian values. That may be a long-term plan and intention of the church. But in the case of the seminary, the purpose is very clear. We need to stick to that purpose and we have to do it separately. I think if they go together (or if we integrate the two), the Theology program may be swallowed up by the other disciplines and become a kind of religious studies department where anybody can come and study, but that is not the purpose of the seminary. (Interview B)

There is agreement among the leadership that establishing a Christian university and seeking accreditation from the government would make it difficult for the university to function as a Christian university with a clear Christian mission. The leadership is considering other alternatives. One leader pointed out that currently a series of debates is discussing whether the institution should sacrifice its Christian identity for the sake of getting accreditation. He said that they are asking, "What is the value we are adding as a church? Is it just adding another management and leadership college?" (Interview C).

Another leader indicates the direction they want to take the university: "Our mission is to establish Mekane Yesus University. That means we are establishing a university that will become the dwelling place of Jesus. The throne of Jesus will be at the center of the university" (Interview A). They also plan to make biblical and theological courses a requirement for students of all programs and to make it a requirement to pass these courses to graduate from any program. Since that is not possible if the university is accredited by the government, for the reasons given above, the plan is to seek accreditation from other agencies that will allow the institution to function as a distinctly Christian university.

Mekane Yesus Seminary Summary

As discussed above, the Management and Leadership College (MY-MLC) was first established as a department of MYS but eventually was organized as an independent college in order to get accreditation from the government. It is not yet clear whether it is the whole seminary (MYS) or only MY-MLC that is going to transition to a university. However, as discussed above, there is a strong desire among the leaders of MYS to transition the whole seminary to a university rather than just transitioning MY-MLC.

When one looks closely at the changes that took place at MYS as a result of the transition of one of its departments to MY-MLC, one can see a clear shift in some of the eight categories of an institution's life Benne described in his chart.[37] Originally, the MY-MLC was started as a department with the same mission of MYS, which is training leaders for the church. However, the vision and mission statements of MY-MLC were changed to adapt to the government's secular guidelines for higher-educational institutions accredited by the government. While the mission statement of MYS clearly states the *public relevance of its Christian vision*, the only indication of the Christian identity of MY-MLC in its vision and mission statements is that it is owned by EECMY. That has created confusion on the *ethos* of MYS as described by the leaders.

---

37. Benne, *Quality with Soul*, 49.

In the area of *membership requirement*, though for many years the students of MYS used to come almost exclusively from EECMY, in recent years the seminary has started accepting students from different denominations. However, the majority of students still come from EECMY. MY-MLC is open to all students and accepts non-Christians. The future university (MYU) will also be open to both Christians and non-Christians. All the full-time faculty members of the MYS, including MY-MLC, are born-again Christians, and a large majority of them are members of EECMY. However, there are non-Christians teaching on a part-time basis at MY-MLC and MYS's School of Jazz Music.

MYS has a strong *Theology department* and it is growing by adding programs. The number of students in the Theology department has increased during the transition. However, its influence over MY-MLC is very limited. There are no *Bible or Theology courses* in the curriculum of MY-MLC. The seminary has a *chapel* service every morning from 8:00 to 8:30. Though attendance is a requirement for theology students who live on campus, it is not a requirement for the students of MY-MLC.

When it comes to *governance*, there is a close relationship between the MYS and its owner EECMY. The governing board of MYS is appointed by the executive committee of EECMY. All the members of the governing board are members of EECMY. The board also has overall responsibility for the MY-MLC and the future university.

EECMY provides financial *support* for the institution. The support mainly comes from congregations and synods that send their people for training and pay for their fees and living expenses. MY-MLC is also supported by different church bodies and donor organizations that work with the church.

From the above discussion, one can see that the MY-MLC has made a shift during transition from what Benne calls an *orthodox* type of college to an *intentionally pluralist* college in many aspects. If that move is not corrected in time, as suggested by the leaders, it increases the threat of secularization of the institution. If Mekane Yesus University follows the same path that was taken by MY-MLC, the church's desire to establish a distinctly Christian university with a Christian vision could be in jeopardy. Table 4 summarizes the current status of MYS using Benne's categories. MYS's departments, Department of Theology, Department of Theological Education by Extension (TEE), and Mekane Yesus Jazz Music School, function in a similar way and are represented by "MYS." MY-MLC is presented in the second column because it functions as an independent college accredited by the government.

Table 4: Changes Due to the Transition in MYS and MY-MLC

	MYS	MY-MLC
Public relevance of Christian vision	Pervasive from a shared point of view	Assured voice in an ongoing conversation
Public rhetoric	Unabashed invitation for fellow believers to an intentionally Christian enterprise	Presentation as a liberal arts school with a Christian heritage
Membership requirement	Near 100%, with orthodoxy tests	Intentional representation
Religion/theology department	Large, with theology privileged	Large, with theology as flagship
Religion/theology required courses	All courses affected by shared religious perspective	Choice in distribution or an elective
Chapel	Required daily in large church at a protected time	Voluntary at unprotected times, with low attendance
Ethos	Overt piety of sponsoring tradition	Open majority from sponsoring tradition finding private niche
Support by church	Indispensable financial support and majority of students from sponsoring tradition	Important direct and crucial indirect financial support; at least 50% of students
Governance	Owned and governed by church or its official representative	Owned and governed by church or its official representative

Africa International University

Africa International University (AIU) is a Christian chartered university in Kenya and is the successor of Nairobi Evangelical Graduate School of Theology (NEGST). NEGST came into being as a result of the vision of the late Byang Kato, the first general secretary of the Association of Evangelicals in Africa and Madagascar (AEAM), now renamed Association of Evangelicals in Africa (AEA). After Kato's death in a tragic swimming accident, the AEA took the responsibility of establishing an Anglophone graduate theological school.[38] NEGST was originally established to serve as a graduate school that catered to the graduates of existing lower-level evangelical theological schools in Africa.

AIU is currently organized under three schools. The first and original one is NEGST. Currently NEGST has five departments – Biblical Studies, Church History, Mission Studies, Pastoral Studies, and Theological Studies – and has over 500 graduates.[39]

The second school of AIU is the Institute for the Study of African Realities (ISAR). ISAR is organized under four centers: Center for Peace-Building and Conflict Transformation; Center for Law, Ethics, and Governance; Center for Transformational Church Empowerment; and Center for Research.[40]

The third school of AIU is the School of Professional Studies (SPS). Currently SPS runs Bachelor of Business Administration; Bachelor of Arts in Psychology and Counseling; Master of Arts in Education; and Master of Arts in Biblical Translation.

The researcher visited African International University in June 2011 and spent eight days at the university. During that time, the researcher was able to interview four senior leaders of the institution, make observations, attend chapel, collect documents relevant to the research, and hold informal discussions with students of the university.

The researcher interviewed the vice-chancellor (president), the deputy vice-chancellor and head of the Theology Department, the dean of the School of Professional Studies, and the head of the Missions Department. The interviews with the leaders took an average of fifty minutes. The researcher provided the interview protocol to each of the interviewees before the day of the interview and conducted each interview at the office of the interviewee.

Reasons for the Transition

The first research question asks, "What are the reasons for the transition from a theological college to a liberal arts college or university?" This section describes

---

38. ww.negst.edu.
39. www.africainternational.edu.
40. www.africanrealitiesinstitute.com.

the different reasons given by the leaders of AIU as to why NEGST transitioned to Africa International University.

According to the leaders of AIU, the consideration to transition NEGST to a Christian university came out of a review process done on the mission and vision of NEGST as it was preparing to celebrate its twenty-fifth anniversary. With the coming of its new vice-chancellor, Dr Douglas Carew, and its approaching twenty-fifth anniversary, the leadership said, "Let us review NEGST's vision and mission and ask the question where the Lord is leading us for the next twenty-five and even fifty years" (Leader A). A committee comprised of NEGST leadership and faculty and two representatives from AEA (the owners and sponsors of NEGST) was formed to deliberate on the future of NEGST and to look at the whole matter of the possibility of transitioning to a Christian university.

The committee, looking at the vision statement "Promoting Excellence in African Christianity," asked what that meant. A leader said, "We had always defined and understood that to mean training in theological leadership and pastoral leadership. So the question then was, 'Is that all there is to African Christianity?'" (Leader A).

During the same time, a number of the leaders of the institution were reading a book written by Chris Wright, *The Mission of God*. Reading the book and reflecting on the vision and mission of the institution gave the leaders a broader understanding of God's mission in the world and their part in it. Describing the theological reflection they had after reading the book, one leader said, "Part of what that did was give us a fuller understanding of God's mission in our world, a fuller theological and missional understanding of God's purposes, and what God is doing in our world. He certainly is bringing us as individuals to himself but he is also creating a kingdom community which is broader than church leadership. The church plays a vital role in that" (Leader A).

In addition to the theological reflection, the leadership was also asking, "What are the challenges in our society today?" They analyzed the challenges and confirmed two things. The first was that there was still a lack of quality leadership in the church; therefore they still needed to continue training quality leaders for the church. The second was that there was also a lack of quality Christian leadership in wider society. Those two affirmations then became the fundamental pillars for AIU (Interview A). They saw the need for quality theological (pastoral) training for the church and quality professional training for the marketplace and civic society. Then they realized that in order to do both they needed to transition to a full Christian university where they could provide quality leadership for the church and quality professional Christian leadership for the marketplace and civil society (Interview A).

Another leader, describing the driving force for the transition to a university and the future plans, said, "We can't say we are a university that tries to reach Africa if we live out other areas of knowledge. That was another driving force. If we are to change the landscape of Africa, then people trained in Christian institutions should go to all facets of society: business, counseling, law, governance, and politics. We are also thinking of architecture and public health so that we bring Christ into all these disciplines to create a difference" (Interview B).

The committee then presented its recommendations to the governing council of NEGST. The council accepted the recommendation and then mandated a feasibility study. The process took "about two to three years before the final decision was made" (Interview A). Once the decision was made by the governing council, it wrote a formal letter to AEA that explained the process and the decision that had been made. AEA accepted and endorsed the decision (Interview A).

Therefore, the first reason why NEGST considered transition to a Christian university was its realization that fulfilling its vision of "Promoting Excellence in African Christianity" required more than providing quality theological and pastoral training for church leadership – that is, it also required providing quality professional training for the marketplace and civic society.

The second reason NEGST considered transitioning to a Christian university was to build financial sustainability. From the beginning, NEGST was established as a graduate school and did not have a large number of students, unlike those schools that have both graduate and undergraduate programs. That meant it had a narrower source of income from student tuition (Interview A). Therefore, NEGST was heavily dependent on donor funding, especially from the West. A leader said, "Part of our history shows that whenever there was a financial challenge in the West, donations drop and we suffer as a result" (Leader A). When donations were coming well and when there were no financial challenges, attempts to make changes to the institution to make it self-sustaining were met with resistance. Another leader said, "When funding was coming from the West, people were saying, 'Why are you rocking the boat? Our budget is being funded'" (Leader B).

In addition to the drop in funding from the West, the theological and biblical studies departments of NEGST were not getting enough students to remain solvent. It became obvious that transitioning to a university was necessary to keep the theological school alive, and the school was forced to ask serious questions about its survival. As one leader put it,

> Part of the question we were asking was "Does the Lord want NEGST to last or is it time to wind up?" And we came to the conclusion that the Lord wants us to keep going and build an institution that would last. The next question was "How do you build an institution that would last and is sustainable?" That led us to revisiting our model. When we go into a Christian university, we are not just offering other courses, non-theological courses in other disciplines (and we can do that just as a graduate school). But then we said, to build sustainability, we must also go to undergraduate level so that we can build a base. Therefore, our new programs now are undergraduate-level programs like a bachelor of psychology and a bachelor of business administration. So, in a sense, the sustainability issue was the other reason that doing undergraduate programs both theological and non-theological actually allows us to build operational sustainability that would lead us to the point where we are no longer dependent on donation, but NEGST can actually be sustained. (Interview A)

Explaining that finances were the primary reason why the institution considered transitioning to a Christian university, a leader said, "And if it were not for the finances – and we were doing pretty well financially as a seminary – we probably would have said that since all these other schools have started these programs, we will support them rather than begin our own. We cannot ignore the fact that it is going to be difficult to raise funds from overseas forever" (Leader B).

Though there was some resistance about such change in the institution at the beginning, when financial challenges got serious, all agreed that the institution had to make this move to survive. A leader, explaining the process, said,

> Now everyone was on the same page at the beginning. But when you go through difficult situations, it makes you rethink your paradigm. We came to a point where salaries could not be paid, allowances would not be given; and the board was saying, if you are not bringing more students, it means you are not supposed to be here. Faculty-to-student ratio has to be 1 to 25. How do you bring in students? Then there starts some mental transformation and we started to question our core assumptions. Even now there are key people who actually champion this change but we have to drag some people along. (Interview B)

The third reason mentioned by the leaders for the transition to a university was that having only one program (Theology) and not getting recognition from the government made it difficult for the school to market its program to the wider community. The number of students joining NEGST was also decreasing (Interview B). Therefore, NEGST considered transitioning to a university by adding more programs and getting a charter from the government to attract more students and expand its student base.

The fourth reason mentioned by the leaders for NEGST's transition to a university is that the Commission for Higher Education of the Kenyan government was pressuring private higher-educational institutions to transform themselves into universities. Explaining the reason behind the push, a leader said,

> There is another factor: "The Millennial Development Goal," as you understand, requires countries to provide free primary education. As of 2002 [the] Kenyan government started giving free primary education. That means ten years down the line, they are going to have a huge mass of students that they cannot accommodate within their own public universities. Therefore, they were putting lots of pressure on private colleges to transform themselves into universities so that they could have space to accommodate all the students coming to higher education. (Interview B)

Therefore, the demand from the government was also among the reasons mentioned by the leaders of AIU as to why NEGST considered adding other programs and transitioning to a Christian university.

The fifth reason that was mentioned by the leaders of the institution for its transition to a university was the request coming from its own students. Students wanted the institution to get a charter from the government so that they could get certificates recognized by the Kenyan government that would enable them to go out and compete for jobs in any organization. "A group of them could not fit within the church, so they needed to work outside the church. For example, students coming to the Christian education department want to be teachers in public schools. But they will be considered as students coming from a non-chartered school" (Interview B). Students also wanted the school to get a charter from the government because they were not able to get loans from the Higher Education Loans Board (Interview B).

From the above discussion, one can see that there were five main reasons why NEGST considered transitioning to AIU. The first reason was its realization that fulfilling its vision of "Promoting Excellence in African Christianity" required providing not just quality theological and pastoral training for church leadership, but also quality professional training for the marketplace and civic society. The second reason was that by adding undergraduate theological and non-theological programs the institution wanted to build operational sustainability that would free it from dependence on donations from the West. The third reason was that transitioning to a university by adding more programs and getting a charter from the government of Kenya would allow the institution to market its programs to the wider community so that it would attract more students. The fourth reason was the pressure from the Commission for Higher Education of the Kenyan government on private higher-educational institutions to transform themselves into universities. The fifth reason was the request of the students of NEGST that the institution get a charter from the government so that they could get certificates that would enable them to go out and compete for jobs in any organization.

External and Internal Challenges

The second research question asked, "What are the external and internal challenges these higher Christian institutions face as they go through this transition?" Presented below is what the researcher found from the interviews he conducted with the leaders and the materials published by the institution. Since NEGST transitioned to AIU recently, the challenges mentioned below are the ones that surfaced at the initial stages of the transition. Some of the challenges mentioned by the leaders are those they expected to come soon.

The first challenge indicated by the leaders of AIU in implementing the transition to a university was bringing everyone together and owning the vision. It took some time to share the vision and to convince everyone that this was the direction the institution needed to go in. One leader put it this way:

> Perhaps one of the biggest challenges internally has been sharing the vision and bringing people along, not only to accept the vision but to own the vision. You can accept the vision biting your teeth, because you are dragged along, but people need to believe in the vision and say this is what God has for us as a Christian institution, and this is what God is calling us to do. That is a big challenge and it involves change management. (Interview A)

The second challenge that was raised by another leader and which is related to the first one was having mental preparedness in the faculty, administration, and students to adjust to the changes this transition would bring to the institution. NEGST had been a graduate school with no undergraduate programs, and the students that came to study at NEGST were mature students. However, the new undergraduates program of AIU would bring many younger students, and that would bring many changes to campus life. Explaining his concern, a leader said,

> We are in the old paradigm of the school. If 200 teenagers apply to join our programs, all of them Christians, and we admit them, where will we put them? How will we contain them? We just have a few and it was too difficult for us to contain them. One of these young students went to chapel with his hat on. There was a guy who said, "These are students from the School of Professional Studies. Tell them to remove their hats in chapel." Since 1984 we have thought one way. And now our values will be challenged. What we considered to be sacred will be challenged. (Interview B)

The leaders of the institution also needed to be prepared to make adjustments to the new changes. An example of that, according to one leader, was that when there was a function at NEGST, such as a lecture or some kind of presentation, all the functions of the school stopped, and everybody went to attend the presentation. That was something that might need to change in a university setting. It would be difficult to require students of all faculties to stop everything they were doing just because somebody was presenting a theology paper (Interview B). The leader also indicated that the Theology School needed to make a mental adjustment to the new realities because they used to be the only school of the institution, but now they were one of three schools (Interview B).

The third challenge the institution is facing in implementing the transition is a financial challenge. As the institution adds new programs, it needs more resources to meet the growing needs of the institution. The university is now going through a difficult period of financial challenges because of the economic downturn in the West (Interview A).

The fourth challenge raised by the leaders in relation to implementing the transition from a theological school to a university is that, now that they have a charter with the government, they are required to strictly follow the guidelines provided by the Commission for Higher Education. A leader said, "There are rigorous checks and balances, and they have their guidelines that we must follow. Sometimes their guidelines impinge on our vision and mission. So we have to see where the balance is. That oversight poses a challenge for us. In a sense it keeps us on our toes, but, on the other hand, it also puts pressure on us" (Interview D).

One of the issues at stake here is in the area of student recruitment. Though the Kenyan constitution gives Christian higher-educational institutions permission to function with freedom as Christian institutions, they are not allowed to discriminate among applicants based on their religion. The university would not have been able to get a charter with a statement that indicated that the institution discriminated among applicants based on their faith, and that may be a challenge in the future (Interview B). However, the leaders hope that the non-Christians who come will be a minority with a minimal voice, but the louder voice will be from their own peers who are believers. The university does not plan to impose Christianity on those who come as unbelievers, but it would like those who are believers to be witnesses to the unbelievers (Interview B).

The same policy may affect the future hiring policies of AIU. So far, AIU hires only Christians. However, that is seen as discrimination according to the Kenyan constitution. AIU and other Christian private universities in Kenya see this as a challenge. A leader said, "There is an association of Christian private universities that are fighting that at all levels to say that we are Christians and you cannot accept us as Christians without allowing us to operate as Christians" (Interview B).

There are also other phrases that the institution included in its governing documents but which were changed by the Commission for Higher Education. For example, the institution had the phrase "a private Christian non-denominational university" in its establishment clause sent to the government; that was taken out and replaced with "non-profit-making private university." That, however, does not significantly affect how the institution functions because a clear statement of faith and the university's philosophy, which is rooted in theology and mission, is given in the charter. A leader said, "We are participating in God's mission with [a] Christ-centered worldview. That is our philosophy and is in our statement of faith. We also require evangelical commitment from faculty and everyone who is part of the university. This charter was actually signed by the President of Kenya on the 4th of March 2011. Therefore, legally we are a Christian entity" (Interview A).

Therefore the leaders of AIU described four major challenges the institution has faced in its transition from a theological school to a Christian university. The first one is bringing everyone to be convinced of the need for the transition and to owning the vision of the Christian university. The second challenge is having the mental preparedness of the faculty, administration, and students to adjust to the changes that the transition is bringing to the institution. The third one is a financial challenge: the institution needs to have the funds to maintain what it has been doing and to make an investment for its future expansion. The fourth challenge is keeping the regulations of the government and at the same time maintaining its own policies that will help the university to keep its clear Christian identity.

Effects of the Transition on the Mission

As mentioned above, when the leaders of NEGST launched a review process, they reviewed NEGST's mission statement and core values. When asked if there was a change of vision and mission when NEGST transitioned to a Christian university, one leader said, "The core mission of NEGST has not changed because . . . we are still committed to training quality pastoral leadership. We have revised our statements. In terms of substance, the mission has not changed, but it has been enhanced so that it would now include theological training as well as professional Christian training. Actually we never had a vision statement for NEGST, but in this process we came up with a vision statement" (Interview A).

NEGST is now one of the three schools of AIU and it has kept its former mission statement. Its full mission statement, given on its website, says,

> NEGST exists primarily as an evangelical post-graduate theological institution to promote excellence in African Christianity. This over-arching mission is promoted through:
> - training men and women in necessary ministry skills;
> - developing in students a deeper understanding of biblical and theological foundations;
> - studying the major issues and challenges facing Christianity in Africa; and
> - engaging in research and publication to address the concerns and needs of African Christianity.
>
> The above fourfold mission is in turn promoted through:
> - striving to be a godly international community of scholars;
> - encouraging personal spiritual formation to produce servant Christian leaders for the churches and ministries; and
> - offering integrated programmes.[41]

The vision statement of AIU is, "Christ-centered leaders in Africa educated to transform God's people and world"; and its mission statement says, "To educate Christ-centered leaders for the transformation of God's people and world, through innovative programmes, research, and community engagement."[42]

By comparing the mission statements of AIU and NEGST, one can see that the institution has expanded its mission. When asked if the transition has affected the focus of NEGST, a leader said that every effort has been made to protect the core mission of NEGST. Explaining how that was done, he said,

---

41. www.negst.edu.
42. www.africainternational.edu.

> We organized AIU around schools. So NEGST remains intact as a school with its purpose and vision. We now have three schools, NEGST, Institute of African Realities (ISAR) and School of Professional Studies (SPS). Each school will have its distinct mission and purpose statement within the overall AIU mission statement . . . We have broadened the original mission statement we had for NEGST so that it fits the mission of the university, but then NEGST, as a school, retains its vision and mission. (Interview A)

AIU received its charter from the government of Kenya in March 2011; therefore, it is too early to see any clear effects of the transition on the mission of the Theology program. In this short period, no effects on the Theology program can be seen (Leader C). The researcher was also able to talk informally to students of the Theology programs of NEGST. The students he talked to confirmed that they had not seen any real changes to the Theology program since the transition.

ISAR is the second constituent school of AIU, and it works in close partnership with NEGST. The mission statement of ISAR says, "ISAR's mission is to transform persons, churches, and African societies toward greater realization of Jesus' vision of a just and peaceful community through educational initiatives (formal and non-formal) designed to: train trainers, build institutional capacity, form effective leaders of integrity, empower individuals."[43]

ISAR has four centers: Center for Peace-Building and Conflict Transformation; Center for Law, Ethics, and Governance; Center for Transformational Church Empowerment; and Center for Research. These centers are designed to bring an impact in the wider society. The Center for Peace-Building and Conflict Transformation has an agenda "to resolve conflict in Africa at all levels – family, interpersonal, in churches and organizations, between communities, and at national levels."[44] The Center for Law, Ethics, and Governance "seeks to empower and resource Christians who are called to serve in the judiciary, the legislative bodies, and the civil service of African

---

43. www.africanrealitiesinstitute.com.
44. Ibid.

nations."⁴⁵ The Center for Transformational Church Empowerment provides "a variety of non-formal and continuing education opportunities that promote 'Jesus-style leadership' for African churches."⁴⁶ The purpose of the Center for Research is described as follows: "The Center is a learning environment in which Christian scholars and practitioners from all across the continent of Africa (along with international partners) are engaging in a rigorous scholarly examination of the complex issues facing Africans in the 21st century. The Center forms African leaders who are equipped to empower the Christian movement to manifest the 'shalom' of God's Kingdom."⁴⁷

The programs of ISAR attract many students who would not have come to NEGST to study theology. The Theology department plays a key role in the programs of ISAR, and that has expanded its ministry to the wider society (Interview B).

The newest school of AIU is the School of Professional Studies (SPS). The main objective of SPU is printed on its advertisement brochure: "The main objective of SPS is to discover and facilitate the development of ministry and educational potential for the various professionals such as accountants, translators, educators, marketers, bankers, entrepreneurs, counselors, among others, in order to be faithful stewards, light and salt in the world." Currently SPS runs Bachelor of Business Administration, Bachelor of Arts in Psychology and Counseling, Master of Arts in Education, and Master of Arts in Biblical Translation.

One of the things that identifies an institute to the public is its name. The name of the institution was changed from Nairobi Evangelical Graduate School of Theology to African International University. Its first name clearly indicated its evangelical identity while the new name does not. When asked why a name that does not identify the institution as Christian/evangelical was chosen, one leader said, "I think the primary thing is that we are in the continent of Africa. We train people internationally and we had to use "university" not "seminary" because of the expansion. So it was not a deliberate act to conceal that we are a Christian institution. That was not the intention, but we went into a process of choosing a name before we chose this one" (Interview B).

---

45. Ibid.
46. Ibid.
47. Ibid.

The leader also indicated that having the name "Africa International University" is having a positive impact on students coming from countries that are not sympathetic to the Christian faith. Having a degree that reads "Africa International University" is more acceptable in Muslim countries than a degree that reads "Nairobi Evangelical Graduate School of Theology" (Interview B).

Another leader indicated that, though some graduates of NEGST do not support its transition to a university, others fully support the transition and some have even asked that their certificates be changed retroactively to read "Africa International University" instead of "Nairobi Evangelical Graduate School of Theology." They want their degrees to be more acceptable in the public sector.

All the public documents of AIU including its governing documents, its website, brochures, and other publications clearly indicate its Christian identity and what it stands for. AIU's vision statement, mission statement, core values, and philosophy of education all clearly show the Christian commitment of the institution.

When asked if the institution has faced any challenges in stating its Christian identity in its public communications, a leader explained that, as a private chartered university, they are allowed to function within their own vision and mission. The legal framework of the country allows them to do that. Both the old and the new constitutions of the country clearly recognize the freedom of religion. Therefore, they can operate as a Christian institution (Interview A).

Another leader sees that transitioning to a university and getting a charter from the government has made the institution more committed to its mission statement and to living up to its stated vision and mission. He said, "We have now become a university, we are more sensitive to our mission than ever before. This is because we are now exposed and the government has its eyes on us, not in a bad sense, but as the body that awards charters, the Commission for Higher Education, has its eyes on us. So we are now more sensitive to our mission and vision than ever before" (Interview D).

The researcher asked how the institution could fulfill its mission of raising Christ-centered leaders unless it accepts only those who are believers in Christ in the first place. Another leader answered,

> We talked about that, and we asked, "What kind of university do we really want to be?" This is partly where our understanding of God's mission comes in. We want primarily to train Christians, but God's mission is bringing people to himself. So how can we build a sense of mission into who we are? You can still take in only Christians and send them out for mission. That is a valid position and there are universities that do that. But . . . instead of just sending out people to mission, you can allow people who are not Christians to come in and get them exposed to the gospel. That was the option we went for. We didn't go to [a] completely open-door policy where anyone would come. But the key thing for us was in terms of our students, we can have primarily Christian students but non-Christian students also can come in. In terms of our faculty, staff, and governance, we insist that everyone must be a Christian. (Interview A)

Another point raised by the same leader is that there are lots of higher-educational institutions in Kenya. Therefore, people have several choices of higher-educational institutions to attend. Those who come to AIU are students who have some interest in Christianity anyway. Those who come in knowing that this is a Christian institution have to abide by the values and ethos at least while they are there, and they have to sign up to that (Interview A).

Chapel also plays a key role in keeping the Christian identity of AIU. It is a requirement of all students and faculty members of NEGST unless they are part-time. The researcher asked if the same policy applies to the students of the new program, especially those who are non-believers. One leader responded,

> It wouldn't be an option. That is why it says without exception everyone must abide by our ethos . . . A student coming in knows that we are [a] Christian institution, we teach Bible, we are committed to integrate Christian faith and learning, and chapel is an important part of that integration. Therefore, it is not going to be optional. It is going to be expected and required. Now that is an area we are slightly concerned about in the new constitution of Kenya, which talks about not forcing people to perform religious rites and things like that. So that is an area, not just us but also other Christian institutions are looking at. Our position is that

there are secular, non-Christian universities. If you don't want to observe certain religious practices, go to a secular university. But if you choose to come to us, then these are the things that you must commit yourself to. (Interview A)

Effects of the Transition on the Relationship with AEA

AIU is owned by AEA and is governed by a board of trustees that represents AEA. The board is now the legally registered body that represents AEA and is in charge of the institution and responsible for safeguarding the vision and mission of the AIU and appointing the members of the governing council.

As a university sponsored by AEA, AIU does not have a specific church or denominational sponsorship. That has both positive and negative implications on the ministry of AIU. Positively, the fact that AIU is not founded by or affiliated with a specific denomination has allowed it to be broadly evangelical and accept people coming from different kinds of churches (Interview A). The negative impact is that AIU (NEGST) does not have any strong grassroots church connection. The members of AIU's sponsoring organization (AEA) are national association of evangelical denominations of different African countries. Therefore, NEGST does not have a direct link to specific denominations or churches.

Describing what AIU is doing to fill that gap, a leader said, "We value our AEA roots but we are also saying that we must build grassroots connections with churches, churches around here and around the world. I am convinced that it will help us to keep our soul" (Interview A). When another leader was asked how church leaders perceived the transition from NEGST to AIU, he said, "It is a mixed bag. Some of them are endorsing it, and others are saying we have lost it. Some of them are lamenting, while others say that this is long overdue and that they have been waiting for this. People react differently depending on where they have been placed in ministry" (Interview B).

Another leader says that the feedback he received was generally positive. Describing the positive responses, he said,

> Generally speaking, the testimonies I have heard about this transition have been very positive. The reason being, most of the students, when they were here (most of the key churches in Nairobi are led by one of our graduates), kept asking, "Can NEGST train

us to be broader or to be more exposed? Can you train us to know how to manage issues of money? Can you help us deal with the issue of HIV/AIDS? Can't you provide something to beat poverty from a biblical point of view?" So most of our students are happy now that we have opened the gate wider so that the students they recommend to come are more exposed and trained holistically, and that we can give them holistic training. (Interview D)

Another leader also indicated that most of the students coming to the School of Professional Studies are students coming from churches led by the graduates of NEGST. These leaders recommend that their members come and study at AIU (Interview B). Building a strong relationship with churches and being accountable to them is one of the key ways that AIU sees will protect the institution from sliding into secularism (Interview A).

Effects of the Transition on the Theology Program

NEGST has transitioned to a Christian university recently. Therefore, it is too early to evaluate how the transition has impacted the Theology program. However, there are indications of the kind of impact the transition will have on the Theology program. One leader said, "It makes it stronger and more responsive to the issues of the church directly" (Interview B). Another leader said that the opening of other programs in the school would "create a forum whereby we can understand the world around us better so that we can communicate God's message effectively. This transition for us is an ideal opportunity because we can provide courses which we were not able to provide before" (Interview D).

When the discussion about transitioning to a Christian university was taking place, there were some concerns among the faculty about its effects on the future of NEGST. Some were concerned that NEGST would lose its vision and become "a Christian university that has lost its Christian soul like many other universities" (Interview A). In order to safeguard against such dangers, AIU was organized around schools so that the mission of NEGST would remain intact and would not lose its focus on training men and women for ministry.

However, NEGST is playing a key role in the curriculum development of all the other programs, especially in the area of integration of faith and learning.

"NEGST is bringing the Christian worldview into all the other areas" (Interview B). All students of the university, whether they are doing a Bachelor of Theology or Bachelor of Psychology, are required to take core Christian foundation courses. The addition of the other schools also created an opportunity to do integration at NEGST. One leader said,

> Integration takes place even within NEGST. Other schools would challenge NEGST to speak on contemporary issues and theologize there. NEGST would also take different issues from the other schools and prepare curriculum that would enable itself to prepare pastors to speak to these life-and-death issues of society. Hopefully it will be a two-way street with the Christian core as the base for all integration of faith and learning. (Interview B)

There are core courses for all students of AIU that are designed to lay a Christian foundation. They are Foundations of Christian Life and Missions, Bible and Moral Issues, and Hermeneutics. Integration of faith and learning does not happen only by requiring a few Bible and Theology courses in all the programs. Explaining how that is done, a leader said,

> Instead of just adding three courses of theology in these programs, we are laying a foundation for each program that is basically Christian from the very beginning . . . What we are saying is that the thinking that goes into each program right from the very beginning is laying a foundation that is basically Christian . . . But within every course there is Christian thinking. There is Christian thinking about counseling and psychology, there is Christian thinking in education, there is Christian thinking about business. (Interview B)

One of the challenges indicated by one of the leaders of AIU is the lack of qualified Christian faculty members who are able to integrate faith and learning in all the subjects that are taught at AIU (Interview B). To fill that gap, for the next few years, AIU wants to use faculty members from other Christian universities in the West who have done an effective job of integration. Once AIU has graduates who are trained through such programs, they can recruit their own faculty members from those graduates and continue effective integration of faith and learning in all their programs themselves.

Africa International University Summary

The discussion above presented the reasons why NEGST transitioned to AIU, the challenges it faced during the transition, and the effects of the transition on its mission, Theology program, and its relationship with AEA. Since the transition took place recently, it is too early to see the full effect of the transition on the institution. However, the summary below shows where the institution stands according to the eight areas of church-related academic institutions given by Benne.

The transition of NEGST to AIU has not diminished the *Christian vision* of the institution. The vision statement of AIU is "Promoting Excellence in African Christianity." By transitioning to a university, the institution has enhanced its vision by adding professional Christian training in different areas to the theological training which is still the focus of NEGST. Regarding its *public rhetoric*, all the public documents of AIU, including its governing documents, its website, brochures, and other publications, clearly indicate its Christian identity and what it stands for.

Since AIU is not owned by a specific denomination, it does not have specific *membership requirements*. So far it hires only Christians and it wants to keep it that way. However, there is a concern that the government may see that as discrimination and may challenge the policy. The university now accepts non-Christian students because the law of Kenya does not allow discrimination of applicants based on their religion, and the university also sees this as an opportunity to reach out to unbelievers. However, AIU wants to keep believers as the majority so that the evangelical atmosphere remains strong.

AIU is organized around schools so that the mission of NEGST remains intact. NEGST as a *School of Theology* will keep its focus on training men and women for ministry. It also plays a key role in the curriculum development of all the other programs and in the area of integration of faith and learning. There are *required courses* for all students of AIU that are designed to lay a Christian foundation in the life of students. *Chapel* also plays a key role in keeping the Christian identity of AIU. Attendance is a requirement for all full-time students and faculty members of AIU.

When it comes to *governance*, as an institution owned by AEA, AIU is governed by a board of trustees that represents AEA, which is a legally registered body that is in charge of the institution and responsible for safeguarding its vision and mission. There is no direct financial *support* that comes from AEA.

The transition from NEGST to AIU took place recently, therefore, it did not bring a dramatic change in the overall function of the institution. The leaders of AIU are aware of possible challenges of secularization that may come in the future if the government requires AIU not to discriminate regarding the people it hires. Currently, AIU is somewhere between the *orthodox* and *critical mass* categories described by Benne.

Table 5: Changes Due to the Transition from NEGST to AIU

	NEGST	AIU
Public relevance of Christian vision	Pervasive from a shared point of view	Pervasive from a shared point of view
Public rhetoric	Unabashed invitation for fellow believers to an intentionally Christian enterprise	Presentation as a liberal arts school with a Christian heritage
Membership requirement	Near 100%, with orthodoxy tests	Orthodoxy for faculty and staff, not for students
Religion/theology department	Large, with theology privileged	Large, with theology privileged
Religion/theology required courses	All courses affected by shared religious perspective	All courses affected by shared religious perspective and required courses in Christian foundation
Chapel	Required in large church at a protected time daily	Required in large church at a protected time daily
Ethos	Overt piety of evangelical tradition	Open majority from sponsoring tradition finding private niche
Support by church	Not owned by a church; indirect support through sponsored students	Not owned by a church; indirect support through sponsored students
Governance	Owned and governed by AEA	Owned and governed by AEA

Table 5 summarizes the changes discussed above using Benne's categories.[48] However, the table does not show the whole picture. For example, NEGST still receives only Christians while the other new departments accept non-Christian students too. One has to look to the descriptions given above to get the details.

St Paul's University

St Paul's University is an ecumenical private Christian university located approximately 30 kilometers (18.6 miles) from Nairobi, along the Nairobi–Limuru Road. It was founded in 1903 as a school of divinity. The divinity school continued as an institution owned by the Anglican Church of Kenya (ACK) until 1949, when the Presbyterian Church of East Africa (PCEA) and the Methodist Church of Kenya (MCK) joined and brought their ministerial candidates for training.[49]

In 1954 the three churches formed a council that ran the affairs of the college, and in 1955 the name of the college was changed to St Paul's United Theological College.[50] In 1973 a fourth church, the Reformed Church of East Africa (RCEA), formally joined the other three churches as a participating partner. In 1993, the National Council of Churches of Kenya (NCCK) in its corporate identity joined as the fifth participating partner in the ownership of St Paul's United Theological College.[51]

Beginning in the year 2000, St Paul's expanded its academic programs by introducing innovative courses like Business Management, Information Communication Technology, Communication, Community Pastoral Care and HIV & AIDS, and Development Studies.[52] In September 2007, the college was granted a university charter by the government of Kenya to operate as a private Christian university. The university currently runs diploma programs in Leadership, Business Management, Banking, Marketing Management, Logistics

---

48. Benne, *Quality with Soul*.
49. www.stpaulslimuru.ac.ke.
50. Ibid.
51. Ibid.
52. Charles Kilonzo and Wanjira Maganjo, eds., "Up Close and Personal with Dr Timothy Wachira," in *Voice: St Paul's University*, ed. Charles Kilonzo and Wanjira Maganjo (Limuru, Kenya: St Paul University, 2010), 12.

and Supplies, and Theology, which is offered in its affiliated colleges.[53] It offers Bachelor of Arts programs in Communication, Business Administration and Management, Divinity, Business, and Information Technology. It offers graduate diploma and Master of Arts degrees in Christian and Muslim Relations, Community Pastoral Care and HIV & AIDS, Master of Development Studies, and Master of Theology. Currently the university functions under four participating partner churches and the NCCK, with representation in the governing council in the following proportions: ACK 50 percent, PCEA 20 percent, MCK 10 percent, RCEA 10 percent, and NCCK 10 percent.[54]

The researcher visited St Paul's University in June 2011. During that time, he was able to interview senior leaders of the institution, visit the campus, make observations, collect documents relevant to the research, and hold informal discussions with a faculty member of the School of Theology.

The researcher interviewed the deputy vice-chancellor, the dean of the Theology department, and the dean of the Faculty of Business and Communication Studies. He was not able to interview the vice-chancellor of the university because he was busy with council meetings, so he delegated the dean of the Faculty of Business and Communication Studies for the interview. The interviews with the leaders took an average of fifty minutes. The researcher provided the interview protocol to each of the interviewees before the day of the interview and conducted each interview at the office of the interviewee.

Reasons for the Transition

As mentioned above, SPU was first established as a divinity school training people for ministry. There was a discussion to transition to a Christian university around 1980, when the college started offering a bachelor's degree in Theology (Interview A). At the time, the degrees were accredited by the Association of Theological Institutions in East Africa. Around 1985 there was a new government proclamation that made it possible for theological colleges to become universities. That opened the door for private universities to offer higher-education programs that had been offered only in a few public universities. The churches also felt that they could offer much more than just theological education because the public universities were not absorbing

---

53. www.stpaulslimuru.ac.ke.
54. Ibid.

everybody. The council of St Paul's United Theological College decided to make the move at that time (Interview A).

Peter Ensor, who served at the institution from 1985 to 1998 and as its principal from 1995 to 1998, writing about the steps that were taken in the early days to transition St Paul's United Theological College to a Christian university, says,

> Many were the plans discussed in those early days. In the earlier part of 1988, there were serious discussions with the Commission regarding the possibility of creating a "Christian University of Kenya," which would embrace many of the Theological Institutions in Nairobi as well as St Paul's. However, the idea fell apart when many of the Nairobi Colleges (which were more clearly "evangelical" than St Paul's) insisted that the recently formulated "Lausanne Covenant" should provide the doctrinal basis of faith for the proposed Christian University, a stipulation which St Paul's, drawing its support from a wider ecclesiastical constituency, could not accept.[55]

After this attempt failed, there was also discussion about combining St Paul's with denominational colleges of the sponsoring denominations to form St Paul's University with "Constituent Colleges." However, the idea was not implemented because the sponsoring denominations became more interested in establishing their own autonomous universities.[56]

Explaining how St Paul's United Theological College started seeking a charter from the government, and the challenges it faced, Ensor writes,

> The Commission for Higher Education had encouraged the College to develop into a fully-fledged University, and to be "chartered" as such. To begin with, the Staff was not wholly in favor of the idea, fearing that the College would eventually become "secularized" in the process. But since there seems to be no other way to offer legally recognized degrees, it was felt necessary to comply. The college was accordingly registered as a University

---

55. Peter Ensor, "Those Memorable Years (St Paul's 1985 to 1998)," in *For God and Humanity: 100 Years of St Paul's United Theological College* (Eldoret, Kenya: Zapf Chancery Research Consultants and Publishers, 2003), 230–231.
56. Ibid., 231.

(though still under the name of "St Paul United Theological College"), with the right to offer its own degrees in 1990. That was, however, only a temporary provision, as a permanent "charter" awaited accreditation.[57]

Getting accreditation from the Commission for Higher Education took a long time. Ensor indicates that there were three factors in that: staff instability, lack of adequate financial support, and an apparent lack of commitment among the sponsors of the college.[58]

SPU started diversifying its programs beginning in 2000 and eventually was chartered as a private Christian university in 2007. The current leaders of SPU mentioned other reasons for the transition to a university during the interviews.

One of the reasons mentioned for St Paul's United Theological College's decision to get a charter from the government and become a private Christian university was that the degrees it offered would be accredited and its graduates would be able to get government jobs (Interview B). This demand came from students and graduates because they wanted to be able to get jobs anywhere in the country. After the university received its charter, graduates of the institution, even those that graduated with a Bachelor of Theology degree, were able to get government jobs such as teaching positions in secondary schools (Interview B).

The process of seeking a charter from the government led to another reason why the institution decided to transition to a university. Once the college started to seek accreditation, the government demanded that the school have more than one program. The college was not able to get its accreditation with only a Theology program. Therefore, the school started programs such as Bachelor of Business Administration, Bachelor of Information and Communication Technology, and Bachelor of Communications programs. That led to its transition to a Christian university.

A further reason that led the institution to transition to a Christian university was its financial challenges. It was getting hard for the institution to stay viable with few students in the Theology program. One leader said, "An institution cannot be viable with only thirty students. We do not have

---

57. Ibid., 232.
58. Ibid., 233.

other sources of income. Our only income is tuition fees from students and it is the other faculties that can bring many students. We no longer were getting money from outside donors, so we had to depend on money from the students" (Interview B). Another leader added, "One should understand that theological education remained for a long time the work of the church because the church was the recipient of the theologically educated people. So we could not get funding or support from public institutions like the government" (Interview A). Therefore, the institution considered transitioning to a Christian university to enhance its financial viability. By opening up other faculties and increasing the number of students, the institution wanted to increase its income and become financially sustainable. The other faculties enabled the university to generate more funds. A leader said, "Because of the addition of the other faculties, the university is now able to develop, build, and expand using internally generated funds. The Faculty of Business Administration is helping the institution to get more funds because we do not depend on external funding to pay salaries and to do many of our things" (Interview C). Therefore, opening up the other faculties and accepting many students has helped the institution to be financially sustainable.

There are therefore several reasons mentioned above that led St Paul's United Theological College to transition to a university. The main reasons are, first, the institution wanted to offer more than theological education to meet the growing needs of higher education in the country. Second, they were encouraged by the Commission for Higher Education to develop into a fully-fledged university. The third reason is that the students were demanding that the college get accreditation from the government so that they would be able to have government-recognized certificates that would enable them to get jobs anywhere in the country. The fourth reason is that the institution wanted to enhance its financial viability by starting programs that would attract a large number of students, thereby increasing the revenue raised from student tuition.

External and Internal Challenges

The leaders mentioned several challenges that the institution has faced because of the transition. The first challenge raised by the leaders about the transition from a theological college to a university was building a consensus about the change. One leader said,

> Moving away from being a theological college to a private university is not something I would say was smooth and that is why it took so long before they finalized it and got the charter. There were expressions of fear. Some were asking, "What are you going to do with our sacred training of priests? We now know who comes to be trained here because we have vetted their theological positions. What is going to happen to the Theology program in the future? What is going to happen to our position in society when we allow the secular to come into this sacred place? How is that going to impact our ministerial training?" (Interview A)

Although there were people who saw that such a transition would negatively affect the Theology program and lead to secularization, there were others who saw this change as a good thing because the theological students would be trained, not in a guarded setting, but in a setting similar to the one that the students would go to serve in after they graduated. The national staff and students also saw that getting a charter from the government and transitioning to a university was necessary for the survival of the institution because of the financial challenges mentioned above, and to help students get different kinds of job opportunities after graduation because they would graduate from a government-recognized institution (Interview B).

Another challenge the institution faced in the transition was moving all the stakeholders together (Interview A). Since the college is an ecumenical college owned by four major churches and the National Council of Churches, it was not easy to bring all five together to agree on the transition. In addition to that, some of the denominations were focusing on establishing their own denominational universities. As mentioned above, getting a charter from the government was also taking a long time because of staff instability, lack of adequate finances, and lack of sufficient support from the sponsoring organizations.[59]

The transition to a university by expanding its programs has helped SPU to attract more students. However, there is still fierce competition in the higher-educational market in Kenya, and that will continue to be a challenge in the future. In 2003, Godfrey Nguru, a former principal of SPU wrote:

---

59. Ibid.

With the increased number of Christian universities in Kenya, with the competition for students posed by parallel programs recently introduced by public universities and the aggressive marketing by foreign institutions, St. Paul's has to position itself appropriately if it hopes to survive and thrive in the 21st century. Higher education in Kenya and in the continent has become highly liberalized. In this educational environment, St. Paul's has to find its niche. It has to rediscover its distinctive and actively recreate and re-engineer itself as a uniquely Christian ecumenical university like no other in Kenya and in the continent. This has to be done while still maintaining its evangelical character bequeathed to the institution by its founding fathers and nurtured by the African Church throughout the Century 1903–2003.[60]

A further challenge indicated by the leaders is maintaining the Christian ethos of the university. Accepting students who are nominal or non-committed Christians and trying to make them committed Christians by the time they graduate is a major challenge (Interview C). The institution has had to re-evaluate its relevance, rethink its role and make sure it does what it says on paper (Interview A).

Another challenge the institute is facing is that of governance. The board is still in a theological-college mentality, and the administration has to constantly remind the board that the institution is no longer a theological college but a university. When board members are invited to address students, they preach to them as theological students when there are also business students and students of other faculties present. That requires constant training of the governance of the university (Interview A).

Yet another major challenge the institution has is the financial challenge. Transitioning to a private university has not solved the financial challenges of the institution. A leader said,

> The belief is that when you open up as a private university, the finances will not be an issue because there will be people paying you fees. I don't know about other universities, but I have not found that one to be true here. People think that when you become

---

60. Ibid., 267.

> a private university, you are making money. Maybe others do. But that for me is not true and it is a challenge. It is a challenge because you still go into a society that has lots of poor people. They are the ones who need education but they can't pay for it. (Interview A)

The leader also indicated that the institution has never been a donor-driven college, even during the time it was a theological college. The support for the school did not come through donations but through sponsorship of students studying theology. Therefore, the institution has to depend on tuition fees received from students. However, that was not clearly understood by the community, students, and sometimes by members of the governing board. People assumed that the institution received big donations.

Related to that is the challenge of being prudent and good stewards of its limited resources and using them to the further development of the university. In order to be competitive in an environment where there are several private universities, the institution has to develop itself and offer education at a competitive price so that it retains a reasonable number of students and keeps afloat (Interview A).

The transition has also brought external challenges to the institution. While being a university helps the school to keep the quality of education, it brings its own challenges. Explaining the challenge, a leader said,

> As a private university now we are in the limelight and we have to adhere to the standards of the Commission of Higher Education in our hiring, in our writing the curriculum, and in our admission. There is a standard and we have to keep to the quality assurance of that. So there is this external body that is looking into us. Our curriculum must be scrutinized, it must be checked, and it must be stamped even if it is a theological curriculum. They take our theological curriculum and give it to other Christian theologians to scrutinize but the academic standards must be kept and that keeps us on our toes because if we don't, then challenges will come. (Interview A)

Some of the challenges mentioned above are ongoing challenges while the others were only at the initial stage.

Effects of the Transition on the Mission

The motto of St Paul's University has remained the same as it was before the transition: "Servants of God and Humanity." One leader said, "Our primary mission has not changed because we still have Faculty of Theology, and the vice-chancellor and the deputy vice-chancellor are from the Faculty of Theology. The Theology Faculty is like the mother of the university" (Interview B).

Another leader argued that the mission of the institution, which is training godly Christian leaders, has not changed, but instead of just focusing on training leaders for the church, the institution has now expanded its mission and started training godly leaders for the marketplace as well (Interview C). Another leader agrees: "The mission is enlarged to encompass the other faculties. In the beginning we were training people for the church, but now whoever we are training we are training them to be servant leaders because the motto of the university, which has not changed, is 'Servants of God and Humanity.' Out of that motto, the vision was created and the mission was broadened, but the motto has not changed" (Interview A).

The vision statement of St Paul's University that is given on its website is, "A University of academic excellence based on Christian principles, producing graduates in various fields for global service."[61] SPU's mission is "To develop servant leaders by imparting knowledge, skills, and values through creative methods of education, research, and Christian spiritual formation."[62]

Before getting a university charter from the government, SPU used to accept only Christian students from the owner churches or African independent churches. However, after the transition, as a university chartered by the government, St Paul's cannot now discriminate among applicant students based on their religious background, and it accepts students from any background. However, once non-Christians join the university, they are expected to abide by the Christian ethics of the institution. Explaining how that works, a leader said, "We try to build a well-grounded Christian culture here. If you join us, you find people who practice their Christian faith. If you like it you join us or else you will go somewhere else. It is all a question of keeping the Christian culture alive. I see a danger if that culture dies" (Interview C). To keep its Christian

---

61. www.stpaulslimuru.ac.ke.
62. Ibid.

identity, the institution requires that all full-time employees of the university be Christians who fear God and observe Christian ethics (Interview B).

The researcher asked how the university's vision of training godly servants is affected by the fact that it accepts on its programs students who are non-Christians. A leader answered,

> When we say "Servants of God and Humanity," we are not saying that we are training only Christians. Like other universities, we admit Christians and we also admit people from other faiths. At the moment, we have people from Islamic and the Hindu faiths. However, when they come, they know that they are coming to a Christian university . . . While we may not force them to become Christians in our way, we expect them to be faithful to their traditions, but their values are not values that discredit our tradition. And we don't force them to convert, but they have to sign up to our code of conduct that is developed for all students, and that code of conduct, of course, is influenced by Christian principles and values. Has that changed our ethos? No! It hasn't changed our ethos. We are open but we have also kept our values and ethical standards as we should. We believe that as they study here, we will be a witness to them to be better servants of God and humanity even with their own traditions. (Interview A)

Another leader, arguing that the transition to a university has not changed the ethos of the institution, said,

> Our motto is developing servants of God and humanity. Adding twenty programs or more will not stop us from developing servants of God and servants of humanity, which is a basic norm in this institution. However, if we stop developing servants of God, then I can tell you everything has crumbled whether we are training theologians, engineers, computer scientists, or business people, because we will not be living our norms, value systems, and our statement of faith to develop godly Christian leaders. (Interview C)

The leader also argued that opening up the university for non-Christian students has given the institution an opportunity to spread the gospel. All students from all religious backgrounds are required to take Bible-based courses, whether they study business, communication, or information technology (Interview C). How accepting non-Christians is affecting SPU, especially the Theology program, is discussed later.

The motto, the vision, and the mission statements of St Paul's University clearly indicate the institution's Christian identity. Its website and publications clearly display the motto of the university "Servants of God and Humanity."

The official magazine of the university, *Voice*, describing the progress the institution made during the years it was led by Dr Timothy Wachira (2004–2010), says,

> In his third year of service, Dr Wachira attained another of his goals. The former theological college was chartered by the Kenyan government to what it is now, St Paul's University. This was the climax of a long relationship that the theological college had enjoyed with the Commission for Higher Education since its registration as a university in 1989. Next, Dr Wachira set his sights on the diversification of academic programs. New programs in non-theological fields began changing the image of the university as an institution that only trains priests.[63]

Because of the transition, therefore, the institution is no longer seen as an institute that trains only priests. It is a place where training is given for communicators, business managers, accountants, IT professionals, development specialists, experts in Christian–Muslim relations, and specialists in community care and HIV/AIDS. There is also a plan to start training teachers, social workers, advertisers, and other professionals.[64]

When asked if there is going to be a challenge of secularization in the future of SPU, a leader said,

> As one currently here, my conviction is that we continue to witness to what we believe as right, and that is the Lordship of Jesus Christ. The future largely depends on the leadership that comes, and hence it also depends on what the board does because it is the board that appoints people who lead the university. I do not see secularization happening in the near future . . . What I see is that

---

63. Kilonzo and Maganjo, eds., "Up Close and Personal with Dr Timothy Wachira," 11.
64. Ibid.

we all believe there will always be a need for education. That is what we are offering. What I see is that we are putting in place mechanisms that ensure that the Christian ethos will continue to influence. That does not mean that we won't have issues of ethics because we are human beings, we live in a fallen world, and we are fallen creatures. (Interview A)

The institution attempts to hire only Christians who adhere to the Lordship of Jesus Christ both in word and deed, and they are expected to be role models to students in worship and practice of their faith (Interview A). The faculty members come from a wide range of Christian denominations. However, there are some who profess to be Christians just to get the job, but sooner or later the truth comes out and some of them leave (Interview A).

The university does not have a practice of requiring faculty members to sign a doctrinal statement, although the university has a statement of faith in its charter (Interview A). It is during the interview process that the institution tries to find out the Christian standing of candidates.

One of the leaders indicated that they hire non-Christians as adjunct lecturers because of the shortage of teachers they have (Interview C). These people can also be nominal Christians who have no personal commitment to Christ, but they may go to church and do some Christian activities.

When asked what makes the liberal arts programs offered at SPU different from similar programs in other secular universities, the leaders explained that the courses taught at SPU are taught from a Christian perspective. For example, courses in Business Administration include topics about what it means to be a Christian business person. A leader said, "You will be given courses that deal with the Christian faith, in terms of how Christians view the world, view money, and morality" (Interview A).

Though there are similar required courses for students in all programs that are taught from the Christian perspective, there are no Bible courses offered for non-theology programs. Explaining how this is done, a leader said,

> We may not teach Christianity in terms of Scriptures because some of them, for example, would say "Why am I doing Old Testament?" or "Why am I doing New Testament?" We have learned that from experience. So when we review our curriculum, we ensure that is integrated in the teaching. So they don't see Old Testament or

New Testament. They see it as it is mainstreamed and integrated. So when they are doing business ethics, we say Christian business ethics. (Interview A)

The leader admitted that the school relies heavily on the lectures for the integration of faith and learning, and that requires lecturers who are convinced that that is the way to go (Interview B). However, there are some who do not necessarily teach from the Christian worldview perspective. The leader said, "We try [to ensure that] the ethos is mainstreamed and the Christian values are not taught separated from the courses they take. They are inculcated in the courses and we do it intentionally. That is why for the first time we teach them all together so they understand the ethos of this university" (Interview A).

The fact that the university does not offer required Bible or Theology courses, and the fact that faculty members are not required to commit to a doctrinal statement, may negatively affect the institution's effort to integrate faith and learning. Moreover, the fact that there are many non-Christian or non-committed part-time faculty members who teach at the institution may compound the challenge because the faculty members are expected to be the key players in the integration effort.

One of the programs the university runs to keep its Christian mission alive is the chaplaincy. It has a chaplaincy team and there is worship and prayer time every day (Interview A). During the theological school days, the institution had a Sunday morning service because all students and faculty used to live on campus. Instead of that, now the school has a Wednesday service for the whole school. The chaplaincy attempts to organize programs that attract young students and meet their needs so that they continue to be interested in the church. Chapel is required for students and faculty of the School of Theology as part of the training and practice of the school. There are people who come to know the Lord because of these programs, and others grow in the Lord (Interview A).

The chapel program runs every morning, Monday to Friday, 8:00–8:30 a.m. On Wednesdays, there is a community service from 9:00–10:30 a.m. Though chapel is required for all students of the university, there is no monitoring system. A leader said, "We don't coerce people to come to chapel but make it a place where they want to come, and our chapel is full especially at Wednesday's community worship service" (Interview A). The requirement for the students of Theology is stronger. They are expected to come to chapel every day because these are the people who lead people in worship, and it is part of their training. The other faculties also participate in chapel in the preaching and the liturgy (Interview A).

Effects of the Transition on the Relationship with Churches

The leaders indicated that there was unanimous agreement among leaders of the sponsoring denominations about the transition from a theological college to a private university, though making the decision took a long time as indicated above. Moreover, the Methodists and the Presbyterians were working towards transitioning their own colleges to universities. They were aware of those necessary changes (Interview B). The government required that the sponsoring organizations show real ownership of the institution. As a result, the sponsoring organizations decided their share in the institution (ACK 50 percent, PCEA 20 percent, MCK 10 percent, RCEA 10 percent, and NCCK 10 percent).[65]

However, the leaders indicated that the relationship with the sponsoring churches is not as strong as they wanted it to be. One leader said,

> That is a sad thing. The churches never come to check the status of the university. In fact, most churches, probably because of their financial situation, do not send students to study here. Very few send students here. Most students come on their own. Even when we were United Theological College, two of the sponsoring churches started their own universities. The churches rarely evaluate what we are doing in this institution. That is a sad thing. For example, they could demand us to do research on a certain topic. They could ask us what we have discovered and ask us how they could change because this is where they have the brains, but they don't. (Interview B)

Another leader also indicated that the relationship of the institution with the founding churches was not that great even when it was a theological college. There were some people who had interest in the college because this was where their pastors where trained, and there were others who did not care

---

65. www. stpaulslimuru.ac.ke.

that the theological college was there. That has continued after the transition to a university. Two of the founding churches have established their own universities, and others may do the same (Interview A). Those who used to visit and support the school before have continued to do so, while others still do not show any concern for the university.

The leader also indicated that the university has become more and more independent of the churches. For example, the churches do not determine which students come to the school. "When the school was a theological college, students needed to pass through all the church interviews. They had to know all the church issues and politics. Now as a private university, the Faculty of Theology receives students seconded by churches and those that are not seconded by churches but come on their own volition to study theology" (Interview A). That has enabled the university to attract students who desire to study theology but would never have had the chance to study in the former setting. Getting students who are not scrutinized by the churches sometimes affects the university because it may get students with questionable characters, and it is hard to evaluate that at the beginning. However, when the churches used to do the scrutiny, they sometimes required the school to accept students who did not meet the academic standards, and in that sense the change can be seen as positive (Interview A).

The sponsoring churches are also not contributing financially to the institution. The only way they support the school is by sponsoring students. If they do not send their students, it means there is no financial support coming from these churches. The fact that the university is not supported financially by the sponsoring churches is seen as positive by one leader:

> Personally, I am happy that they don't give us money. I think there is some independence, not an independence to do wrong, but an independence to think creatively, innovatively, and to be relevant to the society. They may not let us change the Statement of Faith, but they give us space to be innovative and to be creative to enhance the university while sticking to our motto "Servants of God and Humanity." We probably have such a relationship because of the ecumenical nature of the institution. (Interview A)

The sponsoring churches are represented by their leaders, their presiding bishops or moderators, on the board of trustees of the university. There are also experts on the board such as architects and financial experts representing their churches. However, that relationship does not necessarily reach to all levels of the denomination's structure, including local churches. There are some who send their students to SPU, and others who do not send their students to SPU but send them to their own universities.

One leader indicated that there are ways that the leaders of the churches challenge the leadership of the university (Interview A). Church leaders have at different times indicated the problems they see in the institution. Some of them disagree with the theological approach of the school, and they say that they don't want to send students to SPU because they see it to be more liberal. Others do not like the focus on gender issues, which they see as a feminist movement in the university. Some do not like that the school accepts Muslim students into its Christian–Muslim relations program, instead of teaching people to go out and convert Muslims. These examples show that the leaders of the churches challenge the leadership of the university and indicate issues that they perceive as problems.

From the above discussion, one can see that the leaders of the SPU do not see that the university's relationship with the sponsoring churches is strong. The support they get from the churches is minimal. One of the reasons for this is that the institution is owned by several denominations and some of them have their own universities where they send their own students. With minimal involvement of the sponsoring churches, the future of the university depends on the board and what kind of leadership it appoints.

Effects on the Theology Program

The Faculty of Theology was well involved in the discussion and decision-making in the transition from a theological college to a university. The faculty realized that challenges would come in the future, but knowing that the ministry training would continue, they agreed to the transition. In fact, the Theology faculty prided itself as the oldest faculty, and during the first few years it remained the largest faculty. So far the transition has not brought a serious threat to the Theology program. However, the leaders indicated several challenges that the transition has brought to the Theology program.

The first challenge is related to the rapid increase in the number of students in the university. When the institution was just a theological college, it had only 100–200 students. Now there are about 2,000 students. The growth in the number of students has affected the relationship between the faculty and the students. Faculty members used to know students by name and relate to them on a personal level. That is becoming difficult now. When the institution was a theological college, chapel was required, and it was easy to tell who was coming to chapel or not. When the number of students increased, the chapel service was moved to a bigger hall, and with students numbering over 2,000 it has become difficult to keep track of who has come and who has not. Although students are still required to attend chapel, it has become impossible to enforce it.

The transition also affected the campus life of students. Explaining the changes a leader said,

> When we had only the Theology program, we had few students, had good contact with all students, and used to know every student. We used to accommodate all students on campus and had fellowship with them. There was a time when everybody who lived here knew everybody. It was beautiful. It was a residential school. If they came here with their family, they could live here. There was nursery for their children, a dispensary, and a small farm to grow vegetables. We can't do that now with 2,000 students. We can't even accommodate them in our campus, so many of them live outside the campus. Anybody who affords it can live on campus. So we are not able to monitor the behavior of our students. (Interview B)

The leader also sees that the students of theology are facing new challenges that were not there when it was a theological college. The students who come for theological training are those who show commitment to ministry. However, some of them lose their commitment to ministry because of the influence of the students from the other faculties. They are now studying in an environment in which they are the minority, and they don't necessarily live on campus. The chances of distraction and of their losing their focus are high. Describing his observation, the leader said,

> These young people coming for ministry training meet the other students. Sometimes, these other students water down the faith of those priests. Like it or not, they water it down. One can see

the temptation going on. That is affecting the training we give for those who are preparing for ministry. Now they are sleeping out there. You don't know what happens. The students of the other programs are the majority. So inevitably Adam and Eve will start admiring the fruit. Previously that was almost impossible. Everybody respected our rules. We knew everybody. The other thing is since the students of the other programs have become the majority, the compound has become noisy. Previously we had mature students. Most of the students who come for theology (for ministry) are mature. But these other students are adolescents. They are eighteen years or twenty years old. They scream and dance all over. You sympathize with the Theology students. (Interview B)

Expressing his concern, the leader also said, "Now we have about 2,000 students, and out of those, only 400 are Theology students. With time, there is no doubt that theology is going to be a minority here. We received our charter in 2007 and in four years we have seen this. You can imagine what might happen in ten years. I am afraid the church is not growing that fast" (Interview B).

When asked what would be the best way to protect the integrity of the Theology program, the leader said, "What I think will eventually happen is that we will grow as a university. What we have now as the Faculty of Theology will change into a School of Theology within the university so that we have a small group of students that we train properly for ministry instead of treating it just like the other faculties" (Interview B).

Another leader argues that there has not been a significant challenge to the Theology program because of the transition to a university. The academic standards are kept high because of the scrutiny of the accrediting agencies. Though the major tenets of the theological training are there, there are some changes in the practical aspects of the training. For example, each student used to be assigned to go to a particular church every Sunday as part of his or her practical training. That happens now only in a smaller way. Many of the students go to the churches they come from and practice there. Only those who are not ordained are placed in churches around the university. The leader admitted, however, that some see the institution as becoming too academic and less practical. Others also say that the school is not spiritual enough. These views are dependent on the theological background of those who hold them. Some also criticize the institution's critical approach to theology. That approach was there before the transition to a university.

In terms of the number of students on the Theology program, a leader said that they are happy about it, even though the number of students on the Theology program will always be less than that for other faculties. In the past there were fewer theological colleges, but at present there are many, and only those students who like the approach of SPU's theological persuasion come there (Interview A). The number of students coming to join the Theology program depends on the demography of churches in the country because most of those who study theology go on to full-time ministry in the churches (Interview A). There are also churches that do not consider theological training as necessary for ministry.

Currently the vice-chancellor and the deputy vice-chancellor of SPU are both from the Faculty of Theology. When asked if there could be a negative effect on the Theology program if the top leadership positions were held by people from the other faculties, a leader answered,

> It is [only] this year that we have Theology people in the leadership. Even before we were chartered, our vice-chancellors were not theologians. Starting from 1998 we had non-theologians. It was theological school but was led by non-theologians. When we were chartered, it was a veterinary doctor who was our vice-chancellor. It is only since last year that we have a theologian as our vice-chancellor. The academic dean was a theologian. Now the Faculty of Theology has theologians leading it. The Faculty of Business has non-theologians leading it. The senate is composed of the vice-chancellor, who could be anybody but now happens to be a theologian. The deputy vice-chancellors are not all theologians. So far we have stayed firm and continued our work. (Interview A)

People from the theological school have a strong influence on the overall activities of the university because of the history of the school and because the people in the Theology faculty have been with the institution for longer. There is also a perception that the school is still a theological school, even though it has transitioned to a university.

When a leader was asked how the university plans to keep the Theology program strong, he said,

> That is something we have been debating a lot. What we are saying is that we should make sure that we keep our Theology program alive as we continue to develop new programs because the church still needs trained ministers. It is true that the Faculty of Theology may not compete by way of numbers with these other faculties. However, since our foundation is the Divinity program, we will make an effort that the Theology program is kept alive even if we have five students because that is the foundation of this university. So we will do everything to make sure that is not lost. The Divinity aspect is not lost because that is our foundation and we want to maintain that. It is on that foundation that we built the culture we have right now and we cannot wish away our 100-years of history. We will build on it and develop it. (Interview C)

The Theology faculty also plays a role in the education offered in the other faculties. It is the faculty members of the Theology department who teach the courses that are required for all students. These courses are the Christian Worldview (which takes students through the Old and New Testaments), Christian Business Ethics, Business Ethics, and Social Responsibility. These are courses that are required for business and IT students (Interview C).

The researcher asked if there is integration of faith and learning in the other courses taught in the different faculties of the university. A leader explained that there is an attempt to do that and it depends on the teacher. The institution hires Christians and expects them to integrate their faith with what they teach, but the leadership does not insist that they do the integration (Interview C). The ability to integrate faith and learning in the way one teaches depends on the teacher's level of Christian maturity. A leader said,

> It depends on the level of growth of the teachers as Christians and how they practice their faith. It is not difficult if you are well grounded in the Word. [The] majority of us have studied in public universities. I studied in a public university though there are some who studied in Christian universities. But the fact that I got my foundational knowledge from a public university does not really prevent me from integrating faith with learning because that is up

to the individual. But when you are not well grounded or formed in Christianity, then it will be a big challenge to integrate. (Interview C)

Another leader admits that the leadership was not able to foresee all the challenges that would come to the Theology program when they decided to transition to a Christian university. He said, "I think those people who were in leadership at the time did not foresee these challenges. They should have watched what other schools that have transitioned to universities had gone through" (Interview B).

St Paul's University Summary

The section above discussed the reasons why St Paul's United Theological College transitioned to St Paul's University, the challenges it faced during the transition, and the effects of the transition on its mission, Theology program, and its relationship with the sponsoring denominations.

The motto, the vision, and the mission statements of St Paul's University clearly indicate the institution's Christian identity. Its website and publications clearly display the motto of the university, "Servants of God and Humanity," and that clearly shows the *public relevance of the Christian vision* of the institution. The *public rhetoric* of the institution indicates that it is a Christian school but inclusive of others.

When it comes to *membership requirements*, the institution does not require staff and students to be members of the sponsoring denominations. It attempts to hire Christians, though sometimes nominal Christians or non-Christians are hired because of failures in the vetting process. The institution also hires non-believers as adjunct lecturers because of the shortage of teachers who meet the faith requirements.

The *Theology faculty* is still a strong faculty in SPU, though it is not growing as fast as the other faculties. The faculty also plays a role in the education offered in the other faculties and its members teach required courses to all students. There are no *required Theology or Bible courses* per se, but the Faculty of Theology offers required courses for all students that give Christian perspectives to students.

SPU runs a *chapel* program every morning and, once a week, there is a community service for all members of the university. Students of Theology are required to attend chapel, but students of the other faculties attend voluntarily.

As mentioned above, SPU is owned by four denominations and NCCK and is *governed* by a board of trustees whose members are leaders of the sponsoring churches. According to the leaders, the relationship of SPU with the sponsoring churches is not as strong as they wanted it to be. There is no direct financial support coming from the churches to SPU and the only way they support the school is by sponsoring students. Though it is hard to put SPU in one of Benne's categories of church-related colleges, in many aspects SPU falls under the *critical mass* category. Table 6 summarizes the changes discussed above using Benne's categories.

Table 6: Changes Due to the Transition from SPUTC to SPU

	SPUTC	SPU
Public relevance of Christian vision	Pervasive from a shared point of view	Christian school but inclusive of others
Public rhetoric	Unabashed invitation for fellow believers to an intentionally Christian enterprise	Presentation as a liberal arts school with a Christian heritage
Membership requirement	Near 100%, with orthodoxy tests	Orthodoxy for faculty and staff, not for students and part-time faculty
Religion/theology department	Large, with theology privileged	Large, with theology as flagship
Religion/theology required courses	All courses affected by shared religious perspective	Two or three, with dialogical effort in many other courses
Chapel	Required in large church at a protected time daily	Voluntary at high-quality service in large nave at protected time once a week
Ethos	Overt piety of evangelical tradition	Open majority from sponsoring tradition finding private niche
Support by church	Owned by denominations, indirect support through sponsored students	Owned by a church, indirect support through sponsored students
Governance	Owned and governed by churches	Owned and governed by churches

Uganda Christian University

Uganda Christian University (UCU) is located in Mukono, Uganda, 23 kilometers from Kampala. UCU is a private university, chartered and fully accredited by the president of the Republic of Uganda, through the Ministry of Higher Education and Sports, and the National Council for Higher Education. It is owned by the Province of the Church of Uganda and has campuses in Eastern, Western, and Northern Uganda.[66]

The university was born out of the Bishop Tucker Theological College that was founded in 1913 in response to a growing need for pastoral training in the Church of Uganda.[67] When UCU was founded in 1997, the college was named Bishop Tucker School of Divinity and Theology. UCU was inaugurated with Bishop Eriphas Marri as its first vice-chancellor and Archbishop Livingston Nkoyoyo as its chancellor.[68]

In addition to the Bishop Tucker School of Divinity and Theology, UCU currently has several faculties (schools) that have several departments under them. The faculties are Faculty of Social Sciences, Faculty of Business Administration, Faculty of Education and Arts, Faculty of Law, and Faculty of Science and Technology.

The researcher visited UCU in June 2011. During his visit, the researcher was able to interview the vice-chancellor, the dean of the School of Theology, the dean of the Faculty of Social Sciences, the chaplain, and two senior faculty members of the School of Theology who have in-depth knowledge of the transition to a university. The interviews with the leaders took an average of fifty minutes. The researcher provided the interview protocol to each of the interviewees before the day of the interview and conducted each interview at the office of each interviewee. The section below describes the findings of the researcher that relate to the five research questions of this study. In addition to doing the interviews, the researcher was able to visit the campus and make observations and collect documents that are relevant to the research, and hold informal discussions with faculty members.

---

66. www.ucu.ac.ug.
67. Ibid.
68. Ibid.

Reasons for the Transition

The leaders of the institution described the main reasons why Bishop Tucker Theological College transitioned to Uganda Christian University. According to the leaders, the first reason was that the proprietors of the theological college were offering high-school-level education, and they had a long-time dream of establishing a university so that the church could also have a Christian influence at a higher-educational level (Interview A) by providing higher education to the church and the whole community (Interview C).

The second reason for the transition was that the theological college was becoming difficult to sustain on its own. The bishops of the church were not able to send enough students and pay for their fees. It became obvious that the college "needed the larger intake so that it remained part of that larger body to enable its viability. Otherwise, it would have been easily fizzled out" (Interview A). Transitioning to a university became necessary to get more students who would pay fees onto different programs so that the institution would be financially sustainable. One of the founding leaders of the university said, "I think it was caused by economic challenges because at one point bishops had problems sending enough students to the seminary. At one point we said, 'Now we don't even have enough money to run this institution, and this institution is big, and it could be of great use if we expanded it. We could have a place for theology and other courses, too.' So the idea started boiling in our minds and we had a series of talks" (Interview G).

The third reason that led the leaders of the church to consider establishing a Christian university is what they had seen happening with other religious groups. Muslims, Roman Catholics, and Seventh-Day Adventists in Uganda had started universities so that they could train people in higher education. Seeing these developments, the Church of Uganda also felt the need to participate in the development of higher education from a Christian point of view. In order to do that, it was necessary to transition one of the colleges to become a fully-fledged university (Interview E).

The fourth reason mentioned by one of the leaders, which is related to the first one, is that the church wanted to have an influence in the political world. The leader said, "As a church we believe that at the moment you have highly educated Christians, then your church is stable. You do that by having a university where you will have your religious traditions passed on to the next generation. So the church looked around and found that the most ideal place was Bishop Tucker Theological College, which is located near a main road and close to Kampala" (Interview E).

The Church of Uganda initiated the transition of the Bishop Tucker Theological College to a Christian university, and that was led by a strong vision from the archbishop of the church at the time, Archbishop Livingstone Nkoyoyo. He presented the vision to the supreme leadership of the church, the Provincial Assembly, and the vision of starting a university was supported unanimously (Interview A).

External and Internal Challenges

The researcher asked the leaders of the institution about the challenges the institution had faced during the transition from a theological college to a Christian university. The first challenge mentioned was that when the institution was only a theological school, most of the students were mature students who were preparing to go into ministry in the church. However, after the transition, students coming to the university were much younger and were recent graduates of high school. These students tended to behave differently from those in the School of Theology. Managing such younger students was a new challenge that came with the transition to a university (Interview A).

This was a challenge especially for clergy who were studying at the School of Theology. A leader said, "If someone who was here fifteen years ago as a student comes back to do a master's degree or some other degree, he will find that, instead of single-room dormitories, he now has to share a dorm with a student from another faculty who may not even be a committed Christian. It becomes a little hard for them, but others look at it as an opportunity to preach the gospel" (Interview E).

The second challenge mentioned by a leader was attracting enough well-qualified academic staff to the university. The leader said, "That has been a challenge we had to go through because most people do not want to go into a new venture because they are settled in their own jobs and they are comfortable. What we can offer them is an opportunity to innovate, but most people do not want to be innovative. They want to go to an established place where they can work and get paid well" (Interview A). In order to meet its needs, UCU had to use many part-time teaching staff from Mekerere University. In addition, since the faculty members who were full-time at the university during the transition were from the School of Theology, they were heavily engaged in administration work in addition to their responsibilities in the Theology department (Interview D). UCU now has a staff-development program, and it is working to meet the challenge of having its own teaching faculty.

The third challenge was financial. Transitioning to a Christian university did not necessarily enable the institution to overcome its financial challenges (Interview A). A leader said, "The financial challenges particularly become more pronounced because when we add more students, we must add more staff, more physical structure and more other things" (Interview A). Keeping up with the pace of growth is a challenge because the institution does not have an endowment for such expansion (Interview A).

A further challenge of the transition was the competition that was created between the Faculty of Theology and the other faculties. Being the oldest faculty, the Theology Faculty claims ownership of the buildings and expects to be given prominence in everything that takes place in the university (Interview E). The problem is in part caused by a lack of clarity during the transition. Explaining the problem, a leader said,

> At the initial stage, the plan was to start a university education alongside the theological and ministerial formation programs. There were different views at the time. Some people were saying, "We should have a college separate from the university although they share the same premises." There were also others who were saying, "Let us do the whole thing together so that the theological education and the ministerial formation program can also have an input in the other programs in developing a Christian mission." The two groups could not agree, but they agreed to move along. (Interview C)

Though there was consensus on the establishment of the university, there was not a clear agreement on its implementation. As seen above, one of the reasons why the transition to a university was considered was because the financial sustainability of the college, and the livelihood of its faculty, was in question (Interview A). However, when the transition was implemented, it became a challenge for the college that was well established, with its own standards and rules and having all the premises to itself, to share these with the new faculties and become an equal with them. One leader said, "Defining the School of Theology within the university was not easy" (Interview C).

An additional challenge raised by the leaders that has come as a result of the transition to a university by getting a charter from the government is the scrutiny of its programs by the National Council for Higher Education. Describing the change, a leader said,

> When we were Bishop Tucker Theological College, we used to be affiliated with Mekerere University so we got degrees and diplomas from Mekerere University. When we became a university, we started offering our own degrees even for programs offered at Bishop Tucker College. Because of that, we must meet the standards which are set by the government (the National Council for Higher Education). Even the small colleges that Bishop Tucker oversees in the entire Province of Uganda have to meet the standards of the National Council for Higher Education. (Interview E)

Another leader said that this is a good challenge and helps the university to keep a high standard of education (Interview A).

Another challenge that was mentioned by one of the leaders was that there were some who were not happy about the transition. Some of these people were missionaries who used to work at the Bishop Tucker College and who supported it financially. Some were afraid that the changes would kill the ministry training. Others were upset when the old buildings that they had raised money for were demolished to make way for the new library that is being built (Interview E).

Effects of the Transition on the Mission

The institution changed its mission and vision statement when it transitioned to a university. The current motto, vision statement, and mission statement of UCU are as follows:

> **Motto:** Alpha and Omega: God the Beginning and the End
>
> **Vision:** A Centre of Excellence in the Heart of Africa
>
> **Mission:** Uganda Christian University is dedicated, through teaching, scholarship, service, spiritual formation, student

development, and social involvement, to preparing students for thoughtful, productive lives of Christian faith and service in their respective professions and places.[69]

The former vision statement was "Called to Serve," and that is still used by the School of Theology. When asked if the original mission of the theological college has been changed because of the transition, a leader said, "The mission of the college was preparing people for ordained ministry. Now we have to incorporate these other programs into the mission to take care of these other disciplines in the mission of the institution. So yes, in terms of incorporating the other disciplines of training the mission has changed a bit" (Interview E).

The original mission statement of the theological college fits within the overall mission of the university, and the theological college has found its space within the university (Interview A). Although the mission of the School of Divinity and Theology has not changed and it still trains church ministers, the setting where it does the training has changed. One leader, explaining the change, said,

> I think what has changed is the monastic kind of training for ministry that was done in a place which was set apart. Now a Theology student shares a room with students of other programs and I think, for the first students who experienced this, it was tough because they were not used to that kind of setting. For example, students of Theology were not happy with the girls wearing trousers, but with time things change. However, the mission of the school did not change, except I think we are now training church ministers within the university context instead of that monastic kind of training. Our Theology students develop their ministry skills by ministering to the very students who are here as their parishioners. (Interview E)

One of the founding leaders of the university, who nominated the name "Uganda Christian University" for the institution, describing the desire of the leaders for the university at the time it was founded, said,

> It is going to be Christian in formation, Christian in vision, and Christ will be at the center. That was it, and I hope they are

---

69. Ibid.

following that because the vision of this institution is that Christ would be the center of the university, a center of excellence not only in sciences and liberal arts but in promoting God as a prime mover of all things. If members who are there now do not promote Christian virtues, Christian ideals, for us who are founders, that would be greatly disappointing. (Interview F)

The official publications, website, and the legal documents of the UCU clearly state its Christian identity. The UCU Charter, which is its legal document approved by the government, stating the Christian identity of the university, says, "The Christian identity of Uganda Christian University is summarized in the motto 'God the Beginning and the End' and is articulated in its Instruments of Identity. The Instruments of Identity, which include a Rule of Life, shall be consistent with the teaching of the Church of Uganda and shall be approved and maintained by the Proprietors of the University through the University Council."

The "Instruments of Identity" that is mentioned in the charter was written after the institution transitioned to a university and presented to the House of Bishops of the Church of Uganda, who actually passed it. Therefore, its authority is from the proprietors of the university. The "Instruments of Identity" has three parts. The first part, "The Rule of Faith," is like the institution's statement of faith that one can "find in the creeds of the early church and in the Lausanne Covenant" (Interview A). The second part is "The Rule of Conduct," which describes how members of the community should conduct themselves (Interview A). The third part is what is called "The Rule of Worship," which describes what kind of worship is acceptable in the university.

A leader, explaining how the "Instruments of Identity" protects the Christian identity of the institution, said, "This document is not spelled out in the charter, but the charter refers to it and it is so enshrined in there that you cannot change it easily. Of course, there is nothing you can never change, but anybody who is trying to change it will have a big battle. You have to fight hard to change it" (Interview A). The first paragraph of the "Instruments of Identity" of the UCU makes it very clear what the institution stands for. It states, "Uganda Christian University is an established institution of the Church of the Province of Uganda. As such, it is committed to the catholic and apostolic faith, practice and piety. It is religious and explicitly Christian in its name, in its mission statement, and in its motto: 'Alpha and Omega: God the Beginning and End.' Its public worship is conducted according to the Prayer Book tradition of the Anglican Communion."[70]

In addition to the governing documents, there are several things the institution has put in place to promote its Christian mission. The governing council (board of trustee) members are selected carefully, and they have to be committed Christians (Interview A).

UCU also have a strong and well-established chaplaincy that has a central role in the life of the university (Interview A). The chaplaincy is directly under the vice-chancellor's office. The chaplain has direct access to the vice-chancellor so that he will not be impeded by any other person, and he can arrange spiritual programs for the university. There is community worship for all twice a week, Tuesdays and Thursdays, from 12:00–1:00 p.m. It is not compulsory, but all service centers like the library and the computer lab close, except the sections that deal with emergency services, like the clinic, and few staff members stay there. On Monday mornings from 8:00–8:30, there is a prayer meeting for teaching and non-teaching members of staff.

In addition to the regular chapel services, the chaplaincy also prepares a week-long conference every semester (three times a year) on particular subjects. In the September semester the focus is on evangelistic mission. During the week the focus is to call people to accept Jesus Christ as their personal Lord and Savior. In the January semester, the university normally has a mission and ministry conference, and in the May semester, it runs a leadership conference, which is aimed to equip students with leadership skills.

The week the researcher visited the campus, UCU was having its mission and ministry conference. He was staying at the guest house on campus and was able to hear and observe what was going on in the main chapel. The campus had a feel of a church compound where a major conference was taking place. The title of the mission conference for the week was "Extending God's Kingdom: Our Mission." Several messages were presented on different topics, such as "Extending God's Kingdom to the Muslims," "God's Call for Special Ministry," and "The Role of Christian University in Christian Mission." At the meetings, different choirs from the different faculties presented special music.

---

70. Ibid.

The morning meetings had an attendance of about 100 people and the noon meetings had an attendance of over 1,000.

In addition to chapel services and the conferences, the chaplaincy also runs discipleship group meetings that target believers who want to grow in their Christian faith. There are also evening fellowship meetings at the hostels where students live both on and off campus.

Explaining the role of chaplaincy in the overall life of the university and some of the challenges they face, the chaplain said,

> We see ourselves as charged with the responsibility of keeping the Christian identity of the institution. For us spiritual vitality is very central. The challenge is that we have the background of the Anglican, and it is always a struggle to be able to do ministry in such a way that is inclusive to people from other denominations. We sometimes do things which are not really in the Anglican way of doing things, and that always is a problem with divinity and Theology students because some of them think we should not be doing that. But I think it is the only way that we can make our ministry relevant and reach the people rather than just keep the tradition. That aspect is always in our mind that this is our role. (Interview G)

The researcher asked a leader about the percentage of born-again Christians in the student body. The leader indicated that the institution tries to keep a record of the spiritual condition of the applicants by asking applicants to fill in a form at the beginning. Although it is possible that some who are non-Christians fill in the form as Christians, because this is a Christian school, the leader believes that the proportion of committed, born-again believers is around 40 percent, and that the rest are nominal Christians or non-Christians (Interview G). The programs of the chaplaincy are geared toward meeting the spiritual needs of each of these groups.

The university runs two worship services on Sunday mornings. The main Sunday service used to be at 5:00 p.m. That was changed to Sunday morning and now there are two morning services that start at 8:15 and 10:15 a.m., and they are the biggest services of the university (Interview A). The institution also runs a Sunday-school ministry for the children of the university community and the community around the campus. The researcher asked if the university also functions as a church. A leader responded,

> We have been functioning just as chapel, but since last year and even more now we are moving more towards a setup of a church. Actually, this year a bishop officially comes here for us so that we belong to a diocese. We have been having bishops coming and doing different things. However, it has been resolved now that we become like a parish connected to a diocese. Therefore, we are counted as a parish connected to a diocese. Now that has some dynamics because there are things that we cannot [do] exactly as they do. For example, the diocese in Kampala has a theme they follow. Sometimes they do not suit us directly. We had to choose a council recently, and I looked at the guidelines for what a parish council should be. Some of the things couldn't really fit in our context. So I had to talk to the bishop and say that they should allow us to have a council but a bit different. We have some things that are in line with the dioceses, but we may have other positions to cater for different ministries here. So somehow we are moving more closely to having a church here because now we also have people attending here who are not students or staff members. (Interview G)

The chaplaincy has very strong support among the current administration, and that support has enabled the chaplaincy to have a big role in the life of the university. The researcher asked a leader if there are any challenges that the chaplaincy faces at this time or might face with a change of leadership in the future. The leader answered,

> I actually sense some resistance. In the first place, I think it should have been able to stand with or without the current leadership because if the church grasps that this is central, it can go a long way. I realize that there are many challenges that come with growth, [apart from] the administration itself. For example, when we began this, our students had lectures up to 5:00 p.m. so the evening meetings would be well attended. Now you cannot get very high attendance for the evening services because the lectures

are going on at that time, and you will always have lecturers who make it hard for the students to attend. So they can even put tests at this period and the students have no choice. (Interview G)

There are discussions between the university and the Forum for Theological Education and Higher Institution for the Learning for the Church of Uganda, to work out ways in the structure that will make the chaplaincy strong in the future and also enable the church to be involved (Interview G).

The other safeguard the university has to keep its Christian identity is that all the senior administrative positions, like the vice-chancellor and the deputy vice-chancellor, are held by Anglicans or people from churches that are in communion with the Church of the Province of Uganda (Interview E). For the faculty, apart from in Theology, UCU hires practicing Christians, not necessarily Anglican. However, there are staff members and part-time faculty members who are not born-again Christians, but the institution hopes that they will become converted as a result of their exposure to the Christian testimony there. The non-believers are very few. All staff members who are hired must affirm the university's "Instruments of Identity." Those who come to work as part-time staff members or students do not have to accept the "Instruments of Identity" but they must respect it. They cannot speak disparagingly about it or act in a manner that treats it as something that does not matter (Interview A). If those who are even teaching part-time are found disagreeing with the "Instruments of Identity" while teaching or talking to students, that would be a cause for discipline or dismissal.

The challenge the university now has is recruiting men and women who are committed Christians for academic and administrative positions. They are looking for faculty members "who teach courses with passion so that they do not just become other courses but have a real impact on the life of students" (Interview D). Getting committed Christians to teach some courses is a problem. Therefore, the university is forced to use some part-time teachers who are non-believers. It is also the case that some who were hired because they confessed to be committed Christians are found later not to be committed, practicing Christians. A leader said, "I can see in the future that one of our programs may have more non-committed Christians, but at least I know that at the recruitment stage they try very hard to get people that are believers" (Interview G).

In order to fulfill its Christian mission, UCU is also working on integrating faith and learning in its curriculum. A leader said, "We felt that our identity as a Christian institution must not only be expressed in our documents but it must also be expressed in the curriculum" (Interview D). The university offers required courses that build a Christian foundation in all its programs. These courses are known as Foundation Courses and are administered by the Department of Foundations. Every student must do Old Testament, New Testament, Christian Worldview, and Christian Ethics in addition to other required courses, like Introduction to Mathematics and Introduction to Computers, which are offered as part of the foundation courses. The first four courses are designed to bring students to the core of Christianity and are taught by the members of the School of Theology. Students need to pass these courses in order to graduate from the university. A leader said, "People are appreciating this, and even people in the government are saying 'You are doing a good job there.' So long as we are showing that the Christian option is a better option, not an equal option, then we stand a chance" (Interview A).

Other than offering the foundational courses that are required for all students, teachers are encouraged to integrate whatever subject they teach with the Christian faith. A dean of one of the faculties said, "We encourage our staff to integrate faith to their teaching, which is a requirement on our course-outline template. We require them to show how they integrate faith in their teaching and try to help them to know how to do it" (Interview E). In order to do that, the faculty prepares workshops. Faculty members use these forums to share their experiences and exchange ideas.

UCU has gone even further in protecting its Christian identity for the future. According to a key leader, the university is in the process of forming an internal body, named the Institute of Faith, Learning and Service, that reports directly to the vice-chancellor and acts like a watchdog and which has among its other responsibilities making sure that there is integration of faith and learning in everything that is done in the university, including in the classrooms (Interview A). The institute will also have the responsibility of looking at recruitment and vetting staff members. They will vet recruits particularly in the matter of faith and make sure that they fit with the university's ethos. The administrators are also expected to reflect a Christian character in the way they deal with people in their offices.

UCU enjoys freedom to function as a Christian university without restrictions. Explaining how that freedom enabled the institution during the accreditation of its programs, a leader said, "Since our curriculum needs to be approved by the Ministry of Education, the university administration took it to the Ministry of Education. They said, 'You are a Christian university; that is your identity, and we do not mind what else you teach, provided that you cover what we think is essential'" (Interview D). The government also gives freedom for other religious groups to run their academic institutions according to their religious convictions. A leader said,

> First, we are very thankful to God that in Uganda our political leadership and our constitution have allowed freedom of worship. Every religious group has its own university. If you do not want a Christian influence and if you are a Muslim, you can take your children to an Islamic university. If you do not want traditional Christianity, you can take your children to Pentecostal universities and Bible colleges. Even Seventh-Day Adventists have their own institution. So there is a wide [choice] to choose from. If you do not want your children to have any religious education, you can take them to the secular universities, and there are many. I think that has helped a lot and I do not think that the government will intervene because there is no need, and everyone's need can be met in these institutions as long as they meet the academic standards of higher education. That is the blessing we are still having. (Interview C)

Although the university currently enjoys this freedom to function as a Christian institution, it is aware that things may change in the future. That is why they want to establish the Institute of Faith, Learning and Service, so that the institution's Christian identity is firmly established and cannot be easily changed (Interview A).

The researcher also asked if the graduates coming out of UCU are distinct from those graduating from other, secular universities and if they have a good Christian character. A leader said,

> We are receiving very positive feedback. Comparing students who have studied business here and those who have done business

elsewhere, people tell us that our graduates are very different in their character and in the way they approach their job. They may have the same skills, but the Christian influence has changed the way they look at their jobs or the way they deal with other people. That is definitely what people have been saying, and we hear that often. Hearing that makes my heart celebrate, but at the same time it scares me because these are not angels. (Interview A)

One advantage UCU has, of course, is that a good number of the students who join the university are actually born-again students who come from born-again parents. Therefore, they already come as changed people before the school starts contributing anything to their lives. What the university provides for them is an environment that nurtures their Christian faith and an opportunity to be involved in different spiritual programs (Interview H). Some of these students are also active in sharing their faith with unbelieving students. Those who are non-believers feel out of place in the university, and they are more likely to accept invitations to attend spiritual meetings. Many of them become Christians during their time at the university (Interview H).

Effects of the Transition on the Relationship with Churches

The transition from a theological college to a university was the vision of the church; therefore, the church had a very positive and active role in the transition, although the relationship of the Church of Uganda to the university was not clearly defined at the beginning (Interview A). There were "some positions in the university that were ring-fenced to members of the church, like the vice-chancellor, the deputy vice-chancellor and the chaplaincy" (Interview A). When the charter was being written and the university was in the process of seeking accreditation, the charter was written in a way that recognized the proprietors of the university in the governance (Interview A). The charter recognized that within the university council, which is the supreme governing body of the university, the church is heavily represented. Every time there is an election of council members, the church sends its representatives. The relationship between the church and the university is clearly stated in the charter, and it is difficult to change that. Any change made to the charter of the university requires consent from the president of the country.

One of the founding bishops of the university also confirmed the involvement of the church during the transition. However, expressing his frustration about the relationship of the church leaders to the university, he said,

> What bothers me now is that bishops never have a day in the year to come and visit the university and feel welcome. I already told his grace [the] archbishop that something was wrong when we planned this. There must be a clause that says the trustees must have a day, an open day, when everybody in the university knows that this university belongs to the Church of Uganda. That was not addressed at that time, and I am sad about it indeed. I think bishops, the incumbent ones, should have time to come one open day to visit with the students, be shown around, and talk and discuss with the staff, so that students will know who the trustees are. We are only invited for graduation, but that is nothing, and some don't even get invited sometimes. (Interview H)

A senior faculty member of the Theology faculty, expressing his concern about the relationship between the church and the university, said, "The church may start thinking that it is the responsibility of the university to train ministers for the church" (Interview E). That has worked so far because the leadership of the university is committed to the training of ministers for the church. However, the fear is that if the university leadership changes and it gets leaders who do not see it as a necessary program of the university, that may greatly affect the ministerial training for the church. The leader also said, "My conviction is that if you want to kill a church, you first kill the seminary and then the church is done. I have made it very clear to the church leaders that it is detrimental to the Church of Uganda if the seminary does not continue or is weakened in one way or another" (Interview E).

When asked if there was a threat of secularism that could affect the ministerial training that is taking place at the university, a leader said,

> Theological education will continue to grow as long as the church gives theological education and ministerial formation a priority because the church is still the key stakeholder both in the university and in the theological school. So it will depend on the decision of

the church. Once the church leadership has a clear vision of what type of ministerial formation they would like to see happening in the school, it will happen. So it all depends on the church because the churches are the trustees of this university. It also depends on the people that run the theological education. For the rest, this is my personal belief: God will not allow theological education to die. The Spirit of God would not allow that because that is our life and our future. Churches can do without a university but church cannot do without theological education and ministerial formation. (Interview C)

The researcher asked why the students of Theology depend on scholarships while the students of the other faculties find a way of paying for their school fees. A leader explained that it is because of a tradition that their churches inherited from the early missionaries. The tradition is that the church supports its own ministers in preparation and in ministry. When the African leadership took up church leadership, they continued the same manner of doing things. Therefore, theological education has never depended on any parent and it has always been done by the church, and that is what people believe should continue (Interview C).

The leader gave an example to illustrate the point. There are parents who send four of their children to UCU; two of them study Law, one studies Mass Communications, and the other one is in the School of Theology preparing for church ministry. These parents pay for the three children in the other fields but expect the church to pay for their child who is studying Theology. Even those who can afford to pay for their children who are studying Theology expect the church or someone else to pay for them because of what happened there in the past. The understanding is that when one is trained for church ministry, one depends on what the church provides.

Those who study subjects like Law, Education, or Medicine have wider choices to make once they graduate. They can leave one job and go for another one that pays well. However, for those who enter into a church ministry, it is the church that decides what they should do and where they should serve. They could be assigned to rural villages where stipends do not come on time. "Since it is the church that determines what they should do, many people are not willing to have their fate determined by the church if the church is not ready to invest in them" (Interview D). When the parents see that, they expect the church to fully support the studies of their children who have decided to pursue church ministry as their vocation.

Effects of the Transition on the Theology Program

As mentioned above, the establishment of the university was agreed unanimously by the Bishop Tucker Theological College. However, no clear direction was agreed upon as to how the college would fit into the university setting. The first idea was that Bishop Tucker would remain as an autonomous college with its own administration and finances within the university (Interview E). That idea was not accepted by the administration because it could be a cause for conflict. Then "the vice-chancellor and his administration decided that Bishop Tucker would be a school but not independent from the university" (Interview E). Another leader, explaining the situation and how they are still working to resolve it, said, "Those that wanted the transition did not make it clear how the training of ministers would continue. That was never addressed. There was an assumption that the university would work on that and even now, I would say, it is not resolved fully. We are now working backwards on it to make sure of the continuation of ministerial training, and that it would be clearly written down and documented" (Interview F). The ministerial training program is now run as a school, Bishop Tucker School of Divinity and Theology, under the university. Those holding key positions in the university are ordained ministers, and they are committed to it.

The transition to a university also had several positive contributions to the Theology program. A leader said,

> Definitely we try as much as possible to keep it as central, but there is no favoritism here. Theology is not favored here in the sense that their people are paid more, but there is a sense in which we actually try to emphasize it. For example, we introduced scholarships to attract more Theology students. The university setting allowed us to provide scholarships for students that study Theology when churches are not able to pay for the students they send to be trained for ministry. I think in that sense it has been positive for them. (Interview A)

The scholarships that are offered for Theology students have helped to increase the number of students in the school.

The School of Divinity and Theology also added new programs after the transition. Before the transition they had only a Certificate in Theology, Diploma in Theology, and Bachelor of Divinity programs (Interview E). Since the transition, they have added a Master of Arts in Theology, a Master of Arts in Theology and Development, and a Doctor of Philosophy program with four students. The school also has started a Doctor of Ministry program in partnership with a seminary in the US.

The school has also introduced an undergraduate program: Child Development and Children's Ministry. That has increased the enrollment in the faculty. The program admits forty to sixty students each year, and in the three years, in that program alone, there are about 120 students. The number of students in the Theology program has increased from around 100 to 140 in all the Theology programs, not including Child Development and Children's Ministry. A leader said, "Now we have doubled and tripled that number because of programs we have started in theology. We now have students who would want to come and study with us in a university setting but who would not have come in a theological school setting. We are able to attract students from other countries and even those outside of Africa and that has also increased the enrollment" (Interview F). When asked if the School of Theology is still effective in training people for ministry, a leader said,

> Yes, it is very effective in training people for ministry, but with a different focus. In those days we used to train people for rural ministry, but now we want to train students for rural and urban ministry, ministry for the educated and the uneducated. Because of that, we are now able to begin programs like master of divinity. If someone has, say, a doctorate degree, he can now join the master of divinity program, instead of the bachelor of divinity program and can go out and minister. We are able to begin a doctor of ministry program and also a PhD program. That is how we meet the needs of the society now. (Interview E)

There are also other advantages that the School of Theology is enjoying because of the transition to a university. A faculty member of the Theology school said,

> It has been good in one way: in the sense that the welfare of the faculty and the students of the school has greatly improved in terms of remuneration, exposure, and opportunities, and that has certainly been very positive. I think we are better paid than when we were a seminary. We have great opportunities for travel, development, and participation in international conferences, which would not have been catered for by the seminary. There is great opportunity for personal development, academic development, and so on. (Interview F)

There are also other services that the School of Theology now enjoys that the seminary was not able to provide. One of these services is the wireless Internet that is available all over the campus.

The church and the theology school are also benefiting from the university setting because a number of younger students coming to study in the other programs get their first contact with church ministry here. While they are studying at the university, they feel that God is calling them to do ministry. A leader said, "We have seen people coming from different academic backgrounds like law, education, business and mass communication join the graduate programs of the School of Theology for ministerial training" (Interview C).

That has come with its own challenge. The younger people who come onboard sometimes want to be and behave like the rest and at times forget that they have a special ministry. Describing what the school is doing to help them, a leader said, "We are putting in place many discipleship programs and many day and evening programs to explain to them that while they are here and they are young, they are also called for special ministry, and their job is to minister to the rest of the community, but not to be absorbed by the community" (Interview C).

Another leader explained that even the mature students of the School of Theology sometimes fail to see their strategic role in the university. He indicated that the Theology students, who are more mature than the students of the other faculties, do not see themselves as ministers on campus who can minister to the students of the other faculties. He said, "It is unfortunate because it is as if they are waiting until they are ordained and that they will start their ministry to people out there. They want to do out there what they have not been doing here, and I have been challenging them about it" (Interview A).

However, there are other students who are very strong and actually set out to have a good influence on the rest of the university. "Some of them do wonderful things in community worship, in music ministry, prayer meetings, leading groups, discipling, nurturing, and that has gone well" (Interview C).

The researcher also asked how the students of the Theology School relate to the students of the other faculties. One leader indicated that the students of the other faculties do not regard the students of Theology highly. Some see them as less smart. In fact, when it comes to the election of student-body leaders, the students of the other faculties do not even vote for students of Theology. It is more than seven years since the student-body president was elected from the Theology School (Interview A).

The tendency for each faculty to focus on itself rather than considering different ways that it can help other faculties is a problem indicated by one leader, and it is also true of the School of Theology (Interview A). The leader said that there is now a new initiative for faculties to share their expertise with other faculties when they have something that can help others to do well. For example, the education faculty has been helping teachers of the other faculties to improve their teaching skills. The leader also indicated that he is challenging the Faculty of Theology to see its ministry in a broader sense and to minister to all other faculty and staff members.

The other change that affected the programs of the School of Theology that is mentioned by one leader is that, since all the degree programs the school offers are now accredited by the government, they have to strictly follow the standards set by the government. Previously, they had to keep those standards only for those programs that were accredited by Makarere University, but ran their own programs for students that did not meet the required academic standards. However, now, since the whole institution is accredited by the government, all its programs need to meet the government standards, and they cannot accept students whom they want to take because of their ministry experience but who do not meet the academic requirements.

The high standards also apply to the kind of teaching staff the School of Theology recruits. A leader said, "We seem to have fewer faculty members in the Theology School because, first, we do not just admit anybody. Second, we believe that for someone to come and teach Theology, the minimum must be a master's degree and a number of years of teaching experience in a parish setting or other schools. However, our priority is for PhD holders" (Interview D).

The main concern of the people in the School of Theology is the continuation of the training of ministers in the university setting. They are concerned that church leaders may start seeing the training of ministers as the responsibility of the university. That would not be a problem in the current setting because the leaders of the university are committed to ministerial training. However, if a new leadership comes in the future that is not that committed to the training of ministers within the university setting, that would greatly endanger the program and the future of the Church of Uganda. The fear is that the School of Theology might end up as a faculty of divinity detached from the church, as has happened in universities in the West. What the institution has done to avoid that problem for now is "to keep Theology as a school, while the others remain as faculties, because it is vocational and training people for special ministry" (Interview D). A clear written plan is also being prepared to guarantee the continuation of ministerial training in the school.

The School of Theology also works closely with the chaplaincy. Its faculty members are involved in preaching in chapel and in other spiritual programs in the university. During the week-long conferences that take place three times a year, the Theology students participate in it. The School of Theology used to take students to different places to do outreach: evangelistic missions and open-air evangelistic programs. Now the university campus is also considered to be a mission field, and evangelistic meetings are conducted on the field within the university campus. Students from other faculties also join the students of Theology on mission trips (Interview C).

A leader, summarizing the effects of the transition, said,

> Transition is not an easy thing, and we always struggle to maintain our vision. We always make it very clear that we do not want to be consumed in the whole university. And yet, we also feel that we have been privileged to have the mission field close to us, and that is where many of the benefits are experienced both by students and by staff. The church leadership (because this is a church institution) also has been very central in seeing that the ministerial formation continues. (Interview C)

Uganda Christian University Summary

The section above discussed the reasons why Bishop Tucker Theological College transitioned to UCU, the challenges it faced during the transition, and the effects of the transition on its mission, Theology program, and its relationship with the sponsoring denominations. UCU has a clearly stated Christian vision and mission that show the *public relevance of the Christian vision* to the institution. The leadership of the university is committed to the fulfillment of its Christian mission and has put in place mechanisms to protect the Christian *ethos* of the institution.

When it comes to *membership requirement*, the senior administrative positions are held by Anglicans or people from churches that are in communion with the Church of the Province of Uganda. For the faculty positions other than within the School of Theology, UCU hires practicing Christians, but not necessarily Anglicans. However, there are staff members and part-time faculty members who are not born-again Christians, but the institution hopes they become converted as a result of their exposure to the Christian testimony there.

The *School of Divinity and Theology* at UCU has a privileged position and it runs the Foundations Department that offers *required courses* of Bible and Theology to all students. The chaplaincy plays a key role in the spiritual development of the community and the university. The chaplaincy runs a high-quality voluntary *chapel* service twice a week in a protected time.

UCU is established by the Church of Uganda and the church is heavily represented in the university council, which is the supreme *governing* body of the university. Even though there are several areas that UCU still needs to work on to continue to be a strong Christian university, what it has done so far is exemplary for other Christian universities in Africa. Table 7 summarizes the changes that have come due to the transition from Bishop Tucker Theological College (BTTC) to Uganda Christian University (UCU).

Shalom University of Bunia

Shalom University of Bunia (Université Shalom de Bunia, USB) has seen several changes in name and location since its beginning. It was founded in 1961 as the Theological School of Northern Congo (ETCN) in the village of Banjwade, near Kisangani, DRC. Describing the denominations that own

Table 7: Changes Due to the Transition from BTTC to UCU

	BTTC	UCU
Public relevance of Christian vision	Pervasive from a shared point of view	Pervasive from a shared point of view
Public rhetoric	Unabashed invitation for fellow believers to an intentionally Christian enterprise	Unabashed invitation for fellow believers to an intentionally Christian enterprise
Membership requirement	Near 100%, with orthodoxy tests	Critical mass in all facets
Religion/theology department	Large, with theology privileged	Large, with theology privileged
Religion/theology required courses	All courses affected by shared religious perspective	Two or three, with dialogical effort in many other courses
Chapel	Required in large church at a protected time daily	Voluntary at high-quality service in large nave at protected time twice a week
Ethos	Overt piety of evangelical tradition	Dominant atmosphere of sponsoring tradition – rituals and habits
Support by church	Indirect financial support and majority of students from sponsoring tradition	Indirect support through sponsored students
Governance	Owned and governed by church or its official representatives	Majority of board from tradition, some official representatives

the institution, its website says, "In D. R. Congo, Protestant Churches are organized into 'Communities' who have wider membership of the Church of Christ in Congo (Eglise du Christ au Congo). There are five Communities affiliated with USB, and most students also come from these Communities whose representatives oversee the management of the University by meeting twice a year as a Board of Administration. The Communities also provide funding to USB."[71]

---

71. www.unishabunia.org.

Describing the founding "Communities" of the Theological School of Northern Congo, which is now USB, the university's website states,

> The Evangelical Community at the Centre of Africa (CECA-20) and The National Community of Christ in Africa (CNCA-21) with their associated missions, AIM and CrossWorld, were the founding communities of the Theological School of Northern Congo, which has now become USB. They were followed by The Community of Baptist Churches in Congo (CEBC-5) and the Mission WorldVenture in 1969. Then in 1978, The Emmanuel Community (CE-39) and the Mission CMML became the fourth Community member, and shortly afterwards in 1982, The Evangelical Community at the Heart of Africa (CECCA-16) and their Mission WEC became the fifth [member].[72]

The main purpose of the school was to train pastors for church ministry. Teaching at the institution was interrupted due to the war that broke out at the time, so ETCN recommenced its teaching in another location near to Bunia, where it later settled, acquiring its own property that it still uses.[73] In 1972 the institution was renamed the School of Evangelical Theology in Bunia to reflect its new location.[74]

In 1973 the programs of the institution were organized to a university level, and the name of the institution was again changed to Bunia Theological Seminary (Institut Supérieur Théologique de Bunia). In 1986 the institution started a master's program in Pastoral and Biblical Theology. In 2005 the institution opened a Department of Missions and in 2008 a Department of Bible Translation, both offering a master's degree.[75] After five decades of existence, Bunia Theological Seminary made an important transition to Shalom University of Bunia in order to respond to the challenges facing the African churches and communities in general and those of the DRC in particular.

The researcher visited Shalom University of Bunia at the end of June 2011. During that time, the researcher was able to interview four senior leaders of

---

72. Ibid.
73. Ibid.
74. Ibid.
75. Ibid.

the institution, visit the campus, make observations, collect documents that are relevant to the research, and hold informal discussions with faculty members.

The researcher interviewed the rector (president), the academic dean, the dean of the School of Missions, and the director of development. The interviews with the leaders took an average of fifty minutes. The researcher provided the interview protocol to each of the interviewees before the day of the interview and conducted the interviews on the university campus. The section below describes the findings of the researcher that relate to the five research questions of this study.

Reasons for the Transition

For five decades, Bunia Theological Seminary (Institut Supérieur Théologique de Bunia) focused solely on theological training, preparing students for service in different areas such as evangelism, church-planting, and church and development projects (Interview B). However, since 1990 there had been discussions about establishing a university by combining colleges that were owned by the sponsoring denominations of the seminary (Interview A).

As mentioned above, the institution is owned by five different denominations ("Communities"), and some of these denominations also owned other small colleges of nursing and teacher training. Some were raising questions like "Why do we have separate small institutions?" because managing these different institutions was not easy for the leaders of the churches who had to go to separate board meetings, graduations, and manage different organizations although they were owned by the same denominations. The idea was to combine these institutions into one (Interview A). These discussions continued between 1990 and 1994, but no concrete decisions were made (Interview A). At times, some of those who attended the meetings did not really understand the proposed move, while others were suspicious of what the outcome would be (Interview C).

In 2003, a civil war was taking place in the area (Ituri District), and about 50,000 people were killed there. The only place that was not touched by the war was the university's campus. One faction of the fighting group was occupying the land on one side of the university and the other group was occupying the other side, but both sides decided not to attack the university because it provided refuge for the leaders of both groups (especially the civilian leaders) at different times (Interview A).

When it became impossible to function, the seminary was evacuated. The campus was then used as a place of refuge for people from the villages. About 1,350 people were living on campus in the classrooms and different buildings (Interview A).

When the refugees came in, they discovered that the students of the seminary had planted vegetables in their garden. They had also left food and lots of crops. The refugees used those during the time they were there, but they also made sure that they left what they found there. That made the transition smooth. When the members of the seminary returned, they lived with the refugees for about a week and then the refugees left. That created a good partnership between the seminary family and the refugees (Interview A).

Describing what happened to the institution after the people returned to the seminary, the leader said,

> When we came back, we had to ask ourselves what the future of the school was going to be like. The missionaries that supported the school had left. Before they left, some of them asked us to close the school until they came back. We said no. The school does not depend on you; it depends on God. The school was started by missionaries and when they sat for board meetings at the end of the academic year, they would come and ask what the budget was. The budget was about $60,000. There were twelve missionaries and they just shared the burden and that is all. The Congolese were not feeling the pain of raising funds. That is why they told us not to open the school before they returned because they thought we would not make it. (Interview A)

There were at least seven meetings from 2004 to 2005 to discuss the way forward for the school. The changing realities of the continent and the particular challenges facing the DRC inspired the leadership to go through a self-evaluation to measure the effectiveness of the training in solving church and community problems.

This exercise helped the team to list a number of weaknesses. The leaders decided to open the school, but the major problem was money. The other problem that was raised was relevance (Interview B). Students came to the seminary because they had a call to serve, but they had no money and the majority of them were coming from very poor churches. That made it difficult for the seminary to function. A leader said, "It was difficult to teach very poor students whose children were starving" (Interview A).

The leaders decided that they needed to do something to help the students and the churches. In 2006, they organized a research center to address these challenges. The first activity of the research center was to create a project named "Biblical Reflection on Poverty." They invited people from the community to think about poverty and what the Bible says about it. Eventually they decided to open a new department, the Department of Theology and Community Development (Interview A).

The seminary then had two departments, the Department of Theology and the Department of Theology and Community Development. The government gave the institution permission to start the new department but also told the institution that they could no longer be called a seminary if they had departments, and that they could not be a university with only two departments (Interview A). Therefore, the institution was forced to start at least two more programs to get university status.

The other problem that was identified by the leaders during the self-evaluation was a lack of curriculum that would help the church to give a holistic ministry to its members and the communities. As a result, it was noticed that the role of the church as light and salt was diminishing, paving the way for Islamic influence, which had been spreading like wildfire since the troubled moments of revolutionary wars and ethnic clashes, especially in the eastern DRC (Interview B).

There was also a desire to help churches develop. "Many of the pastors did not know what to do in order to get adequate financial resources within their churches. There was the idea that if there were people trained in development, who were then able to help pastors know how to make the church develop financially, whether agriculture or people development or in other ways, that could be beneficial" (Interview B). That was the reason why the seminary started the Faculty of Development. The school wanted to focus not on subjects like Law and Medicine, but on those areas where it was already offering something – courses like Environmental Management and Fishery (Interview A).

Therefore, the first reason Bunia Theological Seminary (Institut Supérieur Théologique de Bunia) made the decision to transition to Shalom University of Bunia (UBS) was to properly respond to the challenges facing the African churches and communities in general and those of the DRC in particular. Describing the new programs that were developed to address these challenges, a leader said,

> In the light of this thinking, new subjects such as Community Development in 2006, then Administration and Management, Environmental Science and Agronomy were added since 2007, followed by Missions and Bible Translation. The main goal is to build the capacity of godly men and women, capable of proclaiming Christ by word and deed so that they may be able to enhance the ministry of the church to its members and the surrounding communities. Since this move, and because of the Christian identity of the university, the institution has been experiencing rapid growth, from 65 students to around 750 within three years. This positive impact is the result of the Christian identity, integrity, and the role of peace-building the institution is playing in the region. (Interview D)

Currently, UBS has five schools, namely the School of Evangelical Theology, the School of Development, the School of Science, the School of Administration and Business Management, and the School of Agricultural Science.[76] Under these schools, the USB runs five graduate programs and twenty undergraduate degree-level (license) programs.

The second reason why the institution considered transitioning to a university was motivated by the institution's desire "to seek financial independence from Western support, and it was felt that other programs could be run profitably and help subsidize the Theology program, which never had [enough] students [to] enable it to be financially independent" (Interview C).

The third reason for the transition to a university was to meet the needs of students. There were a lot of students who wanted Christian education but were not seeking pastoral ministry. There were also many students trained as pastors even though they did not really want to be trained as pastors. Some of them were working for non-governmental organizations on management tasks

---

76. Ibid.

and in other leadership posts. There were also leaders who felt that there was much more to be done than just training pastors and church leaders.

When the researcher asked the leaders if there was unanimous agreement about the transition to a university, they indicated that, though the majority of those who were in leadership supported the move, there were some who had reservations. One of the reasons given by those who opposed the change was that such transition might lead to secularization, as had happened in many Western academic institutions that made similar transitions. However, the decision was made to transition to a university because it was supported by the majority.

The researcher also asked if the members of the governing board who were representing the sponsoring denominations fully supported the transition to a university. The leaders confirmed that they were engaged in the discussions from the very beginning. They supported the transition mainly because they had trusted the leadership of the institution even though they did not fully comprehend the implications of the transition. The members of the governing council are heads of their church denominations and have been elected by the general assemblies of their respective denominations. A leader said, "We tried to explain to them what we wanted, and we had their support mostly because they trust us as the sons of their church denominations. But the board was very helpful at that time and used by God to say 'Let us give it a try'" (Interview D).

The great contribution of the board to the transition process was coming up with fifteen to seventeen points that the university should follow in order to remain Christian. The administration played the key role in the transition of the seminary to a university.

External and Internal Challenges

One of the challenges mentioned by a leader who was involved with the transition was keeping the spiritual vitality of the institution. The vision statement of USB is "Spiritual and academic excellence for the transformation of society through Christ." Explaining the challenge of keeping this vision, the leader said,

> Excellence in spiritual growth to me is the one most affected and the one that will be most affected for good or for ill. Growing spiritually as a university is a challenge, but we are trying hard.

> Aiming for academic excellence is not that difficult. We have official instructions on how to do everything. The main challenge for our vision is keeping spiritual excellence. Are we up to it? I would not say we are at this stage, but we are on the right track. (Interview D)

A second challenge the university is facing is financial, especially when it comes to paying its faculty a competitive salary. A leader said, "The government has increased the salary of the professors at the public universities. The salaries went from $500 to $2,000 a month and that is a big increase. That has not yet created a problem for us, but it will in the future because our salaries are low. That is a lot of money and we can't afford to pay that much here" (Interview A).

Another leader indicated that financial slowdown in the world had affected the university's ability to raise funds for building projects. In addition, a major donor organization that supported the school in the past decided to no longer work in Africa, and that was unexpected. Decrease in incoming funds has affected the operation of the university (Interview B). The university was constructing four buildings at the time and things were going well. However, after the financial slowdown, the progress of the building project has been affected.

Getting qualified faculty members who share the ethos of the university is also another challenge that the institution is facing. A leader said, "When the institution was small, we had enough lecturers. Now the institution is growing in so many departments, we don't have our own well-trained faculty members. We have to depend on other visiting lecturers who come and teach. That is a big challenge because some of them may not even be Christians" (Interview B).

A third challenge the transition brought to the institution is a lack of space to run all the programs. This has been a great challenge for the Faculty of Theology, which had all the space for itself but now has to share it with all the other faculties without much increase in the existing buildings. Illustrating this challenge, a leader said,

> It is like being a father who had two children yesterday and suddenly has ten today without preparing enough space for ten children. We don't have enough room for all. We expected and knew that the number of students coming to the other programs would be bigger than the number of Theology students, but we

> don't have the space now. We have enough land to build on for the future, but for now all the ten children have to live in a house that was built for two. These are internal challenges we face. Even the number of students in a class has changed. We used to have ten students and at most twenty students in a class. But now we have a class of 250 students. When it comes to marking, you can imagine that. Other universities are used to it because they have thousands of students. (Interview D)

The university has student housing, and currently it is only for students of the School of Theology because most of them have families and they have come from other parts of the country. Students of the other faculties live around the university. The university is currently building another campus a few kilometers from the main campus, and all the faculties except the Theology faculty will be moved there once the construction is finished.

The researcher asked if there were external challenges that had come as a result of the transition to a university. One of the challenges mentioned by the leaders was that coming from the government. One leader said,

> Our initial idea was to add one additional program, Development. That was readily accepted and approved by the local leadership, faculty, and board, but when we tried to implement that, the government said, "No, you cannot add just one faculty; you need to add four faculties." That produced a messy outcome which was not exactly what had been planned. So when that word came back, there was some disagreement and discussion as to whether that was too much and how we could do that, and it continued to be a problem in some respects. (Interview B)

The university now has five schools. Another leader indicated that managing these programs in line with the Ministry of Education is another challenge the institution has to deal with (Interview D). They have to meet deadlines and that creates pressure on them, especially on the academic dean's office. This is necessary because the Ministry of Education has to recognize the degrees the university offers. In order to do that, inspectors come to the institution to check the file of every graduating student and to give approval.

A further challenge mentioned by the leader was one that comes from churches. Increasingly, the students coming to the university are coming for the new programs but not for the Theology program. That worries the university leadership about the future of the Theology program. The leaders are constantly examining and analyzing how to maximize the number of students in the Theology program so that the program will continue. The government regulation requires that there be at least twenty-five students in each class (Interview D).

Another challenge of the transition is that the university grew in a very short time without properly preparing for such growth. A leader said,

> We have lost many opportunities to develop from the very beginning. What we had were very small buildings, and it was thought that they were good enough. The vision at the time was very small, and for about thirty years the feeling was that we had reached our goal and everything was OK. However, with God's help we were able to accomplish lots of things within the last four years. We still need to develop our library and expand our collections especially for the new programs. We have a challenge of developing laboratories for the new programs. We have to build more offices and housing for students and faculty. We have lots of challenges, but they are not challenges that would kill us but push us to work harder. (Interview A)

Effects of the Transition on the Mission

The researcher attempted to find out if the mission of the institution has changed because of the transition. One leader said, "The mission has not changed but expanded to reach the needs beyond the church to the larger society" (Interview C). Another leader said, "Yes the mission has changed because before we were preparing couples for Christian ministry, whereas now we are preparing people for serving society as Christians. I think the original mission statement still applies to the Faculty of Theology. So it has become the purpose of the Theology Faculty; in that sense there is no significant change" (Interview D).

Another leader said, "The mission has not changed. In fact, after our self-evaluation, we had to come up with our vision and our mission and to clarify it. That was in 2005 and the university started in 2007. So we tried to clarify our mission, our vision, and our values. We have not changed them but found ways to strengthen them" (Interview A).

The former "Mission Statement" (Objectives) that is given in documents was made available to the researcher during his visit:

> 1. Train students in biblical, theological, and historical areas so that they have personal beliefs on biblical truth to fulfill the ministries of pastor, evangelist, educator, researcher, and translator of the Bible.
>
> 2. Train students as couples so that they can serve the Lord together as men and women.
>
> 3. Help students identify and develop their gifts and capacities to the benefits of the Church, the Body of Christ, and society.
>
> 4. Help students develop a lifestyle balanced and integrated spiritually, physically, emotionally, intellectually, and socially.
>
> 5. Generate a missionary vision.

The current vision statement of USB is "Academic and spiritual excellence for the transformation of society through Christ,"[77] and its mission statement says,

> The Mission of the Shalom University of Bunia is to train men and women with high levels of professional, moral, intellectual, social, and spiritual qualities. The USB is committed to train managers to meet the needs of society. To do this, the university organizes instruction, research, and training in an environment that is conducive to the intellectual, spiritual, and moral development of the student. It offers the student the opportunity to develop an ability to live in harmony with God, with himself, and with others.[78]

One of the changes the transition from a seminary to a university brought to the institution is a change in the student recruiting criteria. The seminary

---

77. Ibid.
78. USB governing documents.

used to accept only students who were born-again believers. Now, the university accepts unbelievers too. That has provided an opportunity for evangelization within the university and many have become believers during their first year (Interview B). However, there have also been negative consequences. A leader said,

> We have seen a deterioration in the ethical quality of our students as the school has gotten bigger. We have seen many cheating problems. We had to expel students for immorality. We are having real world problems that we didn't used to have or rarely had. Before, in ten years, we may have had one student cheat and be expelled, and now we have cheating regularly and that is a big concern. It is very rampant in Congo. The whole culture is full of corruption and cheating. Cheating to pass is common in high schools. So we now have different problems that have invaded from the culture that we fight and it is tiring. (Interview B)

The university has students coming from Catholic and Protestant churches. There are also a few Muslim students. Whatever religious background the students come from, they are all required to sign the Code of Conduct of the university and to attend chapel.

The government does not yet have a law that requires the university not to discriminate among applicants who come to the university based on religion. One leader said that that is a good thing, but it might come in the future (Interview A).

Once the decision was made to transition from Bunia Theological Seminary to Shalom University of Bunia, the Governing Council of the Seminary in July 2007 came up with a list of guidelines the administration needed to follow carefully in order to protect the evangelical Christian identity of the institution. The list included the following points:

> 1. All internal rules and regulations of the university must be respected by all members of the university.

> 2. The recruitment of all administrative and academic staff should require skills, convincing Christian witness, and recommendation from the church.

> 3. There should be a strong and well-structured chaplaincy.

4. There should be an annual assessment of the evangelical stand of the university.

5. The rector (president) of the university must be an evangelical theologian from the sponsoring denominations.

6. The university should not accept gifts from donors who seek to divert USB from its identity as a private Christian university.

7. All staff should be required to sign the Confession of Faith and the Moral Code of Conduct of the university.

8. Students should be introduced to a missionary vision during their training.

9. There should be integration of faith and learning.

10. There should be geographical separation of the Faculty of Theology from the other faculties.

The university is currently doing a revision of the regulations and is in the process of clarifying and strengthening these points (Interview B).

A leader confirmed that the university tries to follow these guidelines by making sure that the mission, the vision, and the values of the institution are kept and protected not only by the staff but also by the students, and also by making sure that the people recruited, both students and faculty, are living in accordance with the vision, mission and values of the institution (Interview C). Another leader said, "To me the question of keeping our Christian identity is very important, and we have to refer back to it all the time to make sure that we are on the right track. The Christian identity has to do with both the way we live the Christian life and the way we teach it to the students and also model and express it" (Interview D).

The university clearly states its Christian identity in its public statements, published documents, announcements and advertisements. There has been no legal problem with its identifying itself as a Christian institution. When asked if there has been a change of ethos of the institution because of the transition to a university, a leader said,

> I don't think you can make the kind of changes we have made without a change of the ethos. We are now a Christian university,

not a Bible college or seminary. Just in that you have a difference. We do not require all students to be Christians in the non-theological faculties. We have non-Christian students on campus. We have Muslim students on campus. Not all of our faculty members are as active as we would like in chapel and in Christian activities and that concerns us. They say they are Christians, but you don't see them coming to our prayer meetings. We don't feel unified as we did because we are much bigger. (Interview B)

The researcher asked about the hiring policy of the institution. The leaders confirmed that they still try to hire Christians and they ask for recommendations from churches. However, a leader indicated that sometimes they find out that the people recommended by their churches are not committed Christians, contrary to what has been indicated in the recommendations (Interview A). Though the university has a Statement of Faith that faculty members need to sign every year, it has not been kept up to date (Interview A).

The university also uses visiting professors to teach courses for two or three weeks. Explaining the challenges the institution has faced with that, a leader said, "When the institution was a theological college, we used to hire only pastors that were well known. Now, especially in our visiting faculty, we take somebody who has the right knowledge without knowing that person very well. That is why we have gotten into trouble sometimes. Usually we have somebody come to give a course or two and we observe them" (Interview B).

For the visiting professors, the university has prepared a document that clearly shows them the vision, mission and core values of the university and the things they can or cannot do while they are on campus. These visiting professors are not necessarily Christians, but they have to sign the Code of Conduct that is prepared for them in order to teach at the university.

During the interviews the researcher asked what makes the education offered at USB distinct from that at other private or public universities that offer similar programs. One leader indicated that there are two main distinctions. The first is that there are required courses that are compulsory for all departments and that are unique to USB. These courses are intended to give students a Christian foundation for all their studies. These courses are Introduction to the Bible, Christian Ethics, Bible, Development and Globalization, Theological Thoughts on Poverty, Christian Home, Biblical Foundations of Environment,

Biblical Foundations of Leadership and Management, Christology and Soteriology, Pneumatology and Ecclesiology, and Evangelization (Interview C).

The second thing mentioned by the leader that makes the education offered at USB distinct from that of other institutions is the chaplaincy. He said, "The chaplaincy focuses on teaching, evangelizing, reaching out to people and making sure that students and staff members are growing spiritually" (Interview C). The programs run by the chaplaincy include morning devotions, prayer sessions, Bible studies, Sunday worship, and spiritual retreats for Theology as well as other students (Interview D).

The teachers also attempt to integrate faith and learning in the courses they teach. A leader admitted that not all teachers are effective at integrating the Christian worldview into their courses (Interview B). Integrating faith with learning is especially a challenge for the teachers in the new schools who have received their training in secular universities.

The university also tries to maintain its uniqueness by giving a high priority to ethics. A leader said, "We have people in this country who are trained, but their goal is self-serving and egotistical, and they don't care how they achieve their ends. So we are definitely trying to teach the youth that how they do something and why they do it is important" (Interview B).

Effects of the Transition on the Relationship with Churches

As mentioned in the introduction, there are five denominations (communities) that are affiliated with USB, and most of the students of USB come from these denominations. Their representatives oversee the management of the university by meeting twice a year as the board of directors of USB. The university has a governmental (presidential) charter as a recognized institution, so it owns its own properties.

The institution relates to the churches through the representatives in the board of directors. The board is made up of church leaders. Each denomination is represented by three people whom it sends to the board. These delegates are usually the president of the church denomination and two other representatives. These board members are delegated by their churches to act when they are sitting on the board, and they do not need to go back to their churches to get approval (Interview B).

Seventeen of the twenty-four board members were pastors, and that brought problems because the board lacked members in other important professions (Interview A). After much discussion, the board has decided to make changes. One of these changes is to lower the membership from twenty-four to eleven. The new board will be made up of five denominational leaders, five professionals and the rector (president) of the university. By reducing the size of the board and making it more balanced between the pastors and the other professionals, the institution hopes to find experts in education, business, and other areas and draw on their abilities in a way that helps the institution. These professionals will also come from the sponsoring denominations. The heads of the denominations will be on the board, and they will bring with them people from other professions. A commission has been assigned to work on these changes (Interview A).

When asked if the board members were involved in the transition process and if they supported it, a leader said, "The board has been with us in this transition. Probably what convinced them was the confidence they started having in the management. They started seeing things done that they had never seen before, like the building of the new library and all the other developments" (Interview A). Because of their concern for the continuation of the theological training and for the protection of the Christian identity of the university, they came up with certain guidelines for the university. These guidelines are given above.

The five denominations also have the responsibility of supporting the university with their finances. However, according to the leaders, they have not been providing funding for USB. A leader said,

> The five churches [denominations] who say this is their school have the responsibility of supporting and sponsoring the programs. However, in practice that is not happening. Money hardly comes from the churches. They plan well and they accept everything, but when it comes to paying the bills, that is a different matter. I think the problem is linked to the general breakdown of the economy and structures, some of them due to war in the past and some because of continued war. But they know that supporting the school is their responsibility because they own it. (Interview D)

Churches, however, do support students who study at the university. Some students' fees are paid by their local churches. Some of the students are sent and supported by their denominations, and it is those denominations that write letters of recommendation for them. The denominations pay for their school fees themselves or raise them from elsewhere (Interview A). There are also students who pay for themselves.

The relationship with the denominations has not changed much since the transition to a university. However, because of the growth of the institution and of its financial needs, the university administration feels that there needs to be "a higher level of commitment from the churches in developing the relationship and giving financial support" (Interview D).

One of the ways the university keeps a close relationship is through the faculty. The faculty members are very much involved in church ministries. A leader indicated that some of the lecturers were too involved in church ministry, to the extent that it was affecting their work at the school, so they had to come up with a policy limiting their involvement in church ministry (Interview A). However, the university wants to make sure that faculty members are actively connected with their churches and minister there in a way that does not affect their ministry at the university.

Another way the university connects with church leaders is through an event that takes place every year. Once a year in May, the university hosts an International Day of Prayer when people from all the churches in Bunia come together. After holding a month of prayer, people from these churches come together on the last day of the month for prayer. A leader said, "That makes the church leaders feel that we belong to them and they belong to us" (Interview A).

Effects of the Transition on the Theology Program

The number of Theology students has not decreased since the transition. In fact, it has shown a small increase, though the number of Theology students is lower than the number of students in the other schools, as mentioned above.

There are courses that the students of Theology now take with the students of the other schools. These classes are large and they are held in a hall. When the institution had only the Theology program, all classes were smaller. Having big classes has affected the quality of education because the teachers cannot give the students the individual attention they used to give before the transition (Interview C).

Another effect of the transition is the change of chapel time. The Theology School used to have chapel from 10:00 to 10:45 a.m., and right after chapel there was time for tea and fellowship. However, chapel has now moved to 7:15 a.m. because the chapel building is used for classes by the other faculties. Since chapel moved to this early morning hour, attendance has been poor "because it is not considered as an essential activity. Staff and students do not attend chapel as they used to" (Interview B). The daily chapel is for the School of Theology. There is chapel for the whole university on Friday mornings. However, the chapel hall is not big enough to accommodate everyone, and that limits the effectiveness of chapel. Many students have to sit outside the hall, and the frequent power outages are becoming a problem. Guest speakers often speak during the Friday chapel, but different faculty members also speak. There are also student choirs that sing during the chapel services. Faculty members of the School of Theology preach in the daily Theology chapels.

The transition has also affected how the theology school runs its program. One of the changes is in the way the higher-level program (Institut Supérieur) is run. Previously, students would do three years of training and graduate with their first degrees. Then they would go out and serve, and come back to do an advanced degree for two more years. However, the university program is such that they go through the five years straight. Students of Theology can also go through the five years without a break. A leader said, "I think we are still graduating some excellent people from that program, and they have more training when they are younger; but on the other hand, they haven't had the challenges and experiences which the older students have had. That has had a different feel and a different way of proceeding" (Interview B). Although finishing the five years straight is not required, more than half of the students of Theology are doing that, whereas in the former days, almost all students did the first three years and then went out to minister, before they returned to finish their studies.

The transition to a university has also brought an opportunity for students of Theology to minister to the students of the other schools while they are in training. That gives them an opportunity to practice their ministry skills. They lead services, preach, lead Bible study groups, and evangelize.

The transition has also given the School of Theology an opportunity to offer Bible and Theology courses for the students of the other schools. There are required Bible and Theology courses in all programs of the university. That makes the non-theology programs distinct from all similar programs offered at other universities in the area. A leader said, "At one point the Ministry of Education said, 'You have too many courses in Bible.' We said, 'Yes, we do. It is because we are a Christian university and that is our identity.' They told us not to go over what we are already doing, and we agreed" (Interview A).

A further change the transition has brought to the Theology program is the introduction of an admissions test for all applicants, which was not there before the transition. Even applicants for the Theology program now have to pass the admissions test, which is in French and Mathematics. This is part of the government's requirements.

The School of Theology focuses on training couples for ministry, as indicated in its objectives. It accepts singles too, but most of the students who are accepted are married with children, and they live in the housing provided by the university. The cost of training couples with children is much greater than that for training single students. The students of the other programs are mostly single, and they live wherever they choose. The enrollment in the Theology program is low because sending students to the new program is cheaper than sending students to study Theology, who come with their families. For that reason, churches have started sending more students to the other programs than to study Theology (Interview D).

As mentioned above, the transition has also affected the student–teacher interaction that used to be strong in earlier years. A leader said, "Life is more chaotic, and there is less individual student–teacher interaction because we are all busy trying to run a university. We don't have enough time for individuals. The staff has grown but not enough in proportion to all the new students. So we are a less cohesive unit than before" (Interview B).

Although the number of students in the Theology program is lower compared with the other programs, the Theology faculty has grown as a result of the transition. There were sixty-two or sixty-three students in 2006–2007, including the seven students who were studying Theology and Development; therefore, there were about fifty-five students studying only Theology. They now have seventy-five students (Interview B).

There are also several other positive impacts for the Theology program as a result of the institution's transition to a university. The degrees that are offered by the university (including the Theology degrees) are now signed by the Ministry of Education. That never happened before. Therefore, the Theology students who graduate now have a better standing in the country than did former graduates. These graduates can now find jobs as chaplains in schools. A leader said, "Formerly, there was always a question whether or not the government would pay their salary as school teachers because they did not have a government official degree. That is no longer a question. They have now thoroughly recognized degrees" (Interview B). The reputation of the school has also definitely grown because it is now a bigger school, with about 770 students (Interview B).

In spite of all the changes, the administration is working hard to strengthen the School of Theology. It is still considered to be the parent of the other faculties. Discussing the plans to strengthen the Theology program, a leader said, "By October this year [2011], the Theology school will have about eight or nine people with PhDs, and this has never happened before. We are even thinking of starting a PhD program in the future. I believe the Theology program will become stronger because there is a plan to strengthen it, and we are still pursuing it" (Interview A).

Shalom University of Bunia Summary

The section above described the reasons why Bunia Theological Seminary transitioned to Shalom University of Bunia, the challenges it faced during the transition, and the effects of the transition on its mission, Theology program, and its relationship with the sponsoring denominations. When one looks closely at the changes that took place at USB as a result of its transition, one can see a shift in some of the eight categories of an institution's life which Benne described in his chart.[79] USB has a clearly stated Christian vision and mission that show the *public relevance of the Christian vision* to the institution. The leadership of the university has put in place mechanisms to protect the Christian *ethos* of the institution. In its *public rhetoric*, USB openly presents itself as a Christian school.

---

79. Benne, *Quality with Soul*, 49.

Although USB does not have specific *membership requirements*, it does require applicants to faculty and staff positions to bring recommendations from their churches. It also hires non-Christians for part-time positions. When the institution was only a seminary, it used to accept born-again Christians only.

The *Theology Faculty* of USB is still strong and focuses on training couples for church ministries. There are *required Bible and Theology* courses that all students of the university must take. The university has a daily *chapel* program, mainly for the Faculty of Theology, and once a week on Fridays for the whole university community. The attendance at daily chapel is low because of the early morning schedule. The early morning schedule for chapel has decreased its effectiveness in the life of the institution.

The five denominations that sponsor USB are represented in the *governance* of USB. They send their representatives to the board of directors, which oversees the management of the university. The denominations give indirect financial support to the university by supporting their students, but there is no direct financial support coming from the denominations.

According to the eight areas mentioned in the above summary, USB can be considered as being in Benne's *critical mass* category. Although it faces many challenges, the leadership is focused on keeping its vision of pursuing "Academic and spiritual excellence for the transformation of society through Christ." Table 8 summarizes the changes.

Evaluation of the Research Design

The research design that was used in this study was qualitative, multi-case-study research and the naturalistic interpretive approach.[80] The researcher used this method of study because the amount of information that exists on the topic of this research is very limited. The qualitative, multi-case-study research method helped the researcher in his attempt to analyze and describe the transitions from a theological college or seminary to a Christian university in the East African context.

---

80. Creswell, *Research Design*, 37.

Table 8: Changes Due to the Transition from ISTB to UBS

	ISTB	UBS
Public relevance of Christian vision	Pervasive from a shared point of view	Pervasive from a shared point of view
Public rhetoric	Unabashed invitation for fellow believers to an intentionally Christian enterprise	Unabashed invitation for fellow believers to an intentionally Christian enterprise
Membership requirement	Near 100%, with orthodoxy tests	Critical mass in all facets
Religion/theology department	Large, with theology privileged	Large, with theology privileged
Religion/theology required courses	All courses affected by shared religious perspective	More than three courses, with dialogical effort in many other courses
Chapel	Required in large church at a protected time daily	Voluntary in large nave at protected time once a week
Ethos	Overt piety of evangelical tradition	Dominant atmosphere of sponsoring tradition – rituals and habits
Support by church	Indirect financial support and majority of students from sponsoring traditions	Indirect support through sponsored students
Governance	Owned and governed by church or its official representatives	All board members from sponsoring churches, some official representatives

The research instrument helped the researcher to have face-to-face, in-depth interviews with the participants, and that provided the opportunity to clarify unclear questions and responses. The qualitative research method also helped to answer research questions that are descriptive in nature that help to analyze the effects of transition in the institutions selected for this study. This method allowed the researcher to present multiple perspectives held by the leaders of the institutions in the study regarding the effects of the transitions in their institutions.

One limitation of the data that was gathered through the interviews is that some of the participants tended to emphasize the positive things that are happening in their institutions because of the transitions, while they gave less emphasis in describing the problems and challenges they face. The data the researcher collected through the documents and observations helped him to triangulate the data that was supplied through the interviews. Another limitation of the research is that the coding of the data depends on the interpretation of the researcher.

5

Conclusion

In this chapter, the researcher presents the potential significance of the findings of this research and suggests areas for further research. The findings of the five research questions presented here provide a better understanding of transitions from a Bible/theological college to a Christian liberal arts college or university in the East African context. The resulting description and analysis of the findings could provide helpful information to those Bible/theological colleges or seminaries that are considering transitioning to Christian liberal arts colleges or universities, or are already in transition.

Research Purpose

The purpose of this qualitative multi-case-study research was to analyze and describe how transitioning from a theological college or seminary to a Christian liberal arts college or university affects the mission of the institution in general and its Theology program in particular.

Research Questions

The research questions that guided this study are the following:
1. What are the reasons for the transition from a theological college to a liberal arts college or university?
2. What are the external and internal challenges these Christian higher-educational institutions face as they go through this transition?
3. In what ways is the mission of the institution affected by the transition from a theological college to a Christian liberal arts college or university?

4. In what ways has the transition affected the relationship between the institution and the sponsoring church(es) or Christian organization(s)?
5. In what ways has the transition from a theological college to a Christian liberal arts college or university affected the Theology program of the institution?

Reasons for the Transition

In this section the researcher presents the summary of his findings for the first research question: "What are the reasons for the transition from a theological college to a liberal arts college or university?" The conclusions were deducted from the analysis of the answers the research participants gave for the interview questions (see appendix 1). Table 9 lists the main reasons given by the participants of this research and how many institutions gave each reason.

Table 9: Reasons for Transition

Reason	Number of Institutions
1. To build financial sustainability	5
2. To have a Christian influence in society by providing Christian higher education	5
3. To be able to offer government-accredited degrees so that graduates can get jobs in governmental and non-governmental organizations	5
4. To fulfill the church's long-time vision of providing Christian education up to university level	2
5. To meet the growing need for trained leaders in churches in different areas (in addition to theological/pastoral ministry)	2
6. To meet the growing need for higher education in the country	2
7. Pressure from the government to get a charter/accreditation	2
8. To compete with other religious groups that have started their own universities	1

The table shows that the institutions in this study gave multiple reasons for their transition to Christian universities. All five institutions indicated that seeking financial sustainability was one of the main reasons why they considered transitioning to a university. Four of the five institutions indicated that they were facing serious financial challenges that threatened their very existence as theological schools. Their financial challenges were caused by the decreasing number of students attending their Theology programs and the dwindling donations coming from the West. By adding additional programs to their Theology program, they aimed to increase the number of students and, as a result, increase their revenue.

A second reason mentioned by the leaders of all five institutions for transitioning to a university is that they wanted to expand their Christian influence in general society by training Christian professionals in different fields who could work in governmental and non-governmental organizations. It is too early to assess if the graduates of these new programs are having the desired influence. However, some of them have indicated that they are receiving good feedback about their graduates.

The third reason given by the leaders of the institutions for their transition to a university is that, by adding more programs and seeking government accreditation, they could offer government-recognized certificates to their graduates. This request came from their students, who wanted to graduate with degrees that did not limit them to working only within churches or in contexts of Christian ministries, but allowed them to compete for jobs in the general marketplace. The institutions also realized that some of their graduates were not able to get employment in churches or Christian organizations, and some of them wanted to be able to compete for jobs in governmental and non-governmental organizations. In addition to that, the institutions also wanted to make their programs marketable to the wider community and to attract more students by offering government-recognized programs. Although the institutions have benefited from their new status as government-chartered institutions, that has also brought several challenges. These challenges are discussed in the next section.

The fourth reason mentioned by two of the institutions in this study for their transition to a Christian university was based on their sponsoring churches' vision of providing education to a higher level. Their founding churches have seen providing formal education as part of their Christian mission.[1]

Although, the other four reasons listed in Table 9 were not mentioned by some of the five institutions as one of their main reasons, they nevertheless were factors in their decision to transition to a university.

External and Internal Challenges

The second research question asked: "What are the external and internal challenges these Christian higher-educational institutions face as they go through this transition?" Table 10 and Table 11 list respectively the main external and the main internal challenges mentioned by the research participants, and the number of institutions that mentioned each as a challenge in their institution.

Table 10 lists the external challenges the institutions faced. Three of the four challenges are related to how the government policies affected the institutions. As mentioned above, getting a charter from the government has brought benefits as well as challenges.

Table 10: External Challenges

External Challenges	Number of Institutions
1. Government policies that impinge on the Christian vision and mission	4
2. Requirement from the government that they should expand programs more than they originally intended	2
3. Competition in the higher-educational market	2
4. Constantly changing government policies	1

As seen in the case of MYS, Ethiopian government policies do not allow government-accredited institutions to include Bible or Theology courses in their curriculums. They are also not allowed to discriminate among potential

---

1. J. Kwabana Asamoah-Gyadu, "Christian Higher Education for Africa: Need, Relevance, and Value," paper presented at the meeting of the International Association for the Promotion of Christian Higher Education, 2007; http://www.iapche.org/gyadu-paper.htm; accessed 10 October 2009.

students based on their religion. These policies have seriously affected the institution's ability to function as a distinctly Christian institution. The constantly changing laws in higher education were also mentioned by the leaders of MYS as a major challenge. For example, the new policy of the Ministry of Education of the Ethiopian government requires accredited institutions to have 70 percent of their programs in natural sciences, with only 30 percent in social sciences. That was not something MYS was ready for (Interview A).

The laws in Kenya do not allow government-chartered institutions to discriminate among employees and students based on their religion. USB in the DRC had to add more programs than it was ready for in order to meet the requirements of the government to get a charter. So far, the laws in Uganda have been very conducive for religious higher-educational institutions. However, the leaders indicate that changes may come in the future.

These challenges are reminiscent of what happened in the UK and many other countries in the West. As discussed in chapter 2, the various laws that were passed by Parliament played a big role in changing the universities from Church of England universities to secular universities.[2] The state also forced the institutions to expand or contract according to the desires of the state and to accommodate any citizens irrespective of their religious background.[3] The Christian institutions that have government accreditation (a charter) in Ethiopia and Kenya are not allowed to discriminate among students based on their religion, and the institutions in East Africa may face more challenges of secularization in the coming years if governments make laws that push for more secular education in the institutions they charter.

Table 11 lists the internal challenges the institutions faced as a result of their transition to a Christian university. The first four are highlighted here. One internal challenge that was mentioned by all the institutions was building consensus about the transition among church leaders, faculty and staff members, and students. Some objected to the transition by expressing their fear that it might lead to secularization, referring to the history of Christian higher-

---

2. D. Bebbington, "The Secularization of British Universities since the Mid-Nineteenth Century," in *The Secularization of the Academy*, ed. G. Marsden and B. J. Longfield (New York: Oxford University Press, 1992), 265.

3. P. Glanzer, "Searching for the Soul of English Universities: An Exploration and Analysis of Christian Higher Education in England," *British Journal of Educational Studies* 56, no. 2 (2008): 178.

educational institutions in the West that started as theological schools but eventually transitioned to universities and slowly became secularized. Others were also concerned about what would happen to the Theology program if it became part of a university. A lack of clear direction about how the transition was going to be implemented and how the seminary would continue to function in a university setting were other challenges some of the institutions faced during the transition.

Table 11: Internal Challenges

Internal Challenges	Number of Institutions
1. Building consensus about the need for the change	5
2. Attracting enough qualified Christian faculty	5
3. Lack of financial resources to expand	5
4. Lack of space to run all the programs	4
5. A lack of clear direction on how the transition should be implemented	3
6. Lack of preparedness for the challenges the transition brings	3
7. Conflict of purpose and competition between the seminary and the other schools	3
8. Maintaining the Christian ethos	2

Another challenge mentioned by all five institutions was finding enough qualified Christian faculty members who share the ethos of their institutions to teach all the courses in the new faculties. The institutions have had to hire part-time non-Christian faculty members to meet their needs. The lack of faculty members who share the Christian ethos of the institution definitely affects the implementation of the institution's desire to integrate faith and learning in all the classes taught.

As mentioned above, one of the reasons why all five institutions considered expanding their programs and transitioning to Christian universities was to generate more income and bring financial sustainability. However, they all indicated that this did not solve their financial challenges. The transition itself brought a need for more funds to expand facilities, to hire more faculty and staff members, and to provide more services to the growing communities of the institutions. Because of the poor economic situation within the countries, institutions could not charge students higher fees that would enable them to overcome their financial challenges. Raising funds from outside these countries has been a continuing problem because of the worldwide economic downturn. These challenges slowed the institutions' plans to expand their facilities to accommodate the new programs. That created a shortage of space and forced the faculties to compete for the limited space that was available.

Effects of the Transition on the Mission

The third research question asked: "In what ways is the mission of the institution affected by the transition from a theological college to a Christian liberal arts college or university?" A clearly stated mission statement is assumed to permeate everything that is done in the college in a way that gives "internal consistency to teaching, scholarship, student life, administration, and community relations."[4]

All five institutions included in this study have made some changes to their former vision and mission statements to reflect the expansion of their programs. The original mission statements have now become the mission statements of the Theology schools or faculties. The vision and mission statements of AIU, SPU, UCU and USB clearly state the public relevance of the institutions' Christian vision. The mission statement of MYS also clearly states the public relevance of its Christian vision. However, the vision and mission statements of its Management and Leadership College (MY-MLC) do not indicate the institution's Christian mission other than stating that it is owned by a church, EECMY. The reason why MY-MLC does not state its Christian mission and vision in clear terms is that as an academic college accredited by the government, it is required to follow the government's secular guidelines and function as a secular institution. That has created confusion regarding the *ethos* of MYS.

Ringenberg, describing how an institution slides into secularization, writes, "The public statements about the Christian nature of the institution begin to include equivocal rather than explicit phrases; these statements often

---

4. Anthony Diekema, *Academic Freedom and Christian Scholarship* (Grand Rapids, MI: Eerdmans, 2000), 57.

describe Christian goals in sociological but not theological terms."[5] The leaders of MYS have realized the problem and are seeking a solution. This researcher believes that, if Mekane Yesus University (MYU) is going to be established as an institution accredited by the government following what has been done at MY-MLC, that will greatly affect MYU's ability to function as a distinctly Christian university with a distinct Christian mission.

Although vision and mission statements are assumed to give consistency to what goes on within the institutions, it is also possible that what is stated on paper does not necessarily reflect what goes on within the institution. As discussed in chapter 2, factors like the public statements the institution makes, its faculty hiring policy, the importance the institution gives to chapel and other spiritual activities, its curriculum, its relationship with founding or sponsoring churches, and its student body are all indicators as to whether the institution is fully committed to its Christian mission or not.[6]

Before their transitions, all the institutions in this study had a policy of hiring Christians only. However, four out of the five institutions have indicated that they have hired non-Christians or nominal Christians as part-time faculty members because they could not find enough committed Christians who could teach all the courses they offer. Some leaders have also admitted that at times they have hired non-Christians to full-time teaching positions because they were not able to vet them properly when they were hired. The leaders of AIU and SPU in Kenya have indicated that, although it is not yet enforced by the government, the law requires them not to discriminate on religious grounds among those they hire as faculty or staff members. If the trend of hiring non-Christians continues and expands, that will be a threat to the institutions' Christian mission and ethos. These Christian universities need to develop their own faculty by training committed and well-qualified Christians in all fields of study who carry the ethos of the institutions.

One can also see that chapel has been given less emphasis after the transition in at least four out of the five institutions in this study. Some of the institutions that used to require chapel attendance for their Theology students do not require it now. Even those that do require it are not enforcing it. The

---

5. William C. Ringenberg, *The Christian College: A History of Protestant Higher Education in America*, 2nd ed. (Grand Rapids, MI: Baker, 2006), 120–121.

6. R. Benne, *Quality with Soul*.

increase in the number of students, and the fact that many of them do not live on campus, makes it hard for the institutions to schedule chapel that is well attended at a protected time.

Another change that took place in all five institutions was that they started accepting non-Christians as students after their transitions, although they intend to keep the ratio very low. The government laws in Ethiopia and Kenya do not allow discrimination of prospective students based on their faith (religion). The institutions want to use this opportunity to reach out to the non-Christian students.

A factor that helps higher-educational institutions to maintain a truly Christian mission is its effectiveness in integrating faith and learning. As Monsma indicated, a truly Christian liberal arts education should not just offer what is basically a secular education with Bible and Theology courses on the side, without properly integrating faith with all the subjects offered.[7] Four out of the five institutions in this study require students of the liberal arts programs to take Christian foundation courses. These courses vary from Bible and Theology courses to courses on Christian ethics or the Christian worldview. The integration of faith and learning in all subjects that are taught is a challenge to all these institutions because they lack experienced faculty members who can do it well. Some of the leaders indicated that they want to train their faculty by partnering with other Christian universities that have faculty members experienced in integrating faith and learning.

Effects of the Transition on the Relationship with Churches

The fourth research question asked: "In what ways has the transition affected the relationship between the institutions and the sponsoring church(es) or Christian organization(s)?" One of the key factors in helping higher-educational institutions to remain faithful to their Christian mission is their maintaining a close relationship with their founding or sponsoring churches. If an institution reduces or drops its church affiliation to become an independent organization, or if it reduces its interest in being identified with interdenominational and

---

7. Stephen V. Monsma, "Christian Worldview in Academia," *Faculty Dialogue* 21 (1994): 146.

parachurch organizations, that may be an indication that it is becoming secularized.[8]

In all five cases in this study, the sponsoring churches or denominations of the institutions have supported the transition of the institutions to Christian universities. In fact, one of the main reasons why two of the institutions transitioned to Christian universities was to fulfill the churches' long-time vision of providing Christian education up to university level. The role of the churches in the governance of all five institutions has not changed greatly since the transitions to Christian universities.

However, serious concerns have been raised by the leaders of the institutions regarding their relationships with their sponsoring churches. A fear was expressed by the leaders of UCU that church leaders might think that training ministers for the church is the responsibility of the universities (seminaries within the universities). That will be a great problem if the universities appoint leaders who do not have a heart for theological education or pastoral training. Leaders of MYS have expressed a concern that the new programs in the Management and Leadership College are no longer in line with the sponsoring church's vision of providing holistic ministry. The leaders of SPU, which is sponsored by several denominations, are concerned that the churches are not engaged enough in the life of the institution because they have established their own denominational universities, and they are not sending enough students to SPU. The sponsoring churches' financial support of the academic institutions in this study comes in mostly through sponsorship of students sent by the churches to the institutions.

Effects of the Transitions on the Theology Program

In this section, the researcher presents the conclusions that were derived from the fifth research question: "In what ways has the transition from a theological college to a Christian liberal arts college or university affected the Theology program of the institution?" The conclusions are deducted from an analysis of the answers given by the subjects of this research.

As described in chapter 4, when the idea of transitioning to a university was raised at each institution in this study, it was met with resistance at some

---

8. Ringenberg, *The Christian College*, 120–121.

institutions, and concerns were raised at others. Those who resisted the idea of transitioning referred to the history of higher-educational institutions in the West that were started by churches to give theological training but eventually transitioned to universities and over time became secularized. They expressed their fears that the same might happen to their institutions.

However, in at least three of the five schools in this study, those who resisted the change gave up their objections when they saw that the very existence of their institutions was challenged by the lack of finances and shortage of students. They were convinced that the only viable way for their institutions to survive was by adding other programs that would bring more students to the school and increase their income. Although the concerns were still present, the institutions moved on with their plans of transitioning to universities. The transitions have impacted the Bible/theological colleges or seminaries both positively and negatively.

Positively, in all five institutions, the number of students on the Theology programs has increased since the transition. The transition has also brought an opportunity for the Faculty of Theology to require students of other faculties to take Bible/Theology or Christian foundation courses. Some of the Theology schools (faculties) added more programs in ministry-related fields and started offering graduate programs in Theology, and as a result attracted more students. The fact that they are now in a university setting has enabled them to get students who would not have come if they had stayed as a seminary or Bible college.

The transition to a university has also brought opportunities for students of Theology to minister to students of the other faculties. Those students who are being prepared for ministry now have a chance to practice their training while they are still in school.

The transition has also strengthened the financial capacity of the institutions so that they can pay reasonable salaries (UCU, SPU) and provide services, such as a wireless Internet service (UCU), that the theological school could not have afforded. Since the Theology faculties (schools) are now part of government-chartered universities, the degrees that they offer are all recognized by the government. As a result, even graduates with Theology degrees can now find job opportunities outside churches and Christian organizations.

Although the number of Theology students in these five institutions has increased since the transitions, that increase is very low compared with the growth of the other faculties. Since the other faculties are growing very fast in a very short time, there is a fear that the Theology faculties will become relatively small faculties in big universities, and that their significance will diminish in the long term.

The transitions have also brought changes to the campus life of the institutions. Before the transition, the Bible colleges or seminaries had mostly mature students who were preparing for ministry. The new programs have brought younger students with difficult characters, and even some unbelievers. The new situation is described by some of the leaders as "chaotic," "loud," "less cohesive," and "noisy." The students of the other programs at times have "less regard" for the students of Theology. Some of those who have come to be trained for ministry face serious temptations, and some of them drop their desire to go into ministry (SPU). A leader called these challenges "real world" challenges. The institutions have less control over what goes on in the lives of the students because many of them live off campus. The campuses can no longer function as a "sacred" place that trains students for ministry.

Another change that the transitions have brought to the Theology programs is that, since all the degree programs the schools offer are now accredited by governments, the schools are now required to strictly follow the standards set by those governments, and they have to seek government approval for all their programs. Although these standards help the institutions to keep high academic standards, they also force them to give less emphasis to ministry experience and limit their flexibility.

The transition has also made it difficult for the Theology schools to maintain the ways of doing ministerial training they had before the transitions. The Theology faculties are struggling to define themselves as part of the universities. They are struggling to adjust to the new realities and to use the new opportunities. This is mainly due to a lack of clear direction that was agreed upon as to how the Theology program should fit in the new university setting. The theological schools that had all the facilities for their exclusive use now have to share them with other faculties that are growing faster than they are. That creates tensions. Some of the theological schools now want to have their own space within the university or have a separate campus in order to function in a way that they see appropriate for training ministers for the church.

Theology faculty members are concerned that if the universities get leaders who do not see the importance or centrality of theological programs in a university setting, the Theology faculties may be affected negatively and may become unable to train ministers for the church.

Research Implications

As indicated in chapter 1, several theological colleges and seminaries in Africa have transitioned or are considering transitioning to Christian universities. Five of these institutions are included in this multi-case study. The implications of this research could help leaders of theological colleges or seminaries that are transitioning or are considering transitioning to universities to understand the potential challenges they may face due to the transition, and the possible impacts of the transition on their overall mission, their relationship with churches, and their Theology program.

The first implication of this research is that, although one of the main reasons why all the institutions in this study considered transitioning to Christian universities was the financial challenges they were facing, transitioning to a Christian university does not necessarily solve the financial challenges. The transition itself brings a need for more funds to expand facilities, to hire more faculty and staff members, and to provide services to the growing communities of the institution. The poor economic situations within the countries did not enable the institutions to charge students high fees that would enable them to overcome their financial challenges.

The second implication of this research is that transitioning to universities by getting a charter (accreditation) from the government helps institutions to market their programs to the wider community. Since they can offer degrees that are recognized by the government, their graduates can compete for jobs in governmental and non-governmental organizations in addition to churches and Christian organizations.

However, by getting accreditation (a charter) from the government, these institutions are required to abide by government laws and regulations that apply to all government-accredited academic institutions. These government laws may greatly influence how the institutions function as Christian universities. As seen in this research, government policies may influence institutions' faculty and staff recruitment policies, student recruitment policies, the curriculum, and even the very mission of the institute. Once the theological college or seminary becomes part of a university, it may also be subjected to stricter government regulations that apply to all the university programs. Theological colleges, which are considered as religious institutions attached to churches, have more freedom to function without much interference from the government than government-accredited universities. Those who desire to transition should carefully consider these risks in light of government regulations and check if the legal framework of their context allows them to function as distinctly Christian universities.

The third and related implication of this study is that transitioning from a theological college to a university may require an institution to move from what Benne calls an *orthodox* institution to what he calls *critical mass* institution.[9] The institutions in this study made changes to adjust to the new realities and to comply with the government regulations. Although it is too early to see a clear sign of secularization in the institutions of this research, government policies on higher education that are motivated by political agendas may limit Christian universities from functioning as distinctly Christian institutions.

The threat of secularization that exists in Christian higher-educational institutions accredited by the governments in East African countries has some similarities with what Glanzer, Carpenter, and Lantinga described as happening in Eastern Europe:

> Secularization did not spring from the natural march of social history but from political efforts to control the production and dissemination of knowledge. If the phenomenon of secularization is the result of a power struggle between individuals and institutions with particular worldviews, religious institutions more closely controlled and financially supported by the state face a common danger. The leaders of nation-states, whether conservative or liberal, are usually more interested in political rather than religious goals. When religious institutions possess few ways to resist powerful state leaders, these leaders will usually transform the institution from one that serves the church to one that first and foremost serves a secularized state agenda.[10]

---

9. Benne, *Quality with Soul*, 49.
10. P. L. Glanzer, Joel Carpenter, and Nick Lantinga, "Looking for God in the University: Examining Trends in Christian Higher Education," *Higher Education: The International Journal of Higher Education and Educational Planning* 61, no. 6 (2011), 175.

The government's laws in the countries in this study are not necessarily anti-Christian but they follow the anti-discriminatory laws of their constitution. In Ethiopia, the government does not recognize religious institutions because of its policy of separation of church and state. Therefore, institutions that seek government accreditation may be pushed to function as secular institutions.

Research Applications

The applications of this research could help theological higher-educational institutes that are in transition or are considering transitioning to Christian liberal arts colleges or universities. The first application of this research is that it could help the institutions by pointing out the possible external and internal challenges they may face as they transition, so that they can prepare for them in advance.

The second application of this research is that theological colleges or seminaries that are considering transitioning to Christian universities need to ask if the setting of a university is the best setting for training ministers for the churches. Since these theological schools are the main and sometimes the only higher-educational institutions that train ministers for their sponsoring denominations, it is critical that they remain strong and committed to their mission of training ministers for the church. A theological-education (ministerial-training) model that requires a small community setting where chapel, small-group fellowship, one-to-one interactions between students and faculty, and mentoring are considered very important would definitely face a serious challenge in a university setting with thousands of students, bigger classrooms, limited space, and less teacher–student interaction. Theological schools in two of the five institutions in this study now prefer to have their own campus where they can function freely as they used to, while the other three want to have a clear boundary between the theology school and the rest of the university. Those who desire to make the theology school part of a Christian university have to adjust their philosophy or model of training to the new realities of a university context.

The third application of this research is that, despite all the challenges, theological colleges and seminaries can be foundations for strong Christian universities if the legal context in the country is conducive and if the institution works on the crucial factors that make universities distinctly Christian. The theology school can play a central role by requiring students of all programs to take courses in Bible and Theology, and by working closely with the other faculties in the integration of faith and learning in all subjects that are taught. The theology school can also play a big role in chapel and the overall spiritual development of the university community. The university setting allows the theology school to train its own students in a "real-world"-like environment that allows them to practice their ministry skills right there while they are still studying. A well-qualified committed Christian faculty and close relationship and partnership with founding or sponsoring churches are also important.

Research Limitations

As is noted in chapter 1 under the delimitations of this research, the findings of this research may not necessarily apply to all theological colleges or seminaries that are transitioning or have transitioned to a liberal arts college or university in Ethiopia, Kenya, Uganda, and DRC. The study is limited in its representation because all transitions are different and dependent on the nature of the institutions and their specific contexts.

This study is also limited in its representation to Protestant evangelical Bible or theological colleges that have transitioned or are transitioning to liberal arts colleges or universities. The findings, therefore, do not generalize to all church-affiliated institutions that belong to other Christian traditions.

Further Research

This research study focused on five institutions that are in transition or that transitioned to Christian universities in the last ten years. One possible area of further research is to do the same study in the same institutions ten years from now to see how the transitions have impacted the Christian mission of the institutions in general and their Theology programs in particular. That would help to see if secularization is taking place in these institutions.

Transitioning from a Bible college to a Christian university is a phenomenon that is taking place in many other African countries. This study focused only on a few institutions in East Africa. Similar kinds of research could be done in other African countries and regions.

This study also focused on institutions that started as theological colleges or seminaries but are now Christian universities or becoming such. A possible area of further research is comparing and contrasting the effectiveness of these universities with those that were founded as Christian universities from the very beginning.

Appendix 1

Semi-structured Interview Questions

Directions: This is a semi-structured interview, and the purpose of the interview is to allow you (the interviewee) to express your perception on how the transition from a theological (Bible) college to a Christian liberal arts college or university has affected the overall mission of the institution in general and the Theology program in particular. I will record some notes during the interview to help in understanding your responses and for asking follow-up questions when necessary. The interview will also be audio-recorded for the purpose of accuracy and review of your responses. Once the interview is transcribed you will get a chance to review the accuracy of your responses. Do you agree with the recording of the interview? I appreciate your willingness to participate in this study.

Agreement to Participate: The research you are about to take part in is designed to provide an analysis and description of the reasons and challenges of transitioning from a theological college or seminary to a Christian liberal arts college or university and how such transitions affect the institution, its theological program, and its relationship with the founding or sponsoring church or Christian organization. As a leader of an institution that is chosen for this study, you will be asked to complete a one-on-one interview on questions related to such transitions. The research is being conducted by Semeon Mulatu for the purpose of doctoral dissertation research. By completing this interview, you are giving your consent for the use of this interview in the research.

Signature: _____ Date: _____

The following questions will serve to facilitate the flow of the interview.

Reasons for the Transition

1. What were the reasons that your institution considered transitioning to a Christian university or Christian liberal arts college?

2. Who initiated the consideration of this change? Explain how it happened.

3. Do you believe there is (was) a general consensus about this change in your institution? Explain.

4. What role did the board play in the transition?

5. What role did the administration take in the transition?

6. What was the role of the church or sponsoring organization in the decision-making process for this transition?

Effects on the Mission of the Institute

7. Has the mission of the institution changed because of this transition? Explain.

8. Does the college clearly state its Christian identity in its mission statement, public announcements, and published documents? Explain.

9. Has there been any change in the way the institution presents itself as a Christian institution since the transition?

10. How does your institution's Christian identity influence its perspective and practices?

11. What makes your institution distinct from other secular higher-educational institutions that offer the same programs you do?

12. In what ways is the education offered in your liberal arts programs different from that of other secular universities?

External and Internal Challenges

13. What are the biggest challenges in implementing the transition?

14. What were the internal challenges the institute faced due to the transition? Which ones were anticipated and which ones were not?

15. What were the external challenges the institute faced due to the transition?

16. What are the new influences that this transition has brought on your school from outside organizations?
    a. From government oversight
    b. Donor organizations
    c. Accrediting agencies
    d. Others?

Effects on the Theology Program

17. In what ways has the transition affected the Theology program of the institution?

18. How is the Theology program integrated into the overall program of the institution? Are there any Bible/Theology courses required for all students?

19. How has the transition affected the chapel program?

20. How has the transition been received by the faculty and students of the Theology department?

21. How has the transition affected the student enrollment of the Theology program?

Effects on the Relationship with the Church

22. How has this transition affected the institution's relationship with the founding or sponsoring church(es)?

23. Has there been any change in the church membership (faith) requirement for those in administration, faculty, staff, and prospective students because of the transition?

24. Are there stated moral expectations of the faculty and students for specified Christian reasons that are different from those in secular institutions?

Appendix 2

Expert Panel Selection

The expert panel consisted of:

Robert D. Benne, PhD, Director of the Center for Religion and Society and Lecturer of the Department of Religion/Philosophy, Roanoke College, Salem, VA, who has expertise in Christian higher education.

Perry L. Glanzer, PhD, Associate Professor of Educational Foundations, and Faculty Fellow in the Institute of Church–State Studies and the Institute for the Study of Religion, Baylor School of Education, Baylor University, Waco, TX, who has expertise in Christian higher education and in devising, refining, and using survey instruments.

John Jusu, PhD, Dean of School of Professional Studies at Africa International University, Nairobi, Kenya, who has expertise in Christian higher-education curriculum in Africa.

Reference List

Abagi, O. "Private Higher Education in Kenya." In *New Trends in Higher Education: Growth and Expansion of Private Higher Education in Africa*, edited by N. V. Varghese, 75–94. Paris: International Institute for Educational Planning, 2006.

Altbach, P. G. "Academic Freedom: International Realities and Challenges." *Higher Education* 41, no. 1–2 (2001): 205–219.

———. *The Knowledge Context: Comparative Perspectives on the Distribution of Knowledge*. Albany, NY: State University of New York Press, 1987.

Anthony, Michael J., Warren S. Benson, Daryl Eldridge, and Julie Gorman, eds. *Evangelical Dictionary of Christian Education*. Grand Rapids, MI: Baker Academic, 2001.

Arthur, J. "Faith and Secularization in Religious Colleges and Universities." *Journal of Belief and Values* 29, no. 2 (2008): 197–202.

Asamoah-Gyadu, J. Kwabana. "Christian Higher Education for Africa: Need, Relevance, and Value." Paper presented at the meeting of the International Association for the Promotion of Christian Higher Education, 2007. http://www.iapche.org/gyadu-paper.htm. Accessed 10 October 2009.

Badley, Ken. "The Faith/Learning Integration Movement in Christian Higher Education: Slogan or Substance?" *Journal of Research on Christian Education* 3, no. 1 (1994): 13–33.

Banya, K. "Are Private Universities the Solution to the Higher Education Crisis in Sub-Saharan Africa?" *Higher Education Policy* 14 (2001): 161–199.

Bebbington, D. "The Secularization of British Universities since the Mid-Nineteenth Century." In *The Secularization of the Academy*, edited by G. Marsden and B. J. Longfield, 259–277. New York: Oxford University Press, 1992.

Benne, R. *Quality With Soul: How Six Premier Colleges and Universities Keep Faith with Their Religious Traditions*. Grand Rapids, MI: Eerdmans, 2001.

Bertrand, J. Mark. *(Re)Thinking Worldview: Learning to Think, Live, and Speak in This World*. Wheaton, IL: Crossway, 2007.

Bloom, David, David Canning, and Kevin Chan. *Higher Education and Economic Development in Africa*. Washington, DC: World Bank, 2005. www.arp.harvard.edu/AfricaHigherEducation/Reports. Accessed 15 October 2009.

Budde, M., and J. Wright, eds. *Conflicting Allegiances: The Church-Based University in a Liberal Democratic Society*. Grand Rapids, MI: Brazos, 2004.

Burtchaell, James T. "The Decline and Fall of the Christian College (II)." *First Things* (May 1991): 24–41.

———. *The Dying of the Light: The Disengagement of Colleges and Universities from their Christian Churches*. Grand Rapids, MI: Eerdmans, 1998.

Carlberg, Judson R. "The Evangelical Vision: From Fundamentalist Isolation to Respected Voice." In *The Future of Religious Colleges*, edited by Paul J. Drove, 224–245. Grand Rapids, MI: Eerdmans, 2002.

Carpenter, Joel A. "Universities on the Mission Field? Part I: New Evangelical Universities: Cogs in a World System, Or Players in a New Game?" *International Journal of Frontier Missions* 20, no. 2 (2003): 55–65.

———. "Universities on the Mission Field? Part II: New Evangelical Universities: Cogs in a World System, Or Players in a New Game?" *International Journal of Frontier Missions* 20, no. 3 (2003): 95–102.

Carpenter, Joel A., and Kenneth W. Shipps. *Making Higher Education Christian: The History and Mission of Evangelical Colleges in America*. St Paul, MN: Christian University Press, 1987.

Central Statistical Authority. *Ethiopian Statistical Abstract 2004*. Addis Ababa: Central Statistics Authority, 2004.

Creswell, J. W. *Research Design: Qualitative, Quantitative, and Mixed Methods Approaches*. 3rd ed. Thousand Oaks, CA: Sage, 2009.

Cuninggim, M. *Uneasy Partners: The College and the Church*. Nashville, TN: Abingdon, 1994.

D'Costa, G. *Theology in the Public Square: Church, Academy, and Nation*. Malden, MA: Blackwell, 2005.

Diekema, Anthony. *Academic Freedom and Christian Scholarship*. Grand Rapids, MI: Eerdmans, 2000.

Dockery, David S. *Renewing Minds: Serving Church and Society through Christian Higher Education*. Nashville, TN: B&H, 2007.

Dockery, David S., and David P. Gushee, eds. *The Future of Christian Higher Education*. Nashville, TN: B&H, 1999.

Dovre, Paul J., ed. *The Future of Religious Colleges*. Grand Rapids, MI: Eerdmans, 2002.

Ensor, Peter. "Those Memorable Years (St Paul's 1985 to 1998)." In *For God and Humanity: 100 Years of St Paul's United Theological College*. Eldoret, Kenya: Zapf Chancery Research Consultants and Publishers, 2003.

Erickson, Millard J. *Introducing Christian Doctrine*. Grand Rapids, MI: Baker, 1992.

Gaebelein, F. E. *The Pattern of God's Truth: Problems of Integration in Christian Education*. New York: Oxford University Press, 1954.

Gall, M. D., W. R. Borg, and J. P. Gall. *Educational Research: An Introduction.* White Plains, NY: Longman, 1996.

Gangel, K. O., ed. *Toward a Harmony of Faith and Learning.* Detroit, MI: William Tyndale College Press, 1983.

Glanzer, P. L. "The Role of the State in the Secularization of Christian Higher Education: A Case Study of Eastern Europe." *Journal of Church and State* 53, no. 2 (2011): 161–182.

———. "Searching for the Soul of English Universities: An Exploration and Analysis of Christian Higher Education in England." *British Journal of Educational Studies* 56, no. 2 (2008): 163–183.

Glanzer, P. L., Joel Carpenter, and Nick Lantinga. "Looking for God in the University: Examining Trends in Christian Higher Education." *Higher Education: The International Journal of Higher Education and Educational Planning* 61, no. 6 (2011): 721–755.

Gomes, Peter J. "Affirmation and Adaptation: Values and the Elite Residential College." In *Distinctively American: The Residential Liberal Arts Colleges*, edited by Steven Koblik and Stephen R. Graubard, 101–119. New Brunswick, NJ: Transaction, 2000.

Green, Madeleine F., and Fred M. Hayward. "Forces For Change." In *Transforming Higher Education: Views from Leaders around the World*, edited by Madeleine F. Green, 3–26. Phoenix, AZ: American Council on Education/Oryx Press, 1997.

Grudem, Wayne. *Systematic Theology: An Introduction to Biblical Doctrines.* Grand Rapids, MI: Zondervan, 1994.

Guba, E., and Y. S. Lincoln. "Do Inquiry Paradigms Imply Inquiry Methodologies?" In *Qualitative Approaches to Evaluation in Education*, edited by D. M. Feeterman, 89–115. New York: Praeger, 1988.

Gutta, Magarsaa. *From a Humble Beginning to Advanced Standing: A History of Mekane Yesus Seminary 1960–2010.* Addis Ababa, Ethiopia: United Printers, 2011.

Hamilton, Michael S., and James A. Mathisen. "Faith and Learning at Wheaton College." In *Models for Christian Higher Education: Strategies for Success in the Twenty-First Century*, edited by Richard T. Hughes and William B. Adrian, 261–283. Grand Rapids, MI: Eerdmans, 1997.

Hatch, Nathan O. "Evangelical Colleges and the Challenge of Christian Thinking." In *Making Higher Education Christian: The History and Mission of Evangelical Colleges in America*, edited by Joel A. Carpenter and Kenneth W. Shipps, 155–171. St Paul, MN: Christian University Press, 1987.

Hayward, Fred M. "Higher Education in Africa: Crisis and Transformation." In *Transforming Higher Education: Views from Leaders around the World*, edited by Madeleine F. Green, 87–113. Phoenix, AZ: American Council on Education/Oryx Press, 1997.

Holmes, Arthur F. *All Truth Is God's Truth*. Grand Rapids, MI: Eerdmans, 1977.

———. *The Idea of a Christian College*. Grand Rapids, MI: Eerdmans, 1975.

———. "Integrating Faith and Learning in a Christian Liberal Arts Institution." In *The Future of Christian Higher Education*, edited by David S. Dockery and David P. Gushee, 155–172. Nashville, TN: B&H, 1999.

———, ed. *The Making of a Christian Mind*. Downers Grove, IL: InterVarsity Press, 1985.

Hughes, Richard T., and William B. Adrian., eds. *Models for Christian Higher Education: Strategies for Success in the Twenty-First Century*. Grand Rapids, MI: Eerdmans, 1997.

Hull, J. E. "Aiming for Christian Education, Settling for Christian Educating: The Christian School's Replication of a Public School Paradigm." *Christian Scholars Review* 13 (Winter 2002): 203–233.

Kilonzo, Charles, and Wanjira Maganjo, eds. "Up Close and Personal with Dr Timothy Wachira." In *Voice: St Paul's University*, edited by Charles Kilonzo and Wanjira Maganjo. Limuru, Kenya: St Paul University, 2010.

Knight, George R. *Philosophy and Education: An Introduction in Christian Perspective*. Berrien Springs, MI: Andrews University Press, 2006.

Kombo, James. "Christian Higher Education for Africa: Need, Relevance, and Value." Paper presented at the meeting of the International Association for the Promotion of Christian Higher Education, Legon, Ghana, 11 October 2007.

Kotter, John. *Leading Change*. Cambridge, MA: Harvard Business School Press, 1996.

Leedy, Paul D., and Jeanne Ellis Ormrod. *Practical Research: Planning and Design*. 9th ed. Boston, MA: Pearson, 2010.

Levy, Daniel. "A Recent Echo: African Private Higher Education in an International Perspective." *Journal of Higher Education in Africa* 5, no. 2–3 (2007): 197–220.

Litfin, D. *Conceiving the Christian College*. Grand Rapids, MI: Eerdmans, 2004.

Marsden, George M. *The Soul of the American University: From Protestant Establishment to Established Nonbelief*. New York: Oxford University Press, 1994.

Marty, Martin. "The Church and Christian Higher Education in the New Millennium." In *Faithful Learning and the Christian Scholarly Vocation*, edited by Douglas V. Henry and Bob R. Agee, 50–61. Grand Rapids, MI: Eerdmans, 2003.

Mekane Yesus Seminary. *Self-Evaluation Report of Mekane Yesus Seminary, Addis Ababa, Ethiopia*. Addis Ababa: Ethiopia, 2007.

Mixon, Stephanie L., Larry Lyon, and Michael Beaty. "Secularization and National Universities: The Effect of Religious Identity on Academic Reputation." *Journal of Higher Education* 75, no. 4 (2004): 400–419.

Monsma, Stephen V. "Christian Worldview in Academia." *Faculty Dialogue* 21 (1994): 146.

Muoka, Kavita, Paul Karaimu, and Nelisa Gacheri., eds. *Nairobi Evangelical Graduate School of Theology (NEGST) Transitions: NEGST to AIU*. Nairobi, Kenya: AIU, 2010.

Nelson, R. R. "Faith–Discipline Integration: Compatibilist, Reconstructionalist, and Transformationalist Strategies." In *The Reality of Christian Learning*, edited by Harold Heie and David L. Wolfe, 317–339. Grand Rapids, MI: Eerdmans, 1987.

Nettles, Tom J. "Evangelicalism." In *Evangelical Dictionary of Christian Education*, edited by Michael J. Anthony, Warren S. Benson, Daryl Eldridge, and Julie Gorman. Baker Reference Library. Grand Rapids, MI: Baker Academic, 2001.

Ngome, C. "Kenya." In *African Higher Education: An International Reference Handbook*, edited by Damtew Tefera and P. G. Altbach, 359–371. Bloomington, IN: Indiana University Press, 2003.

Noll, Mark. "The Evangelical Mind in America." In *Should God Get Tenure?*, edited by David W. Gill, 195–211. Grand Rapids, MI: Eerdmans, 1997.

O'Conell, David. "Staying the Course: Imperative and Influence within the Religious College." In *The Future of Religious Colleges: The Proceedings of the Harvard Conference on the Future of Religious Colleges*, edited by Paul John Dovre, 63–72. Grand Rapids, MI: Eerdmans, 2002.

Osokoya, Israel Olu. "Privatization of University Education in Africa: Lessons from the Theories and Practices of the United States of America and Japan." *International Journal of African & African American Studies* 6, no. 2 (2007): 1–10. www.ojcs.siue.edu. Accessed 20 December 2010.

Otieno, W. "The Privatization of Public Universities in Kenya." In *Private Higher Education: A Global Revolution*, edited by P. G. Altbach and D. C. Levy, 75–77. Boston, MA: Sense, 2005.

Pattillo, Manning M., and Donald M. Mackenzie, eds. *Church-Sponsored Higher Education in the United States: Report of the Danforth Commission*. Washington DC: American Council on Education, 1966.

Pelikan, Jaroslav. *The Idea of the University: A Reexamination*. New Haven, CT: Yale University Press, 1992.

Pressnell, Claude O., Jr. "The Spiritual Life of the Christian Scholar: Practicing the Presence of Christ." In *The Future of Christian Higher Education*, edited by David S. Dockery and David P. Gushee, 121–136. Nashville, TN: B&H, 1999.

Ramley, J. "Moving Mountains: Institutional Culture and Transformational Change." In *Field Guide to Academic Leadership*, edited by R. Diamond, 59–74. San Francisco: Jossey-Bass, 2002.

Reuben, Julie A. *The Making of a Modern University: Intellectual Transformation and the Marginalization of Modernity*. Chicago: University of Chicago Press, 1996.

Ringenberg, William C. *The Christian College: A History of Protestant Higher Education in America*. 2nd ed. Grand Rapids, MI: Baker, 2006.

Rossman, G., and S. F. Rallis. *Learning in the Field: An Introduction to Qualitative Research*. Thousand Oaks, CA: Sage, 1998.

Ryrie, Charles. *Basic Theology*. Chicago: Moody, 1999.

Schaffer, Regan H. "Service-Learning in Christian Higher Education: Bringing Our Mission to Life." *Christian Higher Education* 3 (2004): 127–145.

Schwehn, M. R. "A Christian University." *First Things* (May 1999): 26–27.

———. *Exiles from Eden: Religion and the Academic Vocation in America*. New York: Oxford University Press, 1993.

Sire, J. *Discipleship of the Mind*. Downers Grove, IL: InterVarsity Press, 1990.

Sloan, Robert B., Jr.. "Preserving Distinctively Christian Higher Education." In *The Future of Christian Higher Education*, edited by David S. Dockery and P. Gushee, 25–36. Nashville, TN: B&H, 1999.

Smith, C. *The Secular Revolution: Power, Interests, and Conflict in the Secularization of American Public Life*. Berkeley, CA: University of California Press, 2003.

Smith, G. T. "Spiritual Formation in the Academy: A Unifying Model." *Faculty Dialogue*, 26 (1996). www.iclnet.org/pub/facdialogue. Accessed 20 November 2010.

Sullivan, John. "Connection without Control: Theology and Interconnectedness in the University." *Christian Higher Education* 6, no. 2 (2007): 143–159.

Tanner, K. "Theology and Cultural Contest in the University." In *Religious Studies, Theology, and the University*, edited by L. E. Cady and D. Brown, 199–212. New York: State University of New York Press, 2002.

Task Force on Higher Education and Society. *Higher Education in Developing Countries: Peril and Promise*. Washington, DC: World Bank, 2000.

Teferra, D. "Private Higher Education in Ethiopia: The Current Landscape." *International Higher Education* 40 (Summer 2005): 9–10. www.bc.edu. Accessed 20 November 2010.

Teferra, D., and P. G. Altbach. "African Higher Education: Challenges for the 21st Century." *Higher Education* 47, no. 1 (2004): 21–50.

———. "Trends and Perspectives in African Higher Education." In *African Higher Education: An International Reference Handbook*, edited by D. Teferra and P. G. Altbach, 3–14. Bloomington, IN: Indiana University Press, 2003.

Thiessen, Henry C. *Lectures in Systematic Theology*. Reprint. Grand Rapids, MI: Eerdmans 2006.

Tumwesigye, G. "Private Higher Education in Uganda." In *New Trends in Higher Education: Growth and Expansion of Private Higher Education in Africa*, edited by N. V. Varghase, 203–229. Paris: International Institute for Educational Planning, 2006.

UNESCO Institute for Statistics. "Trends in Tertiary Education: Sub-Saharan Africa." UNESCO Institute for Statistics, July 2009. www.uis.unesco.org. Accessed 2 February 2011.

United Nations. "Information Technology Should Be Used to Tap Knowledge from Greatest Universities to Bring Learning to All, Kofi Annan Says." United Nations Press Release SG/SM/7502 AFR/259, 2 August 2000. http://www.un.org/press/en/2000/20000802.sgsm7502.doc.html. Accessed 5 October 2009.

Varghese, N. V. *New Trends in Higher Education: Growth and Expansion of Private Higher Education in Africa*. Paris: International Institute for Educational Planning, 2006.

Verweij, Johan, P. Ester, and R. N. Ellison. "Secularization as an Economic and Cultural Phenomenon: A Cross-National Analysis." *Journal for the Scientific Study of Religion* 36, no. 2 (1997): 309–324.

Voye, L. "Secularization in a Context of Advanced Modernity." *Sociology of Religion* 60 (1999): 275–288.

Wondimu, H. "Ethiopia." In *African Higher Education: An International Reference Handbook*, edited by D. Teferra and P. G. Altbach, 316–325. Bloomington, IN: Indiana University Press, 2003.

Wood, R. *Contending for the Faith*. Waco, TX: Baylor University Press, 2003.

Wolfe, Alan. "The Evangelical Mind Revisited." *Change* 38, no. 2 (2006): 8.

Yin, Robert K. *Applications of Case Study Research: Applied Social Research Methods Series*. Newbury Park, CA: Sage, 1993.

———. *Case Study Research: Design and Methods*. 2nd ed. Thousand Oaks, CA: Sage, 2003.

Global Hub for Evangelical Theological Education

Mission

ICETE advances quality and collaboration in global theological education to strengthen and accompany the church in its mission.

Objectives

As a global hub for evangelical theological education, ICETE is recognized for its reliable capacity to:

1. Develop, disseminate, mutually validate, harmonize, and inspire quality in theological education, aimed at fostering reciprocal trust among stakeholders, including the church;
2. Cultivate worldwide relationships, stimulated through gatherings, communications for reflection, interactive dialogue, collaboration, and practice in support of the church's mission; and
3. Train, consult, and provide resources for those involved in theological education, marked by relevance, accessibility, and collaborative effectiveness.

ICETE's mission emphasizes its dual focus on quality *and* collaboration through its constituency to strengthen and accompany the church in its mission. The quality aspect of our work addresses the church-academy gap by requiring theological institutions to build strategic partnerships with churches and ministry organizations. ICETE quality assurance seeks to be an agent for change in theological institutions, and consequently in the lives of the next generation of global leaders.

Through collaborative opportunities, our impact begins with theological educators and extends exponentially to training programs, students, church leaders, and the broader community for the sake of the church. Our work targets theological educators across all sectors who prepare thousands of learners serving in hundreds of ministries.

www.icete.info

Langham Literature and its imprints are a ministry of Langham Partnership.

Langham Partnership is a global fellowship working in pursuit of the vision God entrusted to its founder John Stott –

> *to facilitate the growth of the church in maturity and Christ-likeness through raising the standards of biblical preaching and teaching.*

Our vision is to see churches in the majority world equipped for mission and growing to maturity in Christ through the ministry of pastors and leaders who believe, teach and live by the Word of God.

Our mission is to strengthen the ministry of the Word of God through:
- nurturing national movements for biblical preaching
- fostering the creation and distribution of evangelical literature
- enhancing evangelical theological education

especially in countries where churches are under-resourced.

Our ministry

Langham Preaching partners with national leaders to nurture indigenous biblical preaching movements for pastors and lay preachers all around the world. With the support of a team of trainers from many countries, a multi-level programme of seminars provides practical training, and is followed by a programme for training local facilitators. Local preachers' groups and national and regional networks ensure continuity and ongoing development, seeking to build vigorous movements committed to Bible exposition.

Langham Literature provides majority world preachers, scholars and seminary libraries with evangelical books and electronic resources through publishing and distribution, grants and discounts. The programme also fosters the creation of indigenous evangelical books in many languages, through writer's grants, strengthening local evangelical publishing houses, and investment in major regional literature projects, such as one volume Bible commentaries like *The Africa Bible Commentary* and *The South Asia Bible Commentary*.

Langham Scholars provides financial support for evangelical doctoral students from the majority world so that, when they return home, they may train pastors and other Christian leaders with sound, biblical and theological teaching. This programme equips those who equip others. Langham Scholars also works in partnership with majority world seminaries in strengthening evangelical theological education. A growing number of Langham Scholars study in high quality doctoral programmes in the majority world itself. As well as teaching the next generation of pastors, graduated Langham Scholars exercise significant influence through their writing and leadership.

To learn more about Langham Partnership and the work we do visit **langham.org**

www.ingramcontent.com/pod-product-compliance
Lightning Source LLC
Chambersburg PA
CBHW071739150426
43191CB00010B/1630